Reading *Mount and Mountain* was a moving experience! Not only does this creative dialogue of a Jewish rabbi and a Christian minister yield much new insight into the scriptures, it also points in the direction God beckons for our relationship with one another.

—*E. Glenn Hinson*
Author of *A Serious Call to a Contemplative Lifestyle*

What a treat! Two intelligent and articulate people from different faith traditions engage in a healthy dialogue around key writings in their respective scriptures. The result is both informative and encouraging. Here is a model not only for theological dialogue but for doing life together, something that is needed in our divisive times. We have so much to learn from each other if we are willing to take the time to engage one another as these writers have.

—*Ircel Harrison*
Site Coordinator
Central Baptist Theological Seminary, Tennessee
Coaching Coordinator, Pinnacle Leadership Associates

Dr. Mike and Rabbi Rami have given us a grand theological unraveling of the Ten Commandments from two different traditions. Their insights are shaped by God's Spirit; their words are shaped by their respective faith stances. While representing with integrity their distinctive faiths, they also model for us that we are indeed brothers and sisters in Jehovah God!

—*Bo Prosser*
Coordinator for Missional Congregations
Cooperative Baptist Fellowship

The authors weave together ancient and modern insights on the Beatitudes with sensitivity to the original context of Judaism and Christianity in antiquity as well as to the ethical dilemmas of our own day. You can feel the passion of these learned teachers on every page!

—*Sharon Pace*
Associate Professor of Hebrew Bible/Judaica
Marquette University
Author of *Daniel* (Smyth & Helwys Bible Commentary)

In a Southern Christian culture that tends to prefer public idolizations of the Ten Commandments over actually listening to and heeding them, a Baptist minister sits down with a rabbi—in the heart of Tennessee—to help each other better hear and understand. While remaining true to their respective (and in this case overlapping) traditions, Rev. Michael Smith and Rabbi Rami Shapiro demonstrate humility, honesty, and respect as they plow together the always fertile soil of this most sacred ground. Come. Sit. Listen in. And learn to trust the Divine Author, as do the minister and the rabbi, to water and nurture in you a deeper understanding and appreciation of these words to His children.

—*Bert Montgomery*
Author of *Psychic Pancakes & Communion Pizza* and
Elvis, Willie, Jesus & Me

MOUNT AND MOUNTAIN
VOLUME 2

A REVEREND AND A RABBI
TALK ABOUT THE SERMON ON THE MOUNT

Smyth & Helwys Publishing, Inc.
6316 Peake Road
Macon, Georgia 31210-3960
1-800-747-3016
©2013 by Rami Shapiro and Michael Smith
All rights reserved.
Printed in the United States of America.

The paper used in this publication meets the minimum requirements of
American National Standard for Information Sciences—
Permanence of Paper for Printed Library Materials.
ANSI Z39.48–1984. (alk. paper)

Library of Congress Cataloging-in-Publication Data

CIP information on file

Mount
and
Mountain

VOLUME 2

A Reverend and a Rabbi Talk About the Sermon on the Mount

To Janette and Jim —

with best

wishes . . .

Michael A. Smith

Michael Smith *and* Rami Shapiro

Also by Rami Shapiro and Michael Smith

Let Us Break Bread Together: A Passover Haggadah for Christians

*Mount and Mountain, Volume 1: A Reverand and a Rabbi
Talk About the Ten Commandments*

Dedication

To everyone with the faith and courage to engage
the Word anew. —RS

To E. Glenn Hinson, who taught me the value of
cross-tradition conversation. —MS

Contents

Preface

Go tell it on the mountain . . . or on the mount, if that's your context. Most of us know the phrase and the logic behind it. First, there's the symbolism. Mounts and mountains are arresting, majestic, and eternal, not to mention tough to climb. If someone's speaking to you from a mount or a mountain, you know that what they're saying is serious. Second, there's the sheer drama. Standing atop a mount or mountain makes you look amazing. You're *up there*, raised above the crowd. The wind is whipping your hair and (if you've got one) your robe around, and the light is shining beatifically on your face or maybe casting you in a vivid silhouette. You look authoritative; you're someone to be heard, someone to be reckoned with. Finally, there's the practical end of it: because you're elevated, you can be seen by everybody, and the landscape carries your voice in echoes that not only sound great but also ensure that your audience doesn't miss out on your words. These things count, especially when it's thousands of years ago and you don't have a microphone or a big screen to help you out.

So yes, telling it on the mount or the mountain is a good move. Lots of folks—most famously Moses at Mt. Sinai and Jesus at Mt. Eremos—have had good cause to use it. But there is one drawback to mounts and mountains: they are not conducive to dialogue. They're excellent for delivering moving sermons and for handing down commandments, but they're not ideal for having intimate conversations. And this book, the second in the *Mount and Mountain* series, is all about intimate conversation.

If you've read the preface to the first volume, you already know that *Mount and Mountain* records a two-year conversation between Reverend Michael Smith and Rabbi Rami Shapiro. In that dialogue, the rabbi and the reverend share their ideas about and their understanding of two foundational texts of Judaism and Christianity: the Ten Commandments (discussed in volume 1) and the Sermon on the Mount (the focus of the present volume). Their discussion is wide ranging, at times scholarly, at times humorous, often personal, and always rich, honest, and *engaged.*

In this particular volume, it is especially engaged with the words of Jesus—with questioning them, analyzing them, and interpreting them, and above all being challenged by them because the Sermon on the Mount is a challenging text. It challenges its listeners to live a "whole-hearted" (Mike's word) spiritual life, and it challenges us to live ethically as well. Jesus offers perennial concerns that are as relevant today as they were when first spoken almost two thousand years ago, and so, in addition to interpreting the sermon, Rami and Mike frequently find themselves discussing subjects of contemporary note: tribalism, poverty, injustice in the courts, the abuse of political power, and the use of nonviolence as a mode of social protest, among other pressing issues.

It's a powerful conversation about a powerful text, but here's the thing to remember: none of what appears in this book is delivered from a mountain-top. This book is not a sermon, and neither Mike nor Rami will preach. What they will do is talk. That's all. Just talk. Passionately but also lovingly and with humility. With open minds and open hearts, Mike and Rami explore the text of Jesus' sermon cooperatively, contributing perspectives drawn from their lives and religious traditions and seeking moments of illumination. They are, like all of us, audience members, contemplating the words of Jesus together in the hope that we can discern Truth not only through revelation but also through conversation.

That's the strength of this book. It's less imposing than a mountaintop, but it's also more accessible. And that's where you and I come in. As readers, we can participate in Mike and Rami's dialogue. It's true that we can't speak to them directly (though I'm sure they'd welcome e-mails), but we can and do talk back in our own way. We too are part of their conversation: we think and respond, we question and wonder, we entertain doubt and affirm faith. Reading their discussion, we are encouraged to begin our own—with God, with ourselves, and with friends and family. In fact, it might be fair to say that this book is best read in company, where one can quite literally begin a dialogue to coincide with the one in these pages. However you choose to read the book, though, it is my hope, as it is Mike and Rami's, that you will find in it ideas that—whether you agree with them or not—spur you along your own spiritual path and inspire you to realize a more conscious and meaningful connection with God, with faith, and with life.

And if that sounds a little lofty, keep one thing in mind: I'm not talking about a connection that is possible only at magnificent heights. It's one we can make anywhere, even way down here, sitting and chatting with each other at the foot of the mountain.

I have had the pleasure of "sitting in" on these conversations as the original editor of the blog posts from which they originated. And while you may expect me to be biased (Rabbi Rami is my dad), I believe what we have in these two books is a conversation among equals. I urge you to join in.

Aaron Hershel Shapiro
August 21, 2012

Editor's Note

Mount and Mountain, at its inception, was not a book. It was a blog. A blog that Mike and Rami maintained for two years, and through which they shared their readings of the Ten Commandments and the Sermon on the Mount not only with each other, but with the general public. There are significant advantages to conducting a project like this as a blog, not the least of which is that readers (myself included) could respond directly and even carry on elements of the discussion in the blog's comments section. Yet blogs end, updates stop, and eventually sites that have fallen into disuse are moved off active servers, and even, after a while, deleted from the Internet archive.

Books have another sort of longevity. They remain with us as long as we care about them, and they are passed from parent to child, friend-to-friend, colleague-to-colleague. Books also foster community, and in a way quite distinct from blogs. Online communication enables readers from around the world to meet in a shared virtual space. Books, on the other hand, bring us face-to-face—because while one can certainly discuss a book over email or through social media, there's nothing quite as warmly intimate as sharing a book in person, dog-eared copy in hand.

So it was with a great deal of excitement, and trepidation, that I took on (at Mike and Rami's request) the task of translating their blog into book form. There have been challenges. Sometimes, the blog posts led to discussions in the comments that raised new issues or that illuminated the posts in new ways. Sometimes, offline conversations between Mike and Rami would wend their way into the posts in shorthand form, creating gaps in the dialogue. And sometimes, the wild nature of blogging would lead the pair off topic into interesting, though occasionally ancillary, byways. Of course, there was also the issue of organization. After all, blogs don't have chapters, and blog posts may vary widely in length.

It has been my job as editor, then, to fit the square-peg of the Mount and Mountain blog into the round-hole of book publishing. I have tried throughout to maintain the free flowing quality of the original. Where necessary, I have asked the authors to revise their writing to include points raised in the blog's comments or to clarify and focus the text. My overarching goal has always been to help readers take part in Mike and Rami's discussion fully and effortlessly. But while I am responsible for the readability of this volume, the ideas and opinions expressed here are entirely Mike and Rami's.

And now they are yours: to read, to mull-over, reject, take to heart, to share and talk over. Enjoy the conversation.

Aaron Shapiro
December 2012

Approaching Jesus: An Introduction

Mike: Let's begin with each of us offering a brief statement about our individual perspectives on Jesus. After we've done so, I'll prepare a separate post introducing the Sermon on the Mount, insofar as I am able.

Now for Jesus. As you can imagine, it's difficult for me to summarize my take on Jesus in a brief comment, but I'll try to do so.

Jesus, ideally, is the center of my life. Traditionally, Christians speak of Jesus as "Lord," "Master," "Teacher," "Savior," and the like. The simplest way I know to capture the essence of all such terms is to picture Jesus as the one around whom I orient myself. You'll probably ask, "Which Jesus?" My response is the Jesus we find in the canonical Gospels (in all his complexity and simplicity), the Jesus of Christian reflection, and the living Jesus I know through the Spirit of God.

Of course, while doing so I try to take care not to fall into the trap of thinking I've got Jesus pegged. To paraphrase Carlyle Marney, I try to follow the light I've been given, and I hope for more light.[1]

God and humanity intersect and become one in Jesus. How? I don't know. But I accept the incarnation and resurrection, and when I combine them with the life and teachings and manner of Jesus, I find that I stand in the presence of someone far greater than myself (or any other). He knows me, and indeed he knows the human condition—not in the abstract but as a full participant. Yet he knows God in much the same way, as a full participant in the life of God. I can therefore use language such as "Son of God," "Son of Man," "God-Man," and the like, though I try to be careful in doing so, since such terms are open to any number of interpretations.

I know Jesus as the one in whom we see what life is supposed to be like, both now and in the new creation. He is the one who knows what it means to love God, others, and self as God intends. Self-giving love (*agape*) finds full expression in his life and death, and through his resurrection this love is validated as the ultimately unconquerable way of life.

Strangely enough, if I am to engage Jesus with integrity, I must take seriously that he was a first-century Jewish man. That's the aggravating aspect to incarnation: it refuses to allow you to divorce discourse about the divine from the nitty-gritty of human life and history. The first century matters. I believe there is considerable continuity between Jesus the first-century person and Jesus the Risen One. In fact, I best trust interpretations of Jesus' intent when they are tied strongly to his historical context.

Finally, I find that I must treat Jesus as a living entity. Resurrection matters, too. This involves more than memories and influence. For me, it is an objective reality. Not that I claim to understand all that means; in fact, such a thing is quite beyond my grasp. But I try to operate as if Jesus is alive, well, "at the right hand of God," and taking a healthy interest in the world at large and even in me. This is why I may speak of "a living Lord," Jesus as our "friend," and the like.

All of the above, and considerably more that we'll no doubt unearth, comes into play when I deal with the canonical Scriptures and their account of Jesus.

Rami: I think that was an excellent summary. You are right to note that I would ask "which Jesus," and your answer was quite adequate; especially when you add to the canonical Jesus the Jesus of Christian reflection and the living Jesus revealed to you through the Holy Spirit.

To me this is code for "Jesus as I understand him." If there were one way to understand the Gospels, if all reflecting Christians reflected in the same way, and if the Holy Spirit revealed the same Jesus to every Christian, there wouldn't be hundreds and hundreds of denominations of Christianity. So while I have no problem stating that your Jesus is an authentic Jesus, I also understand that your Jesus is *your* Jesus and that you do not and cannot speak for all Christians. Which, of course, is what makes this dialogue so fruitful—just two lovers of God trying to hear the word and walk the Way.

As for me, I speak for no one but myself. When I think of Jesus, and I do so often—both as an adjunct professor of religion who is called upon to teach classes on the historical Jesus and as a student of Wisdom, which I think the historical Jesus embodies—I think of Jesus as a *Lamed Vavnik*.

In Hebrew the two letters *lamed* and *vav* represent the number thirty-six. Jewish tradition holds that in every generation there are always thirty-six God-realized human beings on this planet who, in my words, recognize the interdependence of life and the nonduality of God in, with, and as all things. *Lamed Vavniks* live out that realization by applying justice, compassion, and humility to the ordinary circumstances of their everyday lives.

In addition, the number thirty-six is two times the number eighteen. Eighteen is represented in Hebrew by the letters *chet* and *yud*, which spell the Hebrew word *Chai*, life. *Lamed Vavniks* not only sustain their own lives but also the life of the world; their righteous deeds tip humanity toward goodness and thereby keep the world from imploding under the weight of human ignorance, anger, fear, violence, and greed.

Lamed Vavniks are also called *Tzadik Nistar*, the Hidden Righteous, and rarely come to the attention of the public. They work quietly behind the scenes, just as Jesus attempted to do in many of the stories told about him in the Gospels. But sometimes the hidden is revealed, and when a *Lamed Vavnik* is forced into the public eye, she or he is almost always seen as a danger to the powers that be. And this too is clear from the Gospels.

If I am correct that Jesus was one of the thirty-six of his generation, the Sermon on the Mount may well represent one of the few clear articulations of the way of the *Lamed Vavnik*. I realize the scholarly problems with the text. I understand that there is no compelling scientific proof that Jesus spoke these words, but like you, I am not overly concerned here with the historical Jesus. Of course we need to place the sermon in its historical setting (or at least the historical setting assumed by Matthew, the only writer to record this talk by Jesus). And, of course, we need to reference life in first-century, Roman-occupied Jewish Palestine. And yes, I believe Jesus lived as a Jew, taught as a rabbi, and was crucified by Rome, but this Jesus is less important to me than the mythic Jesus, the teacher of Wisdom, the *Lamed Vavnik* who, once forced into the public eye, did not shrink from speaking Truth to power.

The question I will ask of the Sermon on the Mount is not "Did Jesus actually preach these words?" but "What is the meaning of the words themselves, and how do they guide me in the way of justice, compassion, and humility that is the heart of the *Lamed Vavnik*?"

I have much more to say about Jesus, and I will allow that to come out as we talk. So let's begin.

Note

1. John J. Carey, *Carlyle Marney: A Pilgrim's Progress* (Macon: Mercer University Press, 1980) 30.

Opening Perspectives (Beginning the Discussion)

Mike: Matthew 5:1–7:29 is the canonical account of the Sermon on the Mount. For our purposes, it matters little whether the existing text reports a condensed version of an occasion or is an edited compilation of various sayings of Jesus. We are interested in exploring the sermon's possible meanings.

The Beatitudes describe those who follow the way of Jesus. The subsequent declaration about "salt and light" defines the nature of his followers' influence in society. The specific teachings that follow provide pointed, though not exhaustive, illustrations of how following Jesus might play out in daily life. It is hoped that the challenge and depth of the sayings will become evident as we deal with them.

Christians have long debated how to apply the sermon. At the risk of oversimplification, I tend to reduce the range of options to a handful.

(1) A considerable segment of Christianity assumes that the sermon applies only to a special class of Christian, perhaps clergy or monks or such. Everyday Christians are not expected to live up to such a standard.

(2) Some Christians treat the sermon as Jesus' agenda for social change. For example, classic American liberal theology assumed that the sermon described what society would be like once the kingdom of God came to maturity within history.

(3) Others maintain that the sermon applies only within a limited time frame. They may differ over the time frame in question. American dispensationalists, for example, traditionally argue that the sermon applies only between the return of Christ and the end of world.

(4) A long-standing approach assumes that the sermon's demands are designed to expose our sin, shatter our pride, bring us to repentance, and draw us to rely on God's grace.

(5) One school of thought argues that the sermon has no application in this age. Instead, it describes the life of the redeemed in heaven or in the new creation.

(6) Christians from a variety of theological stripes take the sermon's demands seriously, assuming that they cannot be fully realized in this life but insisting that we must try. Such Christians believe that they live under God's grace. Generally, they also posit that the sermon is meant to apply to the community of God, though such ideals might positively affect the world at large as well. The sermon always informs the life of the Christian individual and the Christian community. This is my favored approach.

Rami, all of the above represents a drastic simplification of an extremely complicated picture. To borrow and modify your earlier illustration, wherever three Christians gather to discuss the Sermon on the Mount, there shall be six opinions. That being said, I hope I've provided a platform from which to launch our conversation.

Rami: I appreciate the overview, and I can see why you prefer the sixth option, but I am troubled by something. Like the Apostle Paul, you seem to be saying that God and Jesus set humanity up to fail; and that if it were not for God's grace and Jesus' redemptive death on the cross, humanity would be damned for all eternity for failing to do what in fact is beyond our capacity to do in the first place. As you said earlier, the game is rigged and the house always wins.

You and I differ greatly over our understanding of God, but simply to offer a counter-argument would be somewhat prosaic. What I would rather do is hear from you regarding why God, as you understand God, would do this.

Judaism offers a different notion. The Seven Laws of Noah that the rabbis derived from Genesis are the basic ethical precepts by which God judges humanity. The 613 Laws of Torah form the system by which God judges the Jews. The Jews are chosen for this more extreme lifestyle, but there is never any idea that God is setting Jews or Gentiles up to fail. God says, "Keep My laws and My statutes, which a person shall keep and live by them—I am HaShem" (Lev 18:5). ("HaShem" means "The Name" and refers to the Name of God that Jews are not allowed to pronounce: YHVH. "LORD" is the usual translation, but it is not accurate.) Even God assumes that we can do what God commands.

While most rabbis would agree that no one ever lives these laws perfectly, Jews do not believe that people are judged based on a notion of perfection. Regardless of your beliefs, as long as your good deeds outweigh your bad deeds, you are assured a place in heaven. Indeed, we even have Yom Kippur, our annual Day of Atonement, when God forgives all sins arising from our imperfect doing of God's commandments. (Jews are obligated to seek forgiveness from the people they may have hurt during the weeks prior to Yom Kippur.)

This is, of course, somewhat academic since I don't believe in a law-giving God who judges or damns; nor do I believe in a literal heaven. As for what I do believe, I am drawn to your first and second options.

Given my suggestion that Jesus was a *Lamed Vavnik*, a *Tzadik Nistar*, one of the thirty-six hidden righteous, his Sermon on the Mount could be, as your first option suggests, a standard of living restricted to *Lamed Vavnikim* (plural of *Lamed Vavnik*, Thirty-Sixers). But if this is so, it is of limited value. I prefer to see the sermon as your second category does, an agenda for social change rooted not in large social or political movements but in personal transformation. Jesus as a *Lamed Vavnik* is articulating an ideal toward which we can all strive but that few us will ever master. Mastery is beside the point; it is the effort that matters, for it is the effort itself that is transformative.

I am excited to go deeply into this text with you, Mike. I have never had the opportunity to study it formally, and certainly not with someone who seeks to embody it. I look forward to going into this verse by verse.

Mike: Before launching into the first Beatitude, I want to unpack my position on the Sermon on the Mount, mostly in response to your previous comments.

I do not think God sets us up for failure via the Sermon on the Mount (or the Ten Commandments, for that matter). Instead, God uses the sermon to call us to our senses, to open our eyes to the truth about ourselves. Only when we more nearly see our genuine condition may we start to live an authentic human life.

What might we come to see about ourselves? When we attempt to embody the sermon, we quickly confront our finitude, the hard fact that we have limits. We get in touch with the complexity of our motivations. The more attention we pay to our external and internal selves, the more we discern how deeply self-centered or (at best) tribe-centered we are.

Strangely enough, though, we also discover how much we yearn to become the kind of person envisioned in the sermon. It's as if something within us says, "Yes, now that you put the matter into words, that's what I've been searching for all my life. That's the 'me' I want to fashion." To put it another way, the Sermon on the Mount may trigger a deep longing for an alternative life and an alternative community.

We find ourselves caught between a new and realistic self-assessment and an awakened longing. It seems to me that we may react in one of three ways: despair, deceit, or realignment. By despair, I mean we may decide that the entire agenda is hopeless or impractical. If so, we'll usually retreat into some form of self-defensiveness. Deceit is a bit more complicated. Knowing that we cannot achieve perfection, we choose to try to fool others (and perhaps even God) into thinking we do so. We may even fool ourselves part of the time. Realignment involves embracing our limits, which is to say accepting our finiteness. Within our limits, we are called to pursue the way of God, which in my case involves the way of Jesus.

Both pride and despair, though, are discarded. God expects us to walk the way of Jesus, but he does not expect us to do it perfectly. He loves that we choose to walk with him, even as he loves us. To totter along the path turns out to be enough!

Analogies cannot be pressed too hard, but I'll risk one. I have a friend who is a top-notch golfer. I play the game, but bogey golf is about all I can manage. Don't get me wrong. I work at the game. I try to refine my swing, hone my putting, improve my course management, and strengthen my ability to concentrate for the entire eighteen holes. Still, I'm limited. Some days I play better than usual, some days worse.

Now here's the funny thing. My friend wants to play golf with me, though I slow him down and will never come near his level of play. We enjoy one another's company. When I hit a bad shot, we may analyze it a little. More often, though, we simply move on to the next shot. I learn what I can from him, and I'm a better golfer for it. Mostly, though, we savor our time with one another. Fellowship is the main thing. Any other benefit is a bonus.

I think the Sermon on the Mount is a means by which God invites us to try to walk with him. The journey builds fellowship. Along the way we may learn some things and hone our skills at living more nearly in accord with God's intentions, but fellowship remains the main thing.

This is a long comment, so I'll stop. My next comment will take us into the Beatitudes.

Rami: Sometimes I think I critique what you say only to get you to say more. I love your idea that the Ten Commandments and the Sermon on the

Mount "call us to our senses" and "open our eyes to the truth about ourselves."

It is a great turn of phrase, especially when used in the context of contemporary religion. I often get the feeling that biblical Judaism at its best is all about returning to our senses—returning to the physical reality around and within us and seeing that it is good. Our culture is far too Gnostic in the sense that it pits the physical against the spiritual, denigrating the former and elevating the latter so high as to be largely irrelevant to our lives. This is why the Song of Songs is so important both to the canon and to our culture. It's unbridled passion, sensuality, sexuality, and love between two people redeems both the Gnostic anti-body tendencies and the xenophobic violence that plagues so much of the Bible and Western civilization.

When we return to our senses, we realize that we are one with each other in a greater Wholeness. When we return to our senses, we stand in what Rabbi Abraham Joshua Heschel called Radical Amazement at the wonder of life.[1] When we return to our senses, we fall in love with the world and with one another, and can learn war no more.

This is the great truth of the incarnational teaching of Christianity (as I understand it, of course). This is the core truth, the real good news that Christianity offers the world, and which the world so desperately needs: God becomes human to remind us that we humans are God, that nature is God, and that the universe is God. Jesus starts out as a baby, just like us. He burps, he pees, he poops, he laughs, he cries, he rejoices, and he knows fear just like us. There is nothing human that is alien to God. And hence there is nothing human that cannot be made holy.

When we come to our senses, we come to God. And when we come to God, that is, when we realize the nonduality of all things as God, we regain our sanity and engage the world and one another with justice, compassion, and humility. This is what Jesus comes to remind us. The Sermon on the Mount is Jesus' program for achieving Micah's True Religion: "Do justly, love mercy, and walk humbly with your God" (Mic 6:8).

So, if I am following your comments correctly, you seem to be saying that the Sermon is in fact a vehicle for personal transformation. I agree. And the more I measure myself against it, the more work I realize I have to do. And, if I am lucky, I will work so hard as to finally realize that work alone won't do; I need something else. This is when Grace takes over.

There is a Hasidic story about the first angels to come to earth. They climb down the Ladder from Heaven and then, when they seek to climb back up, they find that the ladder has been removed. At first they cry out in despair, but after a while they begin to jump. Their hope is that if they jump hard enough and high enough, they will make it back to heaven. After a while, however, they begin to tire; and one after another the angels quit jumping, convinced that they cannot return home under their own power. All save one. One angel just keeps jumping. No matter how exhausted he becomes, no matter how weakly he leaps, he still jumps. And just when he realizes that he cannot leap even one last time, God reaches down and pulls him home.

That is how it is with us. We have to exhaust what the Japanese Buddhists call *jiriki*, self-power, if we are finally to be surrendered to the grace of *tariki*, other-power.

Of course, it takes a lot of courage to keep jumping when everyone else has quit. That is why a fellowship of like-minded and like-willed seekers is, as you said, so helpful. I'm not sure I would agree that fellowship is the point; that sounds a bit too humanistic to me, but it is a wonderful part of the process. The point is exhaustion. And then, God willing, return.

On to the Beatitudes!

Note

1. Heschel (1907–1972) was one of the most important rabbis of the twentieth century. He was the author of *God in Search of Man* and many other books.

Part 1

The Beatitudes
(Matthew 5:1-12)

Chapter 1

The First Beatitude

When Jesus saw the crowds, he went up the mountain; and after he sat down, his disciples came to him. Then he began to speak, and taught them, saying: "Blessed are the poor in spirit, for theirs is the kingdom of heaven." (Matthew 5:1-3, NRSV)

Mike: So opens Matthew's account. Note that Luke's version is a bit different: "Blessed are you who are poor, for yours is the kingdom of God" (Luke 6:20, NRSV). Generations of commentators found the differences important. They argued that Luke's simpler account was probably older, and they often drew a contrast between what they thought to be Luke's focus on the economically poor versus Matthew's "spiritualization" of poverty. I tend to agree with more recent commentators who argue that both Matthew and Luke have something similar in mind: those who have learned to place their hope in God rather than economics or self-righteousness.

While some in the first century may have seen poverty as a blessed state, most did not. Many viewed wealth as a sign of God's favor and poverty as punishment from God. Jesus' statement runs counter to this strand of popular first-century piety. Certainly, the beatitude challenges our own culture's myth that wealth equals blessing.

"Kingdom of heaven" and "kingdom of God" are interchangeable. Both refer to the active "rule of God." Christian theological language was fluid throughout the first century, and we ought not demand modern standards of precision.

"Blessed" (*makarioi*) is an interesting Greek term. Our term "beatitudes" actually comes from the Latin. The Greek term, though, means "fortunate," "happy," and the like. "Happy" is a fine translation, but it may miscommunicate Jesus' intent. We tend to think of happiness as a feeling. Jesus, I think, had something else in mind. Let's assume he thought in terms of the Hebrew Bible. If I understand correctly, *ashrei* is a Hebrew term that may be translated "blessed" or "fortunate." We find it used, I believe, in Proverbs 3:13: "Blessed is the man who finds wisdom." The section goes on to say of wisdom, ". . . her ways are pleasant ways" (v. 17). The key idea is that a person is blessed or fortunate if he finds and follows the way of wisdom. Genuine happiness is found in taking the right journey or embracing the right perspective.

The first beatitude teaches that real happiness lies in recognizing and embracing our poverty, our need of God. When our eyes are opened, we see the futility of clinging to the lie of self-sufficiency and are freed to accept the help that comes only from God. The old Edenic lie ("you shall be as god" unto yourself, and this will make you complete) dies, to be replaced by an acceptance of our finitude and God's grace. Profound humility before God turns out to be the key to joy.

I want to explore possible implications for personal and community life, but I'll save such things for the next entry.

Rami: Let me begin with some general comments on the language of this beatitude.

First, I love the little detail that Matthew supplies here: Jesus first seated himself and then his disciples came close to him. This is most likely a sign of respect. Rabbinic students stand in the presence of their teachers, sitting only when the master ("my master" being the true meaning of rabbi) sat.

As for the term *ashrei* ("blessed" or "happy"), a term that occurs forty-five times in the Hebrew Bible, twenty-six of these in the book of Psalms, I agree with your notion that "genuine happiness is found in taking the right journey or embracing the right perspective." The idea of "right perspective" parallels the Buddha's teaching of Right View. When we see things as they are, interconnected and impermanent, we are free from selfish desires of control, and we learn to engage life rather than master it—a practice that is a hallmark of the enlightened mind.

I wonder, however, about your notion that wisdom puts the lie to the serpent's claim that eating from the tree of knowledge of good and evil will make you like God (Gen 3:5). In fact, God seems to confirm the serpent's claim when God says of Adam after he has eaten from the tree, "See, the man has become like one of us, knowing good and evil" (Gen 3:22). The problem is in the translation and not the original Hebrew. The Hebrew is *k'achad mimenu*, which means "like one who is distinct or separate from us." The problem with Adam, and humanity as a whole, is that we feel separate from God. God banished Adam from the garden to prevent him from eating from the tree of life and thus becoming permanently stuck in this sense of alienation. The kingdom of heaven, as I understand it, is revealed when we overcome our alienation and reclaim the unity that is God, woman, man, and nature.

The phrase "kingdom of heaven" (Aramaic *Malchuta Dishemaya*) is unique to Matthew, while "kingdom of God" appears in all four Gospels. Since Matthew knows both terms, we might say that they are interchangeable. We might also wonder why only Matthew uses kingdom of heaven, and, since Matthew knows and employs both terms, whether or not he distinguished one from the other in his own mind. We can't know, of course, and our speculation would shed little light on the subject.

As for the textual differences between Matthew and Luke, I disagree with you that they are saying the same thing. In Luke, Jesus is being mobbed by the crowd. Luke says, "Then he looked up at his disciples and said, 'Blessed are you who are poor, for yours is the kingdom of heaven'" (Luke 6:20). In the midst of a sea of poor folk, Jesus singles out his disciples as the blessed poor. Why? Because, unlike the crowd surrounding them, the disciples deliberately chose poverty. In choosing to follow Jesus, they had abandoned their livelihoods. He is assuring them that they will be rewarded for this.

I read Luke 6:20 along with Psalm 41:1: "Blessed are they who consider the poor," that is, blessed are those who take the plight of the poor seriously and do what they can to alleviate it.

We can assume that Jesus' disciples knew the text of Psalm 41, so what were they to make of Jesus' recasting of it? Can it be that Jesus, contra Psalm 41, is telling his disciples to ignore the needs of the poor? I doubt this. Rather, he may be saying something like this: "You cannot be concerned with the poor unless you are free from the system that creates such poverty. So choose poverty and free yourselves from the system of oppression that impoverishes others, and in this way position yourselves to be of service to the poor."

What does it mean to be of service to the poor? In the short term it may be ministering to their suffering, but in the long term it means overthrowing the system of oppression that is the kingdom of Caesar and establishing the system of justice and compassion that is the kingdom of God.

With this in mind, we should add Isaiah 61:1 to our reading of Luke as well: "The spirit of HaShem God is upon me, because HaShem has anointed me [*mashiach*/messiah means "the anointed one"]; He has sent me to bring good news to the oppressed . . . ." The role of the anointed, what I called earlier a *Lamed Vavnik*, is to bring good news to the oppressed. What is this good news? That an unjust world will be made just, and with that will come the end of poverty, oppression, and war.

In Matthew, Jesus is not talking about financial poverty but spiritual poverty. I read Matthew 5:3 in light of Psalm 34:18, "HaShem saves those crushed in spirit." This is something other than financial poverty. Even the wealthy can be crushed or poor in spirit, a fact that is no less true in our time than in Jesus' time.

But what is poverty of the spirit? While in no way disagreeing with your take on humility, let me offer a different slant. The word "spirit" (*Ruach* in Hebrew and *Spiritus* in Latin) also means "breath." A poverty of breath could refer to meditative practices known and practiced by the rabbinic mystics of Jesus' time that slowed the breath as a means to shift consciousness from narrow mind (*mochin d'katnut*) to spacious mind (*mochin d'gadlut*), and in this way overcome the egoic sense of alienation (*achad*) I mentioned a moment ago with regard to Adam and all humankind. Matthew's Jesus may be saying to his inner circle, "Happy are those who cultivate the emptying of the breath, for in this way you will experience the unity with God that is the kingdom of heaven."

I find this compelling. Jesus is offering a political agenda (reading Luke in light of Psalm 41) focused on the ending of poverty, and a spiritual practice (reading Matthew in light of Psalm 34) for those of the inner circle who wish to reenter the Garden of Eden by overcoming the ego's sense of separation from God and creation.

Mike: I want to revisit the matter of spiritual poverty. Such poverty may be experienced by people of any station or circumstance. Spiritual poverty does not require or imply that we denigrate ourselves but instead that we accept ourselves as created beings, specifically women and men created in the image of God. As such, we have considerable potential, but still our reach is limited, finite. The Eden story, in part, is about our tendency to refuse to live within our God-given natures, to long to become God unto ourselves, and to take actions toward that end. To put it another way, we tend toward spiritual pride and the supposed blessing it promises. Jesus counters with a call to embrace the blessing of spiritual poverty: the ability to take joy in exercising our actual gifts and potentials in appropriate humility before God.

The first beatitude calls us to a way of life that may relieve us of an unnatural strain. Consider our fingers. They, along with the thumb, are well formed for grasping and manipulating any number of items. As long as we use our fingers for such purposes, they serve us well. In fact, we're hardly aware of them. Call this the way of spiritual poverty or humility.

Suppose, though, that we bought into the idea that we ought to be able to bend our fingers backwards until they touched our wrists. Go farther and imagine we fall into a state of mind in which we cannot be happy unless we find a way to bring this about. Much wasted time, cracked and broken bones, pain and misdirected longing would ensue! We would make ourselves (and probably others) miserable. Call this the way of spiritual pride.

Appropriate spiritual poverty is crucial to the health of a faith community. When the faith community embraces its God-given nature (worship, service, humility, etc.), it may experience a kind of joy. A faith community that falls to pride, to the wish to be something it was not created to be, forsakes genuine joy for a false promise or hope. For example, each time a Christian church embraces the business model as its measure of success, it sets itself up to experience pain and disappointment, for all institutions ultimately experience decline. On the other hand, a faith community that embraces the way of Jesus, the way of self-giving love, always has reason for joy. Even the "death" of such a community may have meaning.

Of course, there's more to the matter than personal joy or even the faith community's well-being.

When we relax into appropriate spiritual poverty, we become free to step outside whatever economic system may dominate our era. This frees us to use the resources we possess in ministry to the poor and to seek reform or replacement of any economic system that oppresses the poor. I'm not sure all of us are "made" in such ways as to be equally effective at both tasks, but I am convinced that the faith community is called to combine the endeavors.

I am intrigued by the practice you describe, the slowing or emptying of breath. While I am aware of such practices, I do not think any Christian commentator I've read notes the possibility of the practice among first-century Jewish teachers. I would like to know more detail with regard to the first-century setting.

You assume that the beatitudes were addressed only or primarily to the inner circle. Perhaps this is so, but in any case they quickly found their way into broader circulation. It seems clear that the early Christian community thought they applied to all followers of Jesus. Certainly, this is my assumption.

Rami: I mentioned that one way I understand "poor in spirit" is "empty of breath," referring to meditation techniques that lead us out of the false and limiting notion that we are apart from God, and reawaken us to the reality that we are part of God. So the poor in spirit are blessed or, if the original Aramaic was based on the Hebrew *ashrei*, happy because they have overcome the state of *achad*, the sense of being apart from God, and returned to the greater wisdom of *shalem*, the realization that we are a part of God.

As you said, knowledge of first-century Jewish meditation techniques is not widely known, and what we do know is sketchy. The mysticism of the time is called *Ma'asei Merkavah* (Account of the Chariot), and practitioners were called *Yordei Merkavah*, Riders (literally, "Descenders") of the Chariot. One aim of Merkavah mysticism was to induce the vision of God's Chariot given to Ezekiel (1:4-26). How one did this is not at all clear. One method seems to use the mantra-like repetition of a sacred Name of God or Hebrew phrase. Another is a yogic-like inversion posture that places your head below your knees and uses the rush of blood to the head to alter consciousness. Another, which is derived from Ezekiel himself, is water gazing.

Ezekiel opens his book saying, "In the thirteen year, in the fourth month, on the fifth day of the month, as I was among the exiles by the river Chebar, the heavens were opened and I saw visions of God" (Ezek 1:1). The rabbis understood this to mean that Ezekiel, unlike the other exiles who saw nothing, was practicing water gazing, allowing his eyes to rest softly on the flow of the water and the sunlight dancing on its surface, and in so doing entering into a trance state where the limited mind (*mochin d'katnut*) dissolves into the larger mind (*mochin d'gadlut*) that knows itself to be part of God.

We all know something of this trance whenever we sit and watch a body of flowing water, whether it be a river, a sea, or an ocean. I become similarly entranced even when sitting by a small brook or stream. Maybe it is because we are made mostly of water ourselves that water is a powerful tool for expanding consciousness. In any case, these states are always accompanied by and deepened by a slowing of the breath. Jesus, if he is referring to his inner circle, and if those in that circle practice such techniques (which I realize requires a lot of speculation), is saying to them, "There is an intrinsic blessedness, happiness, and joy that comes from practicing poverty of the breath and thereby shifting your awareness from ego to soul and remembering your connection with God."

What is discovered through these practices is not new. You are not connecting to God but realizing you are never disconnected from God. The
rabbis found confirmation of this in the name of the river into which Ezekiel
gazed. *Chebar* is Hebrew for "already" (*kvar*), suggesting to the mystics that
what we see in meditation is what is already and always present. The notion
that Yordei Merkavah, those who descend to the Chariot, in fact experience
their awakening as a descent rather than an ascent suggests that they realized
that heaven was not a place "up there" but rather a state of awareness "in
here," meaning in the human heart and mind. Does this shed light on Jesus'
notion that the kingdom of heaven is within us?

Bruce Chilton, author of *Rabbi Jesus: An Intimate Biography* (New York:
Doubleday, 2000), makes a big deal of Jesus' connection with Merkavah
mystics, and I would suggest that book to anyone who wishes to explore this
more fully.

Chapter 2

The Second Beatitude

Blessed are those who mourn, for they will be comforted. (Matthew 5:4, NRSV)

Mike: The Beatitudes turn normal expectations upside down. Where's the blessing or happiness in mourning? The longer I ponder this beatitude, the more I find the following elements in play.

The Pain and Promise of Awakening. Jesus called would-be followers to die to the life they had known and awaken into a new kind of life. Dying to any kind of life is not easy. It hurts. Just as important, when we wake to the new life, we may well mourn our past sin, misperceptions, and wasted time. All such mourning, though necessary, is a prelude to the kind of joy that comes from knowing we're fully alive as never before—alive to God, others, and even self.

Enhanced Sensitivity to the Pain of the World. The new life comes with a price: vastly increasing and growing sensitivity to the pain of the world. The old life is self-centered, while the new life is centered in God. Much to our surprise, we soon find that being centered in God forces us to look outward and see all others as immediate family. This can be frightening to introverts, to those who have lived in insular communities, and to those who hitherto have been able to treat others as objects. Now when others hurt from hunger, catastrophes, illness, or human meanness, we hurt with them. We mourn our past isolation. Even more, we mourn the plight of those we now know to be brothers and sisters.

The Promise of Participation in the Life of God. Jesus promises "comfort." His version of "comfort," though, may sound a bit strange. He offers the comfort of participating in the life of God, of joining God in the work of releasing the captives, helping the blind to see, and the like. Comfort comes as we find (or rediscover) our place alongside God, take up the kind of tasks for which he created us, and invest ourselves in fashioning a life and a society in which self-giving love is the lead virtue.

Rami: Before I take up the wonderful insights you offer, I want to place the second beatitude in its Jewish context. In a sense, there is nothing new in Jesus' teaching. The first two beatitudes repeat the classic messianic mission set forth by the Prophet Isaiah, whose mantle Jesus may be taking upon himself.

Isaiah tells us that "because HaShem has anointed me [that is to say because God has made Isaiah a messiah, an anointed one], God has sent me to bring good news to the humbled, to bind up the broken-hearted, to proclaim liberty to the captives, and release from bondage to those who are bound . . . to comfort all who mourn" (Isa 61:1-3).

Images of God comforting mourners are fairly common. We find them, for example, in Isaiah 40:1; 57:18; and 60:20. Then there is the notion that suffering, and the mourning it invites, is part of the redemptive process. Psalm 125:5 says, "They who sow in tears shall reap in joy." And Psalm 94:12-13 says, "Happy is he whom You chasten, HaShem . . . that You may give him rest from the days of adversity."

In other words, the Hebrew Bible makes it clear that suffering is often a gift from God and that those who mourn are to be comforted. Again the Prophet Isaiah tells us that "sorrow and sighing shall fly away" (Isa 51:2) and that God will comfort the people (Isa 66:13).

My point is simply this: Jesus is drawing from well-known and well-accepted doctrine in this beatitude, and I don't see where he "turns normal expectations upside down," as so many imagine. On the contrary, Jesus isn't saying anything new, but rather laying claim to something very old. He is identifying himself with the messiah idea of Isaiah. His Jewish listeners may be startled that he is claiming the messianic mantle, but there is nothing about that mantle that is knew to them.

Even with what I just said, you do raise some interesting points that my more Jewish reading might have missed. So let me comment on your teaching.

Jesus is calling us to a new life, and following him requires the death of the old life. I believe this is what all great wisdom teachers teach. The egoic life is rooted in *mochin d'katnut*, the narrow mind that is alienated from God and creation and is a block to the greater life of the soul, *mochin d'gadlut*, that level of consciousness that knows all life to be a part of the One Life that is God. We have to let the old life die, and do so respectfully, which means with authentic mourning.

If our mourning is not true, our transformation is false as well, and no real joy or comfort will arise from it. And because this new life is not egocentric but world-centric, the pain of the world becomes our pain. We become compassionate, literally sharing (*com*) the suffering (*passion*) of the world. The passion of Christ is paradigmatic of the passion through which each of us is to pass as we move from egocentric to world-centric to God-centric consciousness.

What I hear you saying is that when we become part of the Greatest of These (God), we cannot help feeling for and act on behalf of the "least of these," to borrow from Matthew 25:40.

I especially like your closing idea that both takes us back to Isaiah and puts forth the way of the kingdom of heaven. When we fully participate in the Life of God—that is, when we realize that we are manifestations of God, the way God is alive in our time and place—we take on the work of God: "to bring good news to the humbled, to bind up the broken-hearted, to proclaim liberty to the captives, and release from bondage to those who are bound . . . to comfort all who mourn" (Isa 61:1-3).

What began as the work of the Messiah becomes the work of each one of us. While faith may be the way *to* the kingdom of God, action (deeds) is the way *of* that kingdom.

Mike: We appear to be on a similar page with regard to death of the old life, the new life, the necessity of genuine mourning, the paradigmatic passion of Christ, and participation in the life and work of God. In short, we continue to find considerable convergence in our applications of a given Scripture passage, even though we approach it from different starting places.

That being said, I want to try to clarify my take on a few matters.

First, I do not think Jesus propounded a new idea via the beatitude. I apologize for giving such an impression. Isaiah 61 undoubtedly informed his understanding of himself and his mission, as did the other passages you mention. We agree that Jesus was genuinely a first-century Jew who drew from the traditions and teachings of his heritage to frame his message and work.

No doubt I need to clarify what I had in mind when I wrote of Jesus "turning normal expectations upside down." Start with the first century. First-century Judaism, as I understand the matter, was far from monolithic with regard to concepts of the (or "a") messiah's role or the desired results of a messiah's work. Jesus' understanding (label it the Isaiah option) had a long history and could be found among the population.

Other options existed as well. For example, the Zealots seem to have thought in terms of a military/political messiah figure who would defeat the Romans and reestablish the old Davidic kingdom (at least as they imagined that kingdom to have been). The apostles sometimes seemed to embrace a vision of the Messiah that leaves little if any room for suffering, let alone death. The Essenes, insofar as I can tell, seem to have envisioned a great war in which the Children of Light joined with God to make God's enemies (and theirs) suffer! On and on it goes. It seems the more we learn about the first-century Jewish world, the more complicated the picture becomes.

My point, then, is that Jesus' take certainly upended the expectations of a sizable percentage of first-century Jewish listeners, not because it was exclusive to him but because they did not share his perspective. When the Beatitudes moved out into first-century Gentile cultures, they ran counter to normal expectations. As for our own time, it seems to me that the Beatitudes, including the one in question, challenge typical American assumptions about happiness.

Historical matters aside, when taken seriously, this beatitude (and its companions) ought to frighten us a bit. Each vies to replace our survival instinct with something quite different: willing reliance on and identification with God and the ways of God. Such a life makes little sense to most of the world at any time, which seldom takes seriously anything other than defensive or coercive power.

Rami: I have no quarrel with any of this, Mike. One way to understand the different Judaisms under Roman occupation is to see them as different ways of dealing with that occupation.

The Sadducees, the wealthy and priestly classes, collaborated with Rome, both for personal gain and to keep the people from further persecution. The Romans murdered thousands of Jews and violently repressed dissent of any kind. Crucifixion was commonplace and was used to keep the people from resisting, so collaborating with Rome in order to minimize the violence made sense to many.

The Essenes were separatists who, as you say, awaited the coming War of the Sons of Light against the Sons of Darkness. This was, perhaps, the prototype of John of Patmos's Book of Revelation.

The Zealots wanted war as well but had no desire to wait for God to start it. They ambushed the Romans whenever possible, and saw themselves as freedom fighters while the Romans no doubt saw them as terrorists. The Jewish Wars of 66 to 70 and 132 to 135 showed the passion of the people for freedom and their inability to wrest it from Rome.

The Pharisees walked a middle way, collaborating when forced to do so and creating a home-based Judaism alongside the temple. Jesus, I believe, was a Pharisee, which is why much of the Gospel writers' wrath is directed against Pharisees as a way of distinguishing Jesus from his colleagues.

While trained as a Pharisee and thus bearing the title Rabbi, Jesus offered a fifth way to deal with Rome: nonviolent confrontation. He didn't disengage from everyday life, nor did he collaborate with the occupiers or their minions. His teachings about turning the other cheek, walking the extra mile, and giving even one's underwear to the debtor courts are, when understood in the context of the time, brilliant acts of nonviolent resistance that I hope to get to when we talk about the third beatitude.

For now, let me simply say that Jesus was a globalist. Judaism was (and still is) a tribal religion. Of all the world's religions, only Buddhism, Christianity, and Islam see themselves as global faiths. Hinduism and Judaism, for example, are regional religions, spreading only because of the migration of their followers and not because of any internal dynamic of their own.

Jesus saw spirituality beyond tribalism. I think this is clear in his conversation with the Samaritan woman who asks him which people, the Jews or the Samaritans, worship on the right mountain. Jesus replies that while the Jews have the right mountain, a time is coming when mountains (and hence tribal divisions) won't matter, and people will worship "in spirit and truth" (John 4:23). This and other statements turn the tribalism of Judaism on its head.

Jesus is no less radical today, though he has been domesticated by his followers who choose to worship him rather than follow him. People are no less tribal today than they were two thousand years ago. Today's tribes are not necessarily rooted in geography but in creed, denomination, class, race, and ethnicity. But the mentality is the same: us versus them, winners and losers, the saved and the damned.

The Jesus I love would have nothing to do with this. But then, the Jesus I love died on the cross.

Chapter 3

The Third Beatitude

Blessed are the meek, for they will inherit the earth. (Matthew 5:5, NRSV)

Mike: Jesus may have drawn from Psalm 37:11 to fashion the third beatitude. Psalm 37:11 reads, "But the meek shall inherit the land, and delight themselves in abundant prosperity" (NRSV). Jesus substituted "earth" for "land," thus enlarging the scope of the promise. The Greek term used for "meek" is *praeis*. The term appears to be an apt translation of the Hebrew term *anaw* (meek).

Psalm 37:11 helps us grasp what Jesus had in mind. In the psalm, the meek are portrayed as those who are gentle or considerate. They submit willingly to God. The psalm contrasts such folk with "the wicked," those who resist or oppose God.

Jesus described himself as "meek" (Matt 11:29). It is also worth noting that Moses is called "meek" (Num 12:3). No leader or would-be leader in the larger Greco-Roman world would have wished to be so described. In the emerging Roman Empire, meekness was generally regarded as a weakness, not a virtue. I find it interesting that the greatest figures in our respective traditions share the distinction of being called "meek."

Jesus, of course, spoke the words in a particular context: the Roman occupation. Many thanks, Rami, for pointing this out. N. T. Wright, in addition to the two authors you have already mentioned, helps us think through the political implications of Jesus' teachings.[1] In this case ("meekness"), Jesus calls for a nonviolent response to oppression. He will address the matter more than once in the remainder of the Sermon on the Mount, insisting that meekness includes both our attitude and actions with regard to oppressors. Jesus' brand of nonviolence requires that we give up the option of hating our enemies in favor of loving (*agape*) them, even as we turn the other cheek or willingly walk an extra mile.

What about "inherit the earth"? I suppose it is possible that Jesus had a "new earth" in mind. Personally, I think the phrase should be read in the larger context of the meek and their willing submission to God's way or God's rule. Such submission requires that we die to possessiveness, in some way give up what hitherto we've believed to be our due. Strangely enough, when we do so, we find that we can enjoy the earth not because we own a piece of it but simply because it is our common dwelling place, a gift from God. Genuine possession does not involve ownership but instead gratitude, stewardship, and enjoyment.

Like all the beatitudes, the third one calls us to follow Jesus by opting out of the "game of life" as generally understood and buying in to a new way of life.

Rami: You have covered this text fully, Mike, and I don't have much to offer. Let me just add a few comments around the edges.

Regarding Jesus substituting "earth" for "land," the Hebrew word *eretz* is used three times in Psalm 37 (vv. 11, 22, and 29), and in all three "earth" is an accurate translation. We see the same thing in Psalm 24:1: "The earth is HaShem's, and the fullness thereof." The Hebrew is again *eretz*, and it clearly means the whole planet. So Jesus is operating well within the Jewish tradition when he says that the meek will inherit the earth.

Who are the meek? Psalm 37 tells us that to be counted among the *anavim*, the meek, one must trust in God, refrain from competing with those who do evil, avoid anger, practice generosity, cultivate grace, turn from evil and do good, and speak wisdom and justice.

I am drawn to Psalm 37:3, "Trust in HaShem and do good," and verse 27, "Turn from evil and do good." The parallel form suggests that you demonstrate your trust in God by turning from evil and doing good. When surrounded by evil, our temptation is to battle it, and when we do we inevitably come to imitate it. Torah and Jesus offer us an alternative. Torah calls it turning from evil; Jesus calls it nonviolent resistance.

Jesus says, "Do not resist one who is evil. But if anyone strikes you on the right cheek, turn to him the other also; and if anyone would sue you and take your coat, let him have your cloak as well; and if anyone forces you to go one mile, go with him two miles" (Matt 5:39-41). These are bold acts of nonviolent revolutionaries.

Why does Jesus specifically mention the "right cheek"? Because Roman occupation law allowed Roman soldiers to strike Jews backhanded on the right cheek. Slapping someone on the left cheek was done only among equals. Jesus is saying, "Do not acquiesce to being treated like a dog. If they are going to hit you, dare them to hit you like a fellow human."

The same is true of walking the extra mile. Roman occupation law permitted soldiers to force a Jew to carry his gear for up to one mile. Jesus is saying, "Don't resist the first mile, but don't let them treat you like a mule. Carry the gear as a human being by freely going the second mile."

Jesus confronts not only the injustice of Rome but also the injustice of the Jewish courts. In an economic system that exploits the poor and powerless, it was commonplace for the poor to use their clothing as collateral for securing loans. If the loan could not be repaid, the court would force the debtor to give up his clothes. Jesus says, "If they take your outer wear, give them your underwear as well, and walk naked into the street that all may see the moral corruption of the courts and those who uphold them." As we saw with the horrible photos of naked prisoners in Abu Ghraib, being stripped naked has terrible repercussions in Middle Eastern cultures. I think Jesus was drawing on this fact.

This is what it is to be *anav*, meek. Through bold acts of nonviolence, the *anavim* reveal just how immoral the ruling system is, and in this way they bring about its collapse under the weight of its own immorality. The game Jesus challenges us to opt out of, then, is not the game of life in general but the game of exploitation, oppression, suppression, and evil that comes to dominate life in so many societies.

Mike: Thanks, Rami, for the clarification regarding "land" and "earth." You've corrected several Christian commentators with regard to that point!

On to the fourth beatitude!

Note

1. See, e.g., *The New Testament and the People of God*, vol. 1 (Minneapolis: Fortress, 1992); *Surprised by Hope: Rethinking Heaven, the Resurrection, and the Mission of the Church* (New York: HarperOne, 2008); *Simply Jesus: A New Vision of Who He Was, What He Did, and Why He Matters* (New York: HarperOne, 2011); *How God Became King* (New York: HarperOne, 2012).

Chapter 4

The Fourth Beatitude

Blessed are those who hunger and thirst for righteousness, for they will be filled. (Matthew 5:6, NRSV)

Mike: Note Luke's briefer version: "Blessed are you who are hungry now, for you will be filled" (Luke 6:21, NRSV). Whatever else Jesus' vision of God's kingdom entailed, it included satisfaction of plain human hunger. I suspect many of those who heard Jesus' words interpreted them in just this fashion. To my way of thinking, this is a sharp reminder that any theology or religious practice that separates the body's needs from spiritual needs is fatally flawed.

During the latter part of the first century, the Christian movement deliberately made provision for feeding the poor and hungry part of its worship and practice. More often than not, an offering of food was taken, and that food was then distributed to the hungry. Christian communities became known as places where a hungry person could get a meal. Such communities, at the very least, had caught a bit of the vision of Jesus.

Matthew's account expands the saying's reach to include hunger and thirst for righteousness. Many of those who heard Jesus would have had experience with hunger. They knew the kind of physical/mental/emotional yearning genuine hunger or thirst generates. Jesus blessed those who had a similar consuming need for righteousness.

What kind of righteousness? I think the most natural and likely answer is the rule of God, the kingdom of God. It's the kind of yearning that causes one to ache for things to be as they are supposed to be, for God's rule to be fully effective in the world at large and in each individual. That which we've thought to be nourishing food and drink now sticks in our throats. If swallowed, it neither feeds nor waters us. We know we need something more, something real.

Jesus promised that such yearnings would be satisfied. The Greek term *choriasthesoniai* carries the notion of being completely filled. Insofar as I can determine, Jesus believed that he had come to begin the fulfillment of the promise.

Let's step away from language, the first century, and theology for a moment and ask, "How might the beatitude play out in my life?" In my case, I sometimes find that I yearn deeply for God's rule in my life and in the world at large. The simplest way to satisfy (partially) such a hunger is to do something congruent with the active rule of God. Feed a hungry person, intervene in the life of an abused child or spouse, take a loving action toward an enemy—you get the drift.

The world is not the way it ought to be! But each time I act as if God is ruling, I challenge the way of the world. I offer an alternative. Whether the world pays any attention or not, at least for a moment God rules in the small space I occupy, and my hunger is satisfied for a time. Someone else might just experience the loving rule of God through me as well.

Rami: I'm struck by the differences between Matthew and Luke regarding the Beatitudes. Luke doesn't know about the mourners and the meek. He has no idea that Jesus spoke about the merciful, the pure in heart, the peacemakers, or the persecuted. Given the centrality of the Sermon on the Mount to Jesus' message, one would expect all four Gospels to record it with some consistency. But of course they don't.

My sense is that each Gospel writer shaped Jesus in his own image, after his likeness. Matthew's Jesus, for example, is concerned with the poor in spirit (Matt 5:3); Luke's Jesus is concerned with the poor (Luke 6:20). Matthew's Jesus is concerned with those who hunger for righteousness (Matt 5:6); Luke's Jesus is concerned with the hungry (Luke 6:21). In other words, Matthew's Jesus is a revolutionary, while Luke's Jesus is a social worker.

Given this, I think it is crucial that we not skip over Luke's use of the word "now." In Matthew, Jesus puts off the fullness of those who hunger and thirst after righteousness into the future, but in Luke he wants to fill the bellies of the hungry immediately.

The two ideas are not antithetical, however. They are sequential. As any good revolutionary knows, you can't win over hearts and minds until you have won over empty bellies and parched throats. Matthew also realizes this, which is why in Matthew 25:31-46, his Jesus speaks about caring for "the least of these." Because this text brings Matthew's revolutionary into alignment with Luke's social worker, it is surprising to me that Luke doesn't record the speech at all.

You seem to favor Luke over Matthew in your last comments, and I am struck by your notion of playing "as if." When we act as if the kingdom of God were among us, it is.

This reminds me of the response of the Israelites to the reading of all God's commandments by Moses in Sinai: "*Na'aseh v'nishmah*, we will do and we will hear" (Exod 24:7). One would expect the word order to be reversed: "We will hear and we will do," but that isn't what Torah says. Why? Perhaps because we only hear the deeper meaning of the commandments when we are actively doing them. This is a central Jewish concept with which Jesus and the Gospel writers were undoubtedly familiar, and one you, too, seem to have adopted.

When we act as if this were the kingdom of God rather than the kingdom of greed, we actually establish and expand God's kingdom in the world. This is not simply affirming the primacy of deeds over faith, but recognizing that it takes faith in the efficacy of deeds to act for the kingdom of God in the face (and it is often a dazzlingly seductive face) of the kingdom of greed.

So, once again, we are in basic agreement. But lest we be mistaken for clones, let me nitpick your closing comment: "The world is not the way it ought to be!"

On the contrary, given the way we act, the world is exactly the way it ought to be, which is why your suggestion is so compelling. If we don't like the way the world is, and we recognize that the world is the way it is because of our actions, the proper response isn't to wish things to be otherwise or even to have faith that God will, sometime in the future, make it otherwise, but to do things differently here and now. To paraphrase the line from the film *Field of Dreams*, "If we live it, it will come" (dir. Phil Alden Robinson, Gordon Company, 1989).

Mike: Much ink (and considerable electronic space) has been taken up with discussions of the differences between Matthew and Luke. The differences are interesting, but I suspect we moderns make more of them than those in the ancient world. Try as we might, we cannot shed our contemporary assumptions regarding strict accuracy, spin, scholarly review, consistency, and the like. One of the ironies of our time is that both higher criticism and fundamentalism have been shaped in the crucible of modernity.

Here's how I think of the task undertaken by the Synoptic Gospel writers. An old teacher of mine used to tell a fable that went as follows. Once upon a time, a group of tourists took a tour of Yellowstone National Park.

Their guide led them near Old Faithful and explained how heat and pressure built up inside the earth on a fairly predictable schedule to produce an eruption. He assured his group that an eruption was scheduled to occur at any moment.

Just then a man appeared seemingly out of nowhere. He was running for his life. A large, angry grizzly bear was right on his heels. The man leaped over Old Faithful. The bear followed. The geyser erupted, throwing the bear high into the sky and saving the man's life.

My teacher liked to end the story by saying, "To the crowd, the eruption was a predictable event of nature. To the endangered man, it was a miracle. To the bear, it was a catastrophe."

My point is that one may see and hear the same thing, yet focus on various aspects and possibilities of the experience. The differences found in the Synoptic Gospels, for the most part, seem to me to fall within the normal limits one might expect among various witnesses.

Matthew, it seems to me, tended to notice and arrange the teachings of Jesus. Luke, on the other hand, loved a good story, especially if it had a strong human-interest angle. Taken together, they help us see a more nearly complete portrait (not photograph) of Jesus.

Let's shift to playing "as if." You and I certainly agree on this point. I appreciate the Hebrew Bible references. The same idea crops up fairly often throughout Christian history. If you want a modern example, look no farther than Dorothy Day (twentieth century). In her journals she noted how hard it was to love many of the stubborn, cranky, ungrateful persons to whom she devoted her life. She also insisted, though, that the best way to start to learn to love was to act lovingly. I find that this approach works with regard to all kingdom of God matters.

As for your final point, the one you label nitpicking, I suppose we disagree a bit. I do not think that the world as it is accords well with God's dream for creation. Certainly, we agree that we bear enormous responsibility for marring the creation and that subset of creation we call human society. Simply because we mess up a recipe and produce a terrible meal does not mean the recipe has changed. It means we need to learn to read and follow a recipe!

If we practice being kingdom of God people, we get better at it. Eventually, practice produces faith and faith, in turn, sustains practice.

I'm not sure I have much more to add in regard to this beatitude. If you wish, we can move on to the next one.

Rami: I agree we should move on, but I have to say I'm not convinced by your professor's parable. If the point is that no one Gospel has the whole picture, then I prefer the Indian fable of the blind men and the elephant. Each man sought to explain what an elephant is from his own narrow vantage point: one touching the trunk, another the tail, etc. None were wrong, but none were right, either. They each had a piece of the truth, and only by putting all the pieces together do we get a closer approximation of what an elephant truly is.

Using this analogy, each Gospel adds to our understanding of Jesus, but none has a complete picture. I agree with this and would urge people to read noncanonical gospels as well to get even more pieces of the puzzle. But I don't see that the Old Faithful story helps us here at all.

While we can argue that the guide in the story had a piece of the truth, i.e., that the eruption of Old Faithful was a predictable event, and while we can argue that the eruption was catastrophic for the bear, I don't see how we can say it was a miracle, unless we define miracle as a natural event about which people are simply ignorant. This eventually does away with miracles altogether, something I'm not sure your professor meant to do.

I'm also having trouble with your idea that focusing on the differences among the Gospels is a modernist conceit. There were lots of gospels from which to choose when the New Testament canon was formed. Those who did the choosing were clearly concerned about the differences among the gospels, which is why they left most gospels out of the New Testament. The fact that they were less troubled by the differences among the four Gospels they did choose doesn't mean that we should ignore those differences. Indeed, when we see what the canonical Gospels have in common over and against the other gospels, we can see the biases of the church fathers who put the canon together.

For me, differences are everything, and I can't see how "the differences found in the Synoptic Gospels . . . fall within the normal limits one might expect among various witnesses." To take only the example of the Sermon on the Mount, how is it that the witnesses in Luke heard so much less than the witnesses in Matthew? And how come Mark and John (not to mention Paul) know nothing of the sermon at all?

Again, differences are crucial to our investigation. I think this focus on differences may be a Jewish trait: we are trained to look for the discordant in our sacred texts, and we believe that new insight can be found in the place of disagreement and conflict. But then I've never been to Yellowstone National Park.

Mike: Obviously, I managed to push a few buttons!

I agree that the story of the blind men and the elephant works best. That's why, insofar as I know, it's the "standard." The Yellowstone fable works along the same lines, only with a more heavy-handed comedic tone. Like all fables, it breaks down if subjected to "objective" analysis. Fables deal in broad strokes, not particulars.

Differences matter. We agree. Still, I suspect that the modern era (the past few centuries) has taught most of us to analyze and define most everything in terms of differences. I think this works well for science, and it's a handy tool for almost any academic discipline. It's been quite useful for biblical scholars as well. Still, I wonder if we have not become so conditioned to pounce on differences that we sometimes forget that it might be just as helpful to start with something as it is.

Take a good story, for example. The first thing to do with a story is to hear or read it as it is, to enjoy and respond to the whole, to allow it to interface with your imagination as it may. Later, perhaps, there may be good reason to play the critic. While doing so, we may discover or guess at the origin, writing process, and editing of the story. We may even suggest how the plot, character development, or dialogue could be improved. Critics, of course, face a particular danger: they may lose sight of the story itself. I'm not picking on critics (I am one!) but instead merely stating the obvious: all disciplines carry their particular temptations and dangers. Biblical criticism is not exempt.

As for the human capacity to witness the same event yet report it in wholly different fashions, I suppose we simply disagree. After thirty-four years of speaking several times a week to people who have come to know me well and who listen with some attention, I continue to be amazed at their diverse memories. They tend to hear and see everything through their personal filters, including not only basic content but even setting, body language, and intent. Their memories sift through and select pieces of a given sermon or lesson, and they organize their memories in ways that may or may not accord with my memory of the sermon event!

As for Mark, John, and even Paul, I'm not certain it's correct to say that they know nothing of the sermon simply because they do not deal with it *per se.* We could go round and round over whether or how the three incorporated insights from the sermon into their works. For example, I think 1 Corinthians 13 probably owes a great deal to Paul's assimilation of the sermon, which then spills out "in his own words."

All of the above leads me to feel comfortable in choosing to deal with the story of the Sermon on the Mount as we receive it in Matthew, even as I make use of Luke's own version as a supplement. When I focus on Luke's account (sometimes called the Sermon on the Plain), Matthew becomes the supplement.

Great fun! Looking back over this entry, I suppose I must say that you managed to push a few of my buttons as well!

Rami: I can't let this go without one more comment, albeit one that is somewhat tongue-in-cheek.

You mentioned that Luke's version of Matthew's Sermon on the Mount is called the Sermon on the Plain. Even if we were to allow that people hear what they want to hear and that this explains the differences between Matthew and Luke (something I cannot fully accept), it still strikes me as odd that the people listening to Jesus couldn't remember if they were standing on a mountain or a plain. Talk about not paying attention!

All right. Enough. Please lead us to the next beatitude before I start babbling on about how Paul wrote long before any of the Gospel writers and that since he mentions almost nothing of the Jesus narrative (Virgin Birth, parables, Sermon on the Something, etc.), there is a case to be made that these were all narrative flourishes of great writers.

I love the Bible—the Hebrew Bible, the Apocrypha, and the New Testament—and one of the reasons I love it is because it is great fiction, and like all great fiction it is at times deeply and powerfully true. I have no more problem with the differences between biblical texts than I do with differences among Shakespeare's plays. And just as the truth found in Shakespeare has nothing to do with the historicity of his plays, so the truth of the Bible has, for me, nothing to do with historicity of the stories. The story's the thing. Let's get back to it.

Chapter 5

The Fifth Beatitude

Blessed are the merciful, for they shall receive mercy. (Matthew 5:7, NRSV)

Mike: Many Christian commentators of my acquaintance argue that the first four beatitudes deal with the interior life, then go on to say that the fifth beatitude strikes off in a new direction, namely behavior. I think the distinction is too neatly drawn. All the beatitudes assume a vital connection between one's heart, mind, tongue, and hands. They deal with the whole person.

The fifth beatitude calls for those who would live under the rule of God to act mercifully toward others. Micah 6:8 no doubt informed the beatitude. ("What does the LORD require of you? To do justice, and to love mercy, and to walk humbly with your God.") Various commentators note that late in the first century CE, Gamaliel II said, "So long as you are merciful, the Merciful is merciful to you." In short, the core concept was in the air.

That's not to say it was the majority position in first-century Jewish life, let alone broader Greco-Roman culture. The position's call for mercy naturally raised the question of limits. Should such mercy be extended to the Romans—in other words, even to one's oppressors? Did the mercy requirement cross religious and ethnic boundaries (for example, the Samaritans)? Could someone's decisions and actions place him or her beyond the possibility of mercy (think of the parable of the loving father and his two sons)? I think we continue to ask the same questions. Only the examples have changed.

What about justice? If living under the rule of God required that one become merciful, who would ensure that justice was done? A Jewish friend in another part of the USA, pointedly raised this question in a group setting. He said (more or less), "You people [he meant Christians] don't get it. We [he meant Jews] aren't interested in grace or mercy toward those who try to kill us. Only justice will suffice. Mercy changes nothing. In fact, it only encourages the oppressors. Justice, though, strikes the needed blow. The world needs justice, not mercy." He was angry, of course. Knowing him, I think his emotion led him to overstate his point. Still, it was well made, and it gave me pause. I suspect that this kind of question lurks in the backs of the minds of most of us.

Jesus was a visionary. We must keep this in mind as we wrestle with the fifth beatitude. When all live under the rule of God, mercy and justice become one. In the meantime, those who willingly subject themselves to God's rule experience his mercy. As we come to grips with being forgiven by the One who is just beyond our comprehension, our potential for practicing mercy toward others grows. Strangely enough, the more mercy we extend, the more aware we become of the mercy we receive, both from God and from others.

At the personal level, the practice of mercy changes us. Over time it blunts resentment, reduces our thirst for revenge, expands our friendship circles, teaches us to pause before reacting, induces empathy, and fosters humility.

Lest I sound naive, I hasten to add that mercy granting is dangerous in the world as it is. The merciful are blessed, but they may also be victimized by the violent, greedy, or vengeful. The merciful may find that they are prime candidates for martyrdom. Christians, of course, do well to remember a phrase Jesus spoke from his cross: "Father, forgive them, for they do not know what they do."

Rami: Your Jewish friend is not alone in the notion of "no justice, no peace." And he has a point. Peace in and of itself can simply perpetuate the exploitation of the powerless. Justice is the higher value and will in time lead to peace. But I doubt that is what your friend was talking about. He doesn't want justice; he wants revenge.

The primary justice issue for Jews today has to do with Israel's treatment of her Arab citizens and Palestinian neighbors. Many Jews want to blame the Palestinians for all the ills of the region, but any objective observer knows that both sides act wickedly. Mercy might be the more strategic choice, allowing Palestinian anger and fear of Israelis (and Israeli anger and fear of Palestinians) to cool. Then they might be able to work together for justice. There are hundreds of peace groups in Israel involving Israelis and Palestinians, and all of them take compassion and mercy as the first step to justice and peace.

The real challenge I see in this beatitude is to define what we mean, or what Jesus may have meant, by "mercy." I would define mercy behaviorally: "That which is hateful to you, do not do to others," to quote Rabbi Hillel (Talmud, Shabbat 31a); or, in Jesus' formulation, "Do unto others as you would have others do unto you" (Matt 7:12). Every religion teaches this ethics of reciprocity, and because it is so clearly reciprocal it may well be the idea behind this beatitude: be merciful and you will receive mercy.

With this definition in mind we can take up the questions you raise. Should Jews in Jesus' day act mercifully toward their Roman occupiers? Yes, for that is the only way to effect change. Should the priest and Levite violate their legal obligations to avoid dead bodies and look to see if the person they pass on the road is actually dead? Of course, isn't that what they would want of others if they themselves had been mugged and left dying on the roadside?

The parable of the two sons (Matt 21:28-32), however, seems to be a different kind of story. First, there is no reason to assume as you do that the father was "loving." Jesus only says "a man had two sons." Second, there is the assumption that doing the will of the father is the right thing to do. Knowing nothing about this father, I can't say if working the vineyard was the right thing to do or not.

If, of course, the father is God, the vineyard is the world, and working in the vineyard means feeding the hungry, clothing the naked, freeing the unjustly imprisoned, etc., then I would say it is the right thing to do, and doing it, even against one's initial inclination, is superior to not doing it. But where does mercy come into play?

At first I didn't see it. The father isn't merciful; we know nothing of his reaction to his son's decisions. But Jesus is, and his mercy really struck me. Jesus clearly equates the priests with whom he is talking with the son who agrees to work the vineyard but does not actually do so. Rather than condemn these people, Jesus just says, "tax collectors and prostitutes are going into the kingdom of God ahead of you" (Matt 21:31). The priests won't be denied access to the kingdom; they just won't be at the head of the line. This is another stunning act of mercy that most of Jesus' followers have yet to imagine, let alone practice.

Your application of this beatitude to our personal lives was right on target. But let me highlight your reminder that Jesus was a visionary.

It isn't that Jesus saw what the world could be like if people lived the principles he taught in the Beatitudes; it was that Jesus actually saw the kingdom of God as a reality. To pick up and invert an earlier point, it isn't only that we live "as if" we were in the kingdom of God and in so doing bring the kingdom into being. It is also the case that the kingdom of God is here and now, and that by seeing it (being a visionary), one knows how to act in accordance with it.

Both ways work. Jesus embodied the latter: he saw the truth and lived it. But in the Sermon on the Mount he taught the former, knowing that not everyone has the eyes to see. Both the way of the seer and the way of the doer lead to the same reality: a just, compassionate, and peaceful world where all beings are seen as the children of God.

Mike: Rami, I apologize for not providing a Scripture reference for the loving father and his two sons. I had in mind Luke's account of what we used to call the "Parable of the Prodigal Son." If you want to alter your comments in light of this information, have at it!

I especially like the way your interpretation of the beatitude makes room both for the visionary and the doer. In addition, I suspect that you may be right in connecting giving mercy to "Do unto others as you would have them do unto you."

You may be correct. All religions may stress such a teaching. I've never had the resources or time to verify the truism. Like "mercy," we might need to determine the definition of religion in question. For example, if religion is that which brings structure, meaning, and direction to life (the broadest definition I can think of, off the cuff), many "isms" and their ilk come into play. The two of us could generate quite a list! For example, I would argue that raw consumerism, capitalism, communism, and the like give short shrift to mercy. In fact, undiluted versions of such "religions" regard mercy as weakness.

Mercy, it turns out, is highly subversive!

The practice of mercy changes us in a number of ways and quickly teaches us our limits. We run out of steam in short order. In my own experience, I find the practice of centering prayer essential to the ongoing practice of mercy. Giving mercy prompts the development of empathy as well. The more often we grant mercy, the more keenly we come to sense our kinship. All of us fail and hurt others and stand in need of mercy. My hunch is that giving mercy ultimately engenders the growth of God's kind of love within us, both *hesed* (unbreakable love) and *agape* (self-giving love). In fact, the practice of mercy may be the key spiritual discipline required.

Rami: I thought you might be referring to the "Parable of the Prodigal Son," but since there is also the "Parable of the Two Sons" I figured I was wrong. So let me take you up on the offer to comment on the Prodigal Son story, as it is one of the most subversive of Jesus' teachings.

For those who might not remember, the story is of a father with two sons, one who is dutiful and the other wayward. When the latter finds himself at rock bottom, he returns home asking only to be accepted back as a slave. His father welcomes him home with full honors, much to the chagrin of the dutiful son.

The reason the story is so subversive is that the father, who is of course God, neither stops the wayward son from being wayward nor punishes him for the life he has chosen. God is beyond reward and punishment; God simply allows us to reap what we sow. We make our own heaven and hell, and God won't keep us from either. But when we hit rock bottom—that is to say, when we have taken the illusion of our separation from God and godliness so far as to leave ourselves unable to function—and ask to come home, i.e., ask to be reawakened to the radical nonduality of woman, man, nature, and God, God is only too happy to reawaken us.

This kind of God is so *not* the god most people want. Most people want a god who welcomes them and rejects those whom they themselves reject. We create god in our image to justify the lives we want to live and the evil we desire to do. Religion is too often simply an institutional expression of human fear, anger, ignorance, and greed. Religions, especially those that mistake monotheism (there is one God) for monopolistic theism (there is one God and we control him), hate the theology of Jesus. If they can ignore it, they will. If they can't ignore it, they will pervert it.

Obviously I have strong feelings about this, but I'm not that far off the mark.

I agree with you, Mike, that religion provides structure, meaning, and direction, and I agree that many other things do as well. I simply doubt that any institution can be trusted when it comes to questions of justice and mercy.

I prefer to understand religion etymologically. It comes from the Latin *religio*, which itself is a combination of two words: *ligare*, "bind, connect," and the prefix *re*, which gives us the meaning "reconnect." Religion is the way we overcome the illusion of our separation from God and reconnect or, as I put it, realize our unbroken unity with God, the One who manifests as the many. Religion for me is more about contemplative practice than about creed, belief, and the politics of piety.

While I value the need for community, I find little need for organized religion in my life. What I do need are contemplative practices designed to wake me up from the egoic illusion of being separate from God. You mentioned one of these practices, centering prayer, as central to your life, and I would urge people to look into this practice either by finding a community devoted to it or by reading any of the books by Father Thomas Keating, one of the great gurus of contemporary centering prayer practice.

For anyone interested in Jewish contemplative practice, I would recommend two of my own books: *Minyan: Ten Practices for Living a Life of Integrity,* and (for anyone interested in an interfaith approach to compassion) *The Sacred Art of Lovingkindness.*[1] Yes, this is a shameless plug, but I trust that you will have mercy on me for trying to make a living.

Mike: The parable of the loving father and his two sons probably generates more commentary than any other parable, with the possible exception of the good Samaritan. Both speak of "mercy."

We seem to be in broad agreement as to the meaning and necessity of mercy. In God's kingdom, mercy is both given and received. You might say that mercy is the coin of the realm.

We may differ over institutions. Perhaps now is the time to unpack the matter and see if this is so.

Humans build community and institutions. It matters not whether one relies on biblical accounts, evolutionary theory, or historical study; all three suggest humanity's bent in this direction. The same sources, though, also confirm and affirm the importance of the individual. Both individuals and institutions may go bad—that is, become self-centered, defensive, and dedicated primarily to self-protection. Conversely, both may be instruments of grace and mercy. Individuals usually run far ahead of institutions in this regard. The institution may, in time, be reformed by such individuals.

Take the matter of slavery and the Quakers in the United States. Colonial-era Quakers generally supported slavery, and some owned slaves. John Woolman, a Quaker, came to believe slavery was a sin. Over the decades of his life, he traveled throughout the colonies, challenging his faith community to abandon slavery and any economic practices that supported it. To say the least, he often was not well received. Yet by the end of his life, Quakers in the United States had changed, community by community. They adopted Woolman's stance. The institution had been reformed so that it became a force for abolition.

I am not fond of institutions. They are big, given to support of the status quo, often impersonal, and self-satisfied. This is certainly true of organized religions, and I suspect it is true of any institution. God, though, seems to be out to redeem (reconnect, recall, awaken, etc.) the entire creation. Institutions are part of the human world, so I find myself compelled to focus not only on the individual but on institutional redemption.

That's a long way of saying we are called to practice mercy, certainly toward others and most likely toward institutions as well. Our previous discussion about the interplay of justice and mercy should not be forgotten.

Rami: Humans, I agree, are tribal creatures. We run in packs and form clans, tribes, states, nations, etc. I doubt we will ever overcome this drive to huddle together, nor should we. Belonging to a tribe is part of what it is to be human. One of the problems with tribalism, however, is its tendency toward jingoism and exclusivity. When we begin to think that our tribe is superior to others or that other tribes should be subsumed into our tribe, or at least subjugated to it, then community becomes a cancer in the body politic. We need a new sense of tribalism that honors diversity in a greater system of unity.

A second danger inherent in tribalism is its lack of respect for the individual qua individual. The true celebration of individuality is a creation of the Enlightenment thinkers of eighteenth-century Europe and America. They planted the ideas that ultimately grew into the abolition of slavery and women's suffrage, two hallmarks of individual freedom that much if not most of the world has yet to embrace.

Free thinkers from Socrates to Jesus to Mary Dyer, the Quaker who was hung on Boston Common in 1660 by her Christian neighbors because of her faith, all face the same fate. And while I agree that both individuals and institutions go bad, it is the evil of the institution that I fear more deeply. Hitler without the German State behind him was just another anti-Semite.

Your example of John Woolman is heartening, and there are many examples of individuals who have changed and perhaps even revolutionized society. Think of Moses, Jesus, Paul, Marx, Freud, and Einstein, to name but six in the Jewish pantheon of civilization shifters. This is why I am more apt to place my hope in individuals than institutions. But I am really interested in where you bring God into the picture.

God, to me, is the ultimate antiestablishmentarian. God is a force of creative destruction: knocking down the old and giving birth to the new. This is how I understand the death and resurrection of Jesus (as well as Osiris, Isis, Horus, Tammuz, etc.) and the destruction of the temple in Jerusalem some decades later: the death of God and temple is the death of our ideas about God that allows for the truth of God to emerge.

Religions, especially creedal and theologically driven religions, mistake ideas about God for God. They worship what they know, and what they know cannot be the true God for the true God is unknowable. God is like the horizon: we can march toward it, but we will never arrive at it. The death of Jesus and the destruction of the temple are, mythically speaking, God's way of pulling the theological rug out from under us, forcing us to live by faith rather than belief. You cannot create an institution around God, for as soon as you do, God is reduced to "god" and you simply have another idolatry.

But when we face the unknown and unknowable God, we are stripped of all our ideologies and "isms"; we are transformed by grace and made merciful. I believe that mercy, along with compassion, justice, and humility, are the hallmarks of one who knows she does not know, and has learned to live the wisdom of not knowing that is true faith.

People like these, known and unknown, continually reshape our institutions in the light of mercy. It is in them that I place my hope for a better world.

Note

1. *Minyan: Ten Principles for Living a Life of Integrity* (New York: Bell Tower, 1997); *Sacred Art of Lovingkindness* (Woodstock VT: Skylight Paths, 2006).

Chapter 6

The Sixth Beatitude

Blessed are the pure in heart, for they will see God. (Matthew 5:8, NRSV)

Mike: Psalm 24:3-4 may serve as background to this beatitude. The psalmist asks who shall ascend God's hill and stand in "his holy place." The answer is he (or she) with clean hands, a pure heart, and a life given to truthfulness.

In any case, Jesus opts for a briefer statement. The pure in heart will see God. "Heart," in the New Testament, is equivalent to the will. We might paraphrase the sixth beatitude, "Blessed are the pure in will, for they will see God." Jesus, to borrow a phrase from Kierkegaard, calls his followers to choose to "will one thing." They are to cultivate a single-minded devotion to God. Such focus may open our eyes so that we see God.

This beatitude implies that most of us lack such a focus. I think this true. People of faith genuinely want to see (experience, know, etc.) God, but they also want a good many other things. To borrow from another saying of Jesus, we find it hard to sell all we have in order to purchase the pearl of great price. We like to think that we can keep what we have and get the pearl as well. We're like a young man who greatly desires to marry a certain woman but refuses to stop dating other women. A divided heart (will) ultimately leaves us out in the cold.

Perhaps this is why Jesus found it necessary to say, "Seek ye first the kingdom of God . . . and all these things shall be added unto you" (Matt 6:33, KJV).

What happens if we become "pure of heart"? At the very least, we start to "see God." We see what we learn to see. Focused on God, we begin to see the divine in others. Some of us catch a glimpse of God in history, a good story, or nature itself. The longer we focus on God, the more apt we are to see God in ourselves as well. Everything in life becomes a God thing.

Most of us, me included, never achieve sustained purity of heart. Fed by the occasional experience, however, our desire to do so grows. With practice, we get better. A kind of spiritual muscle memory develops. Good worship, both private and corporate, is largely devoted to strengthening our spiritual muscle memory.

Rami: Psalm 24 is, as you say, a likely source for this beatitude. So is Psalm 73:1, "Surely God is good to Israel, to the pure in heart." And I agree with your take on "heart" as the seat of will. We are not talking about feelings here at all. I am curious, though, as to what it means to "see God."

I am a panentheist. I believe that all (*pan*) reality is in (*en*) God (*theos*). This differs slightly from a pantheist who equates God with the universe. While I believe the universe is part of God, I do not believe it is all of God. God is not other than the universe, but God is greater than the universe.

Anyway, as a panentheist, I see God all the time. Everything I see is God. Of course this is an intellectual seeing, and not the transformative seeing that reveals the kingdom of God. To achieve that level of seeing one must be "pure of heart," so it is vital to our understanding of this beatitude that we understand what being "pure of heart" means.

Let's start with the word pure, *bar* in Hebrew. When coupled with the word *lev*, heart, it means "straightforward"; one who is pure of heart is one who is simple, honest, without deceit and conceit. Now, why would this person see God?

To me the answer is this: the simple person sees self and others without labels, just as they are in and of themselves, which means as manifestations of God. It is only when we drape people in "isms" and ideologies, seeing race, religion, creed, ethnicity, and political affiliation instead of the person they are, that we fail to see people as God.

When we do see people as they are—God manifest in time and space—then we see God in, with, and as all people (and I would say all beings as well). This kind of seeing is transformative in that it leads to a deep sense of compassion for all beings; we see our neighbor (mineral, vegetable, animal, human, etc.) as ourselves. This awakening to the nonduality of God in, with, and as all reality is the key to living the kingdom of God. And to do this we have to see with the blinders of belief.

I think this leads easily into your comment on the divided heart (as opposed to the simple or whole heart). A divided heart separates self from others, from nature, and from God. But division has to be learned. So much of what we do as parents, clergy, and teachers clouds the heart, distorts the eye, and promotes and perpetuates the delusion of division and duality that excuses our desires to exploit and control the world and those in it.

I would even go so far as to say that by teaching us to "seek ye first the kingdom of God . . . and all these things shall be added unto you" (Matt 6:33, KJV), Jesus is challenging us to step beyond belief, to cleanse the heart of division, and in doing so to then see the world as it is: the kingdom of God.

Mike: Two additional matters occurred to me as I read your comments.

I agree that we are taught to see and take advantage of divisions. This raises the old question of nurture and nature. To put it bluntly, I'm afraid that were we not taught division, we would invent it anew on our own. This applies both to the external (political, tribal, territorial, etc.) world and to our own hearts. From my perspective, environment reinforces our inborn tendency toward division and fragmentation. We are born into the kind of world our species has created, and we have then created this world out of the inherent turmoil of the human heart. We have made the world in our own marred image.

As to the second matter, I quite agree with your point. We use our divisions in order to justify our drive to control. The ant queen's song in T. H. White's *The Once and Future King* (London: Collins, 1958) comes to mind, the tune by which she incites her subjects to go to war with another ant colony. In essence, the song celebrates the supposed differences between the two colonies, which boil down to "they do not smell like us."

I also think, though, that a divided heart can lead one to withdraw from others and their struggles and become only an observer. Frankly, I've not thought this through well. The possibility only occurred to me as I read what you wrote. Both of us know of legitimate motivations for such a withdrawal. Some, for example, do so out of a sense of vocation to engage in focused worship and prayer, which includes prayer for the creation and humanity. Others, though, learn just enough to see the dangers of the divided heart. They seek to protect themselves from others (and perhaps protect others from themselves) by retreat. This kind of pseudo purity of heart might serve for some as a first step toward what Jesus had in mind, but it must not become a destination.

Well, as I said, I've not thought the matter through—so I look forward to seeing what your fertile mind might do with it!

Rami: Ah, the old "nature versus nurture" gambit. I agree that this is a dead-horse argument. Indeed, I'm not sure nature and nurture are the opposites we claim them to be. Doesn't the way we nurture reflect our nature? So we are in agreement here.

I also agree with you that people would invent divisions if the ones we have already invented disappeared. You mention *The Once and Future King*, and I'm thinking of Dr. Seuss's *The Butter Battle Book* (New York: Random House, 1984) where the Yooks and the Zooks go to war over which side bread should be buttered on. This is just part of human nature.

In Judaism we speak of the two inclinations at the core of human nature: *Yetzer haTov*, our inclination toward altruism, and *Yetzer haRah*, our inclination toward selfishness. Both are necessary, and each must be informed by the other in order to operate to the benefit of the person as a whole. So there is no way we can create a society that is totally good or totally evil. And yet . . . .

If you put a Palestinian baby in a room with an Israeli baby, the two don't go to war. Sure, one may push the other over to get a toy, but it is the desire for the toy that motivates them and not some ontological hatred of the other as other. That level of hatred and fear has to be fed to them over long periods. So while I agree that without the divisions we have now the world would not be perfect, it still might be a lot less violent.

I think the image of wholeheartedness is important. Moving from a divided heart to a whole heart is key to understanding both Judaism and Jesus. When in Matthew 22:37-40 the Pharisees ask Jesus to name the most important *mizvot* (divine commandment), Jesus quotes the two central texts of the Jewish religion: Deuteronomy 6:5, *Love YHVH your God with a whole heart*, and Leviticus 19:18, *Love your neighbor as yourself.* When you love God with a whole heart, which means you direct both *Yetzer haRah* and *Yetzer haTov* "Godward" toward acts of compassion and justice, you realize the nonduality of all life in, with, and as God, and you naturally love your neighbor as yourself.

Just imagine a religious school devoted to making hearts whole! Rather than learning creeds and traditions, kids learn how to live whole and holy lives. With a focus on wholeheartedness, we could share traditions and contemplative practices from our respective religions as means for cultivating wholeness. No religion would be right or wrong, true or false, as long as it worked toward wholeheartedness. Fantastic!

In fact, I think we should start this school right here in Murfreesboro. I would call it the "Dr. Michael Smith Academy for Spiritual Wholeheartedness." Of course, since your name is on the program, you will have to fund it. I assume that the check is in the mail.

Chapter 7

The Seventh Beatitude

Blessed are the peacemakers, for they shall be called children of God. (Matthew 5:9, NRSV)

Mike: Blessed are the *eirenopoioi*—the makers of peace. I sometimes think this the most challenging of all the beatitudes.

Consider the historical context. Simon "the Zealot" was among the closest followers of Jesus, and Judas may have been a Zealot, or at least sympathetic to their position. Peacemaking was not part of the Zealots' agenda, though perhaps they might have said, "We shall have peace. We shall have peace when every Roman is dead or driven from our land, and when those who cooperated with the Romans have been punished." By saying these words, Jesus took a position within the complicated political life of the time. Obviously, peacemaking does not require that everyone agree with or like the peacemaker's position. Ironically, peacemaking may put one at odds with others or a group!

Many evangelical Christians tend to restrict the beatitude's application to interpersonal relationships. The historical context disallows such a limit. At the very least, the beatitude was a political statement. Followers of Jesus, by implication, are called to be voices for peace and workers toward peace in the broader world.

Jesus claimed to reveal the nature of the rule of God, the kingdom of God, and so the priorities of God. Peacemaking is a top-agenda item with God, indeed part and parcel of the character of God. Using God's name, therefore, to invoke or justify violence, division, and war may well amount to taking the Lord's name (character) in vain.

Peacemaking is not restricted to the political arena. Interpersonal relationships do come into play. Reconciliation is the life work of a Christian. I use the term "work" intentionally. Peacemaking should not be confused with passivity, "going along to get along," or the like. It requires active engagement in the lives of others. Theologically, the incarnation underscores

God's commitment to reconciliation and calls Christians to join in God's work.

The seventh beatitude's promise is that such peacemakers shall be called or recognized as children of God. On the one hand, the promise offers a bit of comfort as we struggle to "make peace" in a divided world. The promise also suggests that peacemaking is the mark or identifying characteristic of a genuine follower of Jesus. So much for going to war (in any fashion) over creeds and the like, as if discerning and adhering to the right formulas marks one as a genuine follower of God.

"The devil is in the details," I suppose. It is one thing to embrace all the above in general and quite another to practice peacemaking with regard to particulars. It's much like the well-worn (but quite accurate) saying with regard to love: "I love humanity; it is people who give me trouble." Still, I see no way out. To follow Jesus well requires that we become and remain peacemakers.

Rami: When it comes to matters of peace, two Jewish texts come to mind, both of which would have been known to Jesus. The first is Psalm 34:14, "Seek peace, and pursue it." The second is from Rabbi Hillel: "Love peace, pursue peace, and love humankind" (*Pirke Avot* 1:12).

Before we can talk about loving, seeking, and pursuing peace, however, we have to define peace itself. The Hebrew word for peace is *shalom* and it shares a root (*sh-l-m*) with the Hebrew word *shalem*, wholeness. Peace is what arises when there is wholeness; that is to say, when we realize that all opposites are complements in the greater unity of God.

To achieve *shalom/shalem* (peace/wholeness), we must overcome our sense of separation from God and the consequent alienation from one another and from nature. As I mentioned earlier, when Adam eats from the tree of knowledge of good and evil, God says he has become *k'achad mimenu* (Gen 3:22), not "like one among us," as most English translations put it, but, more accurately, "like one separate from us." Being separated from God means being separated from all things, for God includes all things. It is this sense of separation and alienation, symbolized by our expulsion from Eden, that is the human condition.

The "original sin" in Judaism is a shattering of wholeness, our sense of belonging and place where, as the Prophet Micah puts it, all people have enough to eat and no one is afraid (Mic 4:3-4). The loss of this wholeness gives rise to alienation, which triggers fear, and fear in turn leads the alienated ego to engage the world angrily and violently, seeking to grab what it wants at the expense of both person and planet. To put an end to this violence, we must put an end to fear; and to put an end to fear, we must re-pair ourselves with the world (what Judaism calls *tikkun haolam*), and then re-pair the world with God (*tikkun hanefesh*). We must become, as Jesus said, shalom-makers, makers of the wholeness that gives rise to peace.

Peace, then, is not simply the ending of conflict; it is also the making of wholeness. Peace is learning how to embrace conflict without losing one's sense of wholeness. This, I think, is what Jesus means when he says, "Love your enemies" (Matt 5:44). He still recognizes that we have enemies, but he urges us to encounter them in a way that recognizes the divine within them, and in so doing work toward re-pairing all beings in the greater oneness of God.

How do we do this? How do we seek peace and pursue peace? I think Micah holds the key: "They will beat their swords into ploughshares, and their spears into pruning knives; nation shall not lift sword against nation, nor will they learn war anymore. They will eat, each person under his (and hers!) vine and fig tree, and none will make them afraid . . ." (Mic 4:3-4). Reverse the order of Micah and we have a program for peace: end fear, provide security of place and abundant food, and there will be no need to study war or wage it.

The 23rd Psalm tells us something similar. Fear, primarily fear of not having enough of what we need to survive, drives the alienated ego. The 23rd Psalm tells us that when we surrender to God's guidance—that is, when we learn to act in harmony with the Whole—we "shall not want." We will no longer lack for anything. Without want there is no fear, and without fear there is no need to separate myself from you in order to exploit you to get what I want. Micah and the psalmist are saying the same thing, and so, I suggest, is Jesus.

So, to be as clear as I can, to seek peace is to seek peace within myself: to end my sense of fear, and the anger and violence that accompany it, by realizing my unity with God. To pursue peace is to pursue peace outwardly, to work toward ending fear in the world and thus ending the need for violence, oppression, exploitation, and war.

I want to come back to the second half of this beatitude, "they shall be called the children of God," but let me stop here for a bit and invite your response.

Mike: Beautifully written! The nature and practice of *shalom* appears to be something you've mulled over a great deal.

I agree that *shalom* is the key background concept in question, and your description of the role of separation and alienation resonates with me.

Human violence is certainly driven by fear and want. I suspect that other factors are at play as well. Violence incited by want and fear at least has some semblance of a rational basis, usually related to self-perceived survival issues. What are we to make of pathological violence or irrational violence? I mention this only to suggest that eliminating fear and want might not prove enough to end violence.

You write, "To put an end to violence, we must put an end to fear; and to put an end to fear we must re-pair ourselves with the world . . . and then re-pair the world with God." I might tend to reverse the order. On the other hand, I suspect that if we pick up part of the task, we eventually find ourselves involved in what remains.

I strongly agree that unity with God is the way to find peace within ourselves, thus opening the way to pursue peace in other contexts. From the perspective of my tradition, I probably would speak of unity as becoming aligned with God's nature and purpose, but the result appears to be similar.

I am interested to see what you have to say about "children of God."

Rami: Thanks, Mike. A couple of quick comments before getting to "the children of God" idea.

First, as you well know, I tend to use a broad brush in my thinking, and you are of course right to bring up pathological violence and irrational violence. There will always be violent people who suffer from illnesses that cannot be cured or controlled, and who must be put away for their sake and ours.

Second, thanks for bringing up the order of re-pair. In Hebrew these two efforts are called *tikkun* and *teshuvah*, repair and return. Do I repair the world with godliness and then return to my true nature as a manifestation of God? Or do I return to God first and then engage the world with godliness? The fact is that *tikkun* and *teshuvah* are different ends of the same pole. You may start from either end, but in time the whole pole is engaged.

Last, I appreciate your definition of unity as "becoming aligned with God's nature and purpose." While we differ subtly on this point, we end up in the same place regarding action.

Now on to my thoughts on the "children of God."

I take my starting point from Philo of Alexandria (20 BCE–50 BCE), the Hellenistic Jewish philosopher who read the Torah with an allegorical eye. In his work, *Confusion of Languages* (28, M. i. 426), he defines "children of God" as referring to all those "who have real knowledge of the one Father of all."

The rabbis, and perhaps Philo himself, understood this kind of knowledge as *Imitatio Dei*, Imitation of God: to know God is to act godly. This they linked to Leviticus 19:2, where God says to Israel, "Be holy as I, YHVH, am holy." This is God's correction to the serpent's distorted promise in the Garden of Eden that "you shall be as gods" (Gen 3:5). The serpent's view leads to the alienated god-playing ego. God's version leads to the peacemaking and fearless child of God.

To be holy as God is holy implies that humanity and God share a common essence. Just as Jesus is fully human and fully divine, so each of us is fully human and fully divine. This is like an ocean wave being fully a wave and fully the ocean. It is not that the wave includes all of the ocean but that the ocean includes all of the wave.

When we realize that God embraces and transcends all things, we realize that all things, without giving up their uniqueness, are yet part of the One Thing, God. In short, we realize that "I and the Father are one" (John 10:30).

This makes perfect sense to me. The previous beatitude spoke of the "pure in heart" as those who "see God." Being "pure in heart" means being transparent, allowing the Light of God to shine through us *as* us. When we see this, we are free from fear, free to make peace, and free to reveal the good news that wholeness, not fragmentation, is the true nature of reality.

Mike: Your take on "children of God" strikes me as classic mysticism. Christian mystics use similar language. I've always found such language moving for several reasons, not the least being its reliance on analogies, such as your wave-to-ocean metaphor.

My tradition tends to speak of the matter in one of two ways.

First, you do not have to look long to find Christians who believe that the phrase has to do with heaven and judgment. They believe that the status is conferred by God and that it is received in a final judgment. Those who take this view rely on the passive construction of the phrase ("shall be called"), noting that it suggests the title is something given as the gift of God. Some hold this view, then go on to interpret "blessed are the peacemakers" to mean "blessed are those who share the gospel and lead others to acknowledge Jesus as their savior, and so help others find peace with God." In short, the beatitude is interpreted as a call to practice evangelism. I find this approach reductionist at best and a distortion of Jesus' intent at worst.

A second, and to my mind better, approach draws on an analogy based on the family. I have a son and daughter. Both were conceived and born as my children. Nothing can change their essential status. On the other hand, each has spent well over two decades becoming himself and herself, while remaining my child.

Along the way, they picked up many of my values and some of my practices. We often tease one another gently. With reference to one of their own beliefs, ideas, approaches to challenge, or actions toward others, either of them is apt to say, "Well, I guess that proves I'm your child."

Oceans and waves, fathers (and mothers) and their children—both analogies help us remember who we already are and what we might best do with ourselves. Both preserve our unity with God and our uniqueness. Taken seriously, each conditions us for the work of peacemaking.

Rami: I can't help wincing when listening to the reductionist version of the beatitude. Jesus is so often forced to fit the agenda of those who use him to excuse actions that he himself would condemn.

When we invaded Iraq in 2003, Larry King had a panel of Christian ministers on his show. He asked one of them how she understood "blessed are the peacemakers" in the context of this preemptive war. Without missing a beat she said, "Our soldiers are peacemakers. They will invade Iraq, kill our enemies, and make Iraq a more peaceful place. This is exactly what Jesus had in mind."

True, I'm recalling her words, and they may not be exact, but her message was as I portray it.

A year or so later, I was attending a Christian rock concert in Nashville and heard the MC ask the joyous crowd, "Okay, how many of you are ready to kill for Christ?" At first I thought I misheard him, but when he repeated it, and when the crowd shouted happily that they were ready to do just that, I left. It's never safe for Jews to stand in crowds of Christians ready to kill for Christ.

I don't mean to suggest that this is kind of thinking is unique to Christianity. One can hear much the same sentiment, with different particulars of course, in certain Jewish and Muslim settings as well. It just saddens me to see the Prince of Peace used to excuse acts of violence.

You need not respond to this. I know you feel the same. And there is no need for, or even a way to, excuse the fear, greed, anger, and violence that pass for religion in so many people's lives. All we can say is that this is why we need prophets like Hillel, Jesus, Rumi, Hafez, Kabir, and others who have seen through the veils of human difference and seen the One who is all.

Chapter 8

The Final Beatitudes

Blessed are those who are persecuted for righteousness' sake, for theirs is the kingdom of heaven. Blessed are you when people revile you and persecute you and utter all kinds of evil against you falsely, on my account. Rejoice and be glad, for your reward is great in heaven, for in the same way they persecuted the prophets who were before you. (Matthew 5:10-12, NRSV)

Mike: If we embrace the Beatitudes, in the process opening ourselves to the active rule of God, the focus of our lives shifts. A modern Christian might put it this way: "My life's center has shifted, so that I now want to live in accordance with God's will, as seen in the life and ministry of Jesus." We start to live "in the kingdom of God" in the present moment, while awaiting the fullness of the kingdom. Past, present, and future meet in us.

Tension results. When we try to walk through life playing by a different set of rules than the prevailing culture (whether that of first-century Rome, twenty-first-century America, or even the tiniest subculture—think of one's own family system), trouble ensues. The combined Beatitudes mention three examples: persecution, ridicule, and slander. Such assaults threaten one's inclusion in a culture, reputation, self-esteem, economic well-being, and possibly life.

Where's the blessing or genuine happiness in such a state? We have to be careful at this point. If we experience trouble because we have embraced and are being changed by immersion in the presence and will of God as described in the preceding beatitudes, such trouble verifies that we're on the right track. It means we're in the company of the prophets and Jesus. That's good to know.

The danger is that we may confuse being opposed with being "right." Many a fundamentalist Christian in America has been taught to view opposition as proof positive of his or her personal righteousness. I've known my share of Christian pastors who have bought into the idea that those who differ with them are "of the world and the devil." Such a worldview tends to reinforce self-righteousness and self-centeredness. People who buy into the mindset usually adopt one of two strategies in dealing with opposition: fight or flight. Both do violence to community and violate the peacemaking intent of Jesus.

On the other hand, a healthy willingness to suffer without resorting to violence or escape may be a mark of a Beatitudes person. Beatitudes people do not seek suffering, but they are willing to endure it if need be in order to live in the kingdom of God now. Martin Luther King, Jr., to my mind, exemplifies such suffering. So does an Anglo pastor of that era in southern Georgia who willingly lost his position because he refused to endorse segregation or racism. I suspect that there are many women and men who lose out on career advancement because they are committed to the kingdom of God. The two of us probably could generate a long list of people we've known who fit the bill.

I like the realism of the combined Beatitudes. Becoming a kingdom of God person is the right and best thing to do with our lives, but it's seldom easy or "safe."

Rami: The juxtaposition of these last two beatitudes is interesting. In the first, Jesus blesses those who are persecuted "for righteousness' sake." In the second, he blesses those who are persecuted for his sake, "on my account." Are we to assume that these are the same thing? That is, is being for Jesus the same as being for righteousness? And if he is saying that, why repeat the idea twice in succession?

I suggest that Jesus does not mean to associate himself with righteousness and that he is talking about two different things in these two beatitudes. And I think we can see that in the wording of the text.

Jesus says blessed are those who are persecuted "on my account" rather than "on account of my torah or teaching." This suggests that Jesus is not equating himself with righteousness but with something separate from, though not necessarily opposed to, righteousness. What that something is, I will take up shortly. Right now let's focus on the issue of righteousness.

"Blessed are those who are persecuted for righteousness sake, for theirs is the kingdom of heaven."

The idea here is that you can tell a lot about people by the enemies they make. Do people hate you because you are wicked or because you are righteous? Do they despise you because you stand up for the weak and powerless or because you oppress the weak and powerless? Jesus is saying, as you yourself seem to be saying, that if we live the Beatitudes we will live righteously and in opposition to much of the general society and its unrighteousness. And, again as you just said, this was certainly so in first-century Rome and is no less so in twenty-first-century America.

There is in our time and our culture, and in so many other cultures, plenty of injustice and evil to go around. The question Jesus is posing is this: Whose side are you on?

Some people, I know, would rather not take sides and find talk of sides to be part of the problem. But I see such talk as unavoidable. We have to take sides. We are either on the side of justice or injustice, the side of righteousness or unrighteousness, the side of love or hate.

What becomes challenging is that when you go to choose sides, you find that the lines are not so clearly drawn as my rhetoric would suggest. People on both sides claim to be on the side of justice, righteousness, and love. But how can this be?

The problem with this kind of thinking is that fine words can be manipulated to justify any evil we wish. Once we are convinced that we are on the side of righteousness, we can excuse all kinds of evil in the name of Jesus (though by no means only in the name of Jesus). This is painfully evident in the preaching and pronouncements of so many who claim, I would say falsely, to be righteous followers of Jesus. The vitriol that pours forth from so many pulpits (of many faiths) regarding "the other," whether that other be liberals, conservatives, lesbians, gays, bisexuals, transgendered people, women, Hispanics, blacks, Jews, Arabs, Muslims, Catholics, and Protestants-not-of-our-denomination is frightening. And it is all done, again falsely, in the name of righteousness.

So what worries me about this beatitude and many who claim to uphold it is something that did not come up earlier: the way the idea of righteousness can be used to create, fuel, and grow a vicious "us versus them" culture war that, in the name of Christ, perverts the very nature of Jesus' teaching.

What we need is a clear and behaviorally measurable definition of righteousness, and I think we can easily find it in the texts we have been discussing, as well as others from the Prophets of the Bible to the Qur'an. To be considered righteous, one must live a life that is defined by compassion, justice, humility, peace, patience, love, etc. And these can be further defined by specific behaviors also lauded in many religions.

Without a behavior definition as a safeguard, righteousness simply gets confused with self-righteousness, and Jesus is forced to bless and offer the kingdom of heaven to those who are so filled with anger and fear as to be poster children for the kingdom of hate.

I feel this happening all around the United States today. Humility and doubt are banished, and people are taking up extremist positions in the name of righteousness that cannot help leading to the desecration and destruction of the eighteenth-century enlightenment values upon which this country was founded and which are its very *raison d'etre*.

I feel that I am on a rant. Obviously, this beatitude struck a cord with me. I want to comment on the last text, but I'll stop here for a moment and invite you to jump back into the conversation.

Mike: "Rant" is too strong a term. My guess is that your long-standing concerns and the escalation of hate- and fear-filled political rhetoric during the election season combined to fuel your composition. In any case, each of your comments deserves serious response.

(1) "Why repeat the idea twice in succession?" I might suggest that parallelism is at work here, but how could one know for certain? Persecution is the linkage between the two sayings. How can persecution ever be considered "blessed"? I think our two previous posts answer the question, and that we are in essential agreement.

(2) Jesus and righteousness go together in the Christian tradition. In some sense, for us, he is the righteousness of God made manifest in a genuine human life. The one speaking the Beatitudes is the embodiment of those beatitudes. To be persecuted for pursuing the kind of righteousness defined by the beatitudes is to be persecuted for the sake of Jesus, at least to a Christian.

To pervert the person or teachings of Jesus in support of hate- or fear-driven agendas is the worst kind of heresy (and I do not use the term lightly or easily). From my perspective as a Christian, to do so involves the same kind of evil as is involved in taking the Lord's name in vain. And, yes, this may be the greatest visible sin of the Christian movement in America at this time.

The challenge for those of us within Christianity is how to stand against such perversion without taking up its weapons: slander, double-talk, fear, hatred, violence, and the like. After all, we follow Jesus (however poorly), and he refused to allow his disciples to take up arms in his defense or to advance his cause.

(3) I come back to the beatitudes and to your point about a "behaviorally measurable definition of righteousness." I agree with you that we can find it in the texts before us. We're also forced to consider the matter of the inner life—attitudes and motivations and such. Much of the remainder of the Sermon on the Mount fleshes out the attitudes and behaviors called for by the beatitudes.

As you hint, the problem comes at the point of application. Gray areas become evident, and humility- or even confusion-driven doubts emerge—it's much harder to follow Jesus than many a Sunday school lesson suggests!

At its best, community (whether the community of a few trusted friends or a larger one) has something to offer at this point. Community, whatever else it may do, thrusts us into ongoing conversations with one another. Our ideas and attitudes and actions may be challenged, affirmed, broken, or refined. Communities, of course, can become clans or mobs. But this possibility does not negate their potential to serve as crucibles of reflective righteousness.

Well . . . enough. This is a discussion I would love to have face to face, perhaps over Mexican food.

Rami: I found what you're saying very helpful. Your second point raised a few things on which I'd like to hear your take. You said, "The challenge for those of us within Christianity who oppose such perversion is how to stand against it without taking up its weapons: slander, double-talk, fear, hatred, violence, and the like."

This is the challenge for all of us who oppose the hatred that passes for holiness and patriotism in our time. How do we stand against it? How do we not get infected by fear when the airwaves are dripping with it? How do we hold to truth when the government has mastered Orwellian Newspeak that makes the very idea of truth questionable? And how do we not take up arms when militarism seems to have replaced diplomacy around the world?

I don't think Jesus ever expected there would be such a thing as a Holy Roman Empire or a Christian Nation. Judaism and the Hebrew Bible are replete with rules of war and a warrior God who deploys human troops, but Jesus came at a time of Jewish political and military impotence, and he pointed us in a new and different direction. I cannot imagine Jesus teaching a doctrine of "Just War." And John of Patmos's global holocaust in his book of Revelation, based as it is on the apocalyptic fantasies of the equally impotent Qumran Jews and their War Between the Sons of the Light and the

Sons of Darkness, is anathema to the teachings of Jesus in the Gospels. Are those of us who follow Jesus (and I would count myself in that group as long as it is Jesus we are following and not the Christ for whom I admit no connection whatsoever) supposed to be conscientious objectors, pacifists, and anti-war prophets?

Just imagine what might happen if all Christians suddenly said "no" to war. First, Israel would be attacked from all sides. Second, unless John Hagee is correct and the certain destruction of Israel would trigger the end times and the second coming of Christ, Israel would blow itself up in a nuclear Massada that would decimate the Middle East with nuclear fallout and mass death that would make the region uninhabitable for centuries.

Perhaps I am being a bit apocalyptic here myself, but what do we do with the nonviolence at the heart of Jesus' teaching? It seems to have gone the way of nonviolence in India, and for the same reason: maybe a community when it reaches a certain size cannot function without violence. Maybe Mao is right when he says that all power comes from the muzzle of a gun. Maybe you cannot overestimate the human passion for violence. After all, we are the descendants of Cain not Abel.

I think the author of the Cain and Abel story believed this to be true. After murdering his brother, Cain goes off to found the first city. The Bible is telling us that once we humans move beyond simple agriculturally based communities, we are doomed to murder and, as we organize into larger and larger groups, mass murder. Did Jesus see this and deliberately aim his teaching at individuals rather than at kings and nations as did the earlier prophets? Is this why he used agricultural metaphors rather than urban ones when trying to explain God and godliness?

I'd love to hear your thoughts on this.

Mike: Elijah lamented his fate, claiming to be the only one who had remained faithful to God in all of Israel. God corrected Elijah. There were a few more left, some thousands in fact. Elijah did not know them. They, apparently, had not sought out Elijah. He, though, was not alone. Even in a time when enormous governmental and cultural pressures pushed most people toward idolatry, a significant minority remained faithful.

That kind of story is the only answer I can provide to your question ("How do we hold to the truth," etc.). Some always have, some do even now, and some always will. When all is said and done, evil wins the field for only a day, and even then its victory is never complete.

I might add that John's Revelation is not about the end of the world per se but instead about the possibility of faithfulness under the most trying circumstances. The faithful in Revelation, by the way, are never called into battle. Their only job is to remain faithful to Jesus. The final defeat of evil is left to God. Of course, faithfulness might, in fact will, lead to trouble. One's witness, though, does not involve might and arms but instead a willingness to suffer and even die for the sake of fidelity to the Lord.

Mao said all power comes from the muzzle of a gun. I say that's but one kind of power, and far from the most effective over the long term. The power of love coupled with a willingness to suffer the consequences startles us. It may change us, and it always has within it the potential to change everything. This, of course, amounts to a faith statement. So be it. It's the one I choose to believe.

It's a faith statement that keeps cropping up, though. Jesus certainly thought so. Augustine, in his better moments, does the same. St. Francis makes this the ordering center of his life and work. Paul starts to get it, especially as he ages and reflects more deeply on the intent of Jesus. The perspective lies at the heart of some of the most loved contemporary literature. You'll find it in Tolkien. It seems to me to be at the heart of much of what E. B. White had to say. As for the Harry Potter stories, the power of love relative to that of almost unthinkable, unstoppable evil is the central question addressed.

Love takes root and grows in individuals. Jesus, indeed, directed his teaching, his way of life, at individuals. His community will be composed of individuals, each one of whom makes (and remakes, over and over) the decision to accept the love of God and to become in due measure a living embodiment of that love. All else—theology, actions, institutions, corporate worship, ethics, etc.—becomes a running commentary or expression of this central reality.

Both of us have had quite a run over the past few posts. Let me know if you are ready to press on.

Rami: I agree that Jesus was speaking to individuals. In the end, while I understand the need for community and organized movements, I place my hope in individuals. If we do not transform our selves as selves, there is no hope for transforming society. The individual transformation for which I hope is one that leads us out of the narrow mind of cults, creeds, tribes, etc., and into the spacious mind awake to the One God/Reality giving rise to one world, one humanity, and one moral code—justice and compassion for all beings.

Okay, on to the final beatitude: "Blessed are you when people revile you and persecute you and utter all kinds of evil against you falsely, on my account. Rejoice and be glad, for your reward is great in heaven, for in the same way they persecuted the prophets who were before you."

The key issue for me in this beatitude is Jesus' saying, "on my account." Why would people be persecuted because of Jesus?

The answer I hear most often is that followers of Jesus, then and now, in ancient Israel and in contemporary America, are persecuted because they are pro-life, pro-gun, pro-God, anti-gay, and (according to a couple of my acquaintances) anti-dancing. To impose twenty-first-century culture war values on first-century Jewish society is, however, both silly and anachronistic, and I won't say any more about it.

The second reason I can imagine for people being persecuted on Jesus' account has to do with Jewish life in Matthew's time. When the Gospel of Matthew was written, Jesus had been dead for decades. The early church was emerging and competing with the Pharisees for the loyalty of the Jews. As the rabbis saw it, Jewish Christians were a threat to their power, their authority, and the foundation of Jewish society as they saw it, namely the legal rulings of the rabbis themselves.

In this context, it is not hard to imagine families being torn apart, with some members siding with Jesus and others with the rabbis. Since Peter, James, and the other Jewish Christians continued to attend and preach in the synagogue, conflict between mainstream Jews and Jewish Christians was probably both common and heated.

But this wasn't going on in Jesus' own day. If we are going to take our text seriously, we either have to assume that it was written by Matthew and therefore reflects the situation of his day, or that Jesus was thinking of something else entirely. For argument's sake, I opt for the latter.

The Jews of Jesus' day had four basic options when dealing with the socioeconomic-political-religious tenor they faced. They could follow the path of the Sadducees and collaborate with Rome; they could follow the Pharisees and seek to create their own society within the occupation; they could follow the Qumran model, opt out of Jewish and Roman society altogether, and take up a pure and pious life in the desert; or they could follow the Zealots and take up jihad against Rome.

Jesus, I believe, offered a fifth way: nonviolent engagement with Rome, Sadducees, and Pharisees and on behalf of the poor, the powerless, and the disenfranchised. He challenged the corruption of the priesthood and the sacrificial system, the immorality of the courts, the unjust and brutal occupation by Rome, and the violence preached by those who would wage holy war (in fact, i.e., the Zealots, or in fantasy, i.e., the Qumran community) against Rome.

We have already talked about the politics of "turning the other cheek" and "walking the second mile," and I am referring to this. Jesus, like Gandhi and Martin Luther King, Jr., who modeled themselves after him and who believed in the power of what Gandhi called *satyagraha*, nonviolent truth force, and in the power of prophetic theater to effect social change. He trusted that even the hardest heart, if forced to look at itself honestly, would eventually soften. And his way was to confront that heart with the pain and suffering it caused others.

Elsewhere in Matthew Jesus says, "One who does not take his cross and follow me is not worthy of me. One who finds his life will lose it, and one who loses his life for my sake will find it" (Matt 10:38-39). Imagine what would have happened if the Jews had done just that. What if tens of thousands of Jews presented themselves for crucifixion along with Jesus? Would Rome have slaughtered them all?

As brutal as the regime was, history shows that it had its limits. The mass act of prophetic theater with thousands upon thousands of Jews walking nonviolently to be crucified on Golgotha would have overwhelmed the system of intimidation and caused a revolution that might have changed everything. This is exactly what Christians did when they powerfully and nonviolently (at least on their part) stood for execution in the Roman coliseum. And, it can be argued, their display of faith grew the movement and gained it respect.

Of course, Rome had crucified thousands before (I love the movie *Spartacus*), but never an entire society. Crucifixion was a tool of intimidation, but if everyone picked up her or his cross and volunteered to die on it, there would be no more intimidation left in it. If you are not afraid to die, you are at last fearless enough to live.

The same nonviolent acts of *satyagraha* on the part of the Palestinian people would, by the way, put an end to the Israeli occupation of the West Bank, an end to settlement expansion, an end to the building of the "security wall," and an end to the rationalization for continued Israeli occupation altogether. While the Muslims of India had their "Muslim Gandhi," the Pashtun leader Badshah Kahn, the Palestinians have yet to find theirs.

In any case, *satyagraha* is, I think, what Jesus had in mind. If you are persecuted because you take up your cross and challenge the system of oppression that brutalizes the poor, the powerless, the sick, and the disenfranchised, then you are worthy of standing "with the prophets who were before you."

Jesus was a revolutionary of the highest order. He was among the best Judaism had to offer. How sad that Jews ignore him, Christians spiritualize him, and so few of us truly dare to follow him. And how ironic that those who do are so often condemned by the very people who claim to know and love him the most.

Mike: Once again, we find ourselves in substantial agreement on a number of points.

For the sake of brevity, I'll just say I agree substantially with your first two points regarding the final beatitude. I think that you may underestimate tensions experienced by Jesus within his own lifetime. His own family, for example, appears to have harbored significant doubts about his ministry, not to mention his sanity. Still, we're on the same page.

Your "fifth option" argument is on target, insofar as it goes. Some of the New Testament scholars we've mentioned in earlier posts certainly take similar positions. Collaboration, "ghetto," complete withdrawal, and jihad were the options espoused and practiced by the groups you identify. I often wonder what common folk thought about it all. Jesus' nonviolent approach, coupled with his insistence on the acceptance of the suffering it would bring, challenged all other options.

From my perspective, the resurrection hallowed Jesus' version of *satyagraha*, in effect stamping it as "approved by God" and thus making it both universal and for all times.

Assuming you're ready, we'll now move on and take up the remainder of the Sermon on the Mount.

Rami: I do have one question. You said that the resurrection "hallowed" the *satyagraha* of Jesus. That caused me to wonder, if there were no resurrection, how would your love of Jesus and your commitment to his teachings change?

As you know I take the resurrection as a parable articulating deep truth but not in the context of literal, scientifically provable fact. Given what we know about science and the nature of the universe, if Jesus were literally lifted into heaven, body and soul, even if traveling close to the speed of light, he would not yet have escaped the universe, let alone reached heaven. So I don't take this literally and instead find meaning in it beyond the literal: as a statement that while you can kill Jesus, you cannot kill the wisdom he embodied.

Anyway, my question isn't why or how you understand the resurrection (though that too is an interesting question), but rather if the resurrection never happened, how and why your approach to Jesus and his teachings might change.

Mike: There you go again, posing good questions! Of course, by now I should know better than to drop a loaded term into a sentence. Your sharp eyes miss nothing!

Before I try to answer the question you pose at the end of your post, I think it best to address the matter of "literal" and "myth." "Myth," to my way of thinking, is a story that captures a key truth or insight into reality and/or human nature. Scientific reality has to do with theories that are capable of being verified in some manner, not just once but repeatedly. Both myth and science deal with truth, so to speak. Unfortunately, we do not yet know how or if the two methods and their conclusions can be unified. To use an analogy, we're in a quandary similar to that faced by modern physics when it attempts to create a unified theory of everything.

The resurrection of Jesus, at the very least, is one of the great myths. Taken as metaphor or parable, it provides many a modern Christian with insights and motivation enough to sustain viable faith. Naturally, as myth, the entire matter falls outside the scope of science.

The same is true if the resurrection was a one-time event. Whether "myth" or "fact," the scientific method is not designed to investigate or assess the resurrection.

So, when all is said and done, one's approach to the resurrection boils down to individual decision.

My personal decision is to accept the resurrection as a unique event. With that as my starting point, I see the resurrection as God's validation of Jesus (his teachings, actions, way of life, etc.), hence my use of the term "hallowed." To use theological language, all the "powers" could not kill the way of God, stuff it into the grave, and make it stay there. The way of *agape* love triumphs when all is said and done. As Aslan once said (in C. S. Lewis's

Chronicles of Narnia), this is "deep magic," and the witch does not understand it. Winters come, but they cannot hold forever. Now I'm slipping into literary talk, which is to say drawing on the resource of various sub-created myths, all of which spring from the story of the resurrection.

Would it make a difference to me if the resurrection could be proven beyond doubt to be nothing more than a delusion, a hoax, or a mistake? I suppose the honest answer is, "I don't know." I doubt that it would, mostly because the power of the story long ago gripped my imagination and began to shape my living. I choose to think it would continue to do so.

Rami: I am curious about the idea that resurrection is beyond science. If we say that Jesus was raised bodily from the dead, are we speaking biologically rather than metaphorically or mythically or symbolically? Are we making a scientific claim that is absolutely within the realm of biology? And, if so, just how did that happen? Did Jesus' cells regenerate? What would have happened to his brain function after three days without oxygen? I'm not being factious here. I am taking this quite seriously. Even if it was a unique event, though I am unsure as to the criteria we would use to credit the Christian story while simultaneously discrediting the other resurrection stories, even then we are still making a claim about a physical body, and that puts it clearly in the realm of science.

Given that all we know about biology makes the resurrection of the dead after three days physically impossible, the only answer I can come up with is this: "It was a miraculous act of God." But all that really says is, "Given the nature of human biology, I don't know how it could happen, but since I want to believe it happened, I will take refuge in God." God doesn't answer the question but only allows us to stop asking it.

I guess this is what you mean by it all boiling down to "individual decision." I think I understand that idea, but, since you and I clearly decide differently, I wonder by what criteria we each make our respective decisions. My criteria are a blend of reason, science, and the fact that my formative years were steeped in denial of Jesus as anything but a Jew like myself. I am willing to question this last element of my conditioned thinking, but I am having a hard time with the first two.

When you opt to speak in theological language, however, I am right there with you. The story of the resurrection is a narrative affirming that the powers then and now cannot defeat the way of God, the way of nonviolent confrontation in the pursuit of justice, compassion, humility, love, and peace. This is deep magic, requiring an alchemical transformation of the human ego from fear to love. And that to me is what religion is: not science but alchemy. Not the literal transformation of lead into gold which, like the bodily resurrection and ascension of Jesus violate the laws of physics, but the psycho-spiritual transformation of the alienated and fearful ego into the integrated, loving, and courageous self.

As for the resurrection being a delusion, hoax, or mistake, I did not mean to imply this at all. I find these options offensive, reductionist, and shallow. This is like people who say to me, as one who does not believe Jesus is the Christ, "Then you must believe he was a liar." How shallow that thinking is. Either Jesus is a literalist or a liar? Are these really the only options people of faith are offered? When these people read, "I and the Father are one," they read it as if Jesus were a mathematician rather than a prophet and a poet. That is so sad, and it speaks poorly of their religious education.

What I intended to ask you was this: Why do we need the resurrection to hallow anything? Why aren't the life, teaching, and forgiveness-filled death of Jesus enough? Why isn't the mythic understanding of the resurrection, the notion that the Way of the Jesus transcends the death of Jesus and any who follow him, enough?

I realize this is taking us far off topic, and you may choose to ignore all this and get back to our text, but I find your answers so interesting that I just want to hear more.

Mike: The idea of the resurrection, and its various implications, provoked tension within the early Christian movement, both while it was contained within first-century Judaism and later as it spread and came in contact with ancient religions and philosophies. Within early Christianity, for example, some came to see it as the means through which God elevated Jesus to the status of unique Son of God and Lord. Others, who eventually became the majority, saw the resurrection as confirmation of the Son's preexistence as a member of what eventually came to be called the Trinity. Obviously, I've oversimplified a complicated story, but my only point is that historically the resurrection tends to generate rather intense debates.

With regard to science, my hunch is that we may be misunderstanding one another. When I say that the resurrection is beyond the scope of science, I mean something quite specific: the classic scientific method. The scientific method, as you know, requires the formulation of theories. Theories must be subject to experimental test. Furthermore, the results of such a test must be repeatable in order for the theory to be accepted. The resurrection, on these terms, is not available for scientific verification.

The most we might do is state that the content of current knowledge makes such an event unlikely to the nth degree. Even here a bit of caution is in order. A given theory may be overturned or revised by new data and new experiments. In some cases, perhaps most often in physics, we sometimes find that new theories and experiments require that we expand our picture of the universe to accommodate realties that do not seem to mesh well (think of the classic problems posed by a universe that seems to make room for Newtonian, relativistic, and quantum physics).

So, for example, Einstein's understanding of the universe cannot allow for instantaneous communication between twin particles separated by enormous distances (the old speed of light limit). As it turns out, though, quantum theory plus experimentation confirms that at the quantum level, reality works that way. Why? After decades of multiple theories, it seems to me that no one quite knows why. At this point in time, we simply know that Einstein's theories work at the macro level and quantum physics theories work at the quantum level. The more we discover about the universe, the weirder it becomes.

I think the current state of science encourages a rediscovery of humility before the mystery of the universe. As a result, I tend to treat science as an extremely useful tool among several tools I use to understand and make sense of the universe, including human life.

Being a theist, my worldview posits God as the Creator who remains at work within and from outside creation. We, of course, differ with one another at this point. Given my perspective, I do not so much "take refuge in God" as assume God may work in ways beyond my current comprehension. The resurrection falls into that category. By the way, such an assumption does not stop me from trying to expand our understanding of how the universe works. In fact, it rather pushes me to try to learn more.

All of the above is quite general, but it seemed to me that our conversation required it.

Changing gears, some Christians would argue vigorously that the resurrection understood as an event within history changes the entire equation of history, serving notice to the "powers" that they may not claim it as their realm and that their days are numbered. Those who take such an approach believe that any other approach to the resurrection robs it of such power.

I do not agree. I've known too many people who take your approach and who are empowered by it to follow the way of Jesus. My hunch is that God makes good use of either approach to advance his way in the world. Personally, I find that the two approaches enrich one another as they play out in my mind, heart, and imagination.

If you like, we can continue this particular conversation. Otherwise, I'll move on to the next portion of the Sermon on the Mount.

Rami: To be honest, Mike, I could talk about this kind of thing forever, and I have no doubt there would be a huge audience for that conversation. Whether we are talking about Christianity or Judaism (or any other religion), there are many concepts that people have a difficult time understanding, and I suspect many of them would be enthralled, engaged, and helped by being able to participate in the kind of conversation you and I are having. But that is way beyond the scope of this dialogue. I think we have raised the issues that needed raising and should get back to our text.

Part 2

Salt, Light, and Law (Matthew 5:13-20)

Chapter 9

The Metaphors of Salt and Light

You are the salt of the earth; but if salt has lost its taste, how can its saltiness be restored? It is no longer good for anything, but is thrown out and trampled underfoot. You are the light of the world. A city built on a hill cannot be hid. No one after lighting a lamp puts it under the bushel basket, but on the lamp stand, and it gives light to all in the house. In the same way, let your light shine before others, so that they may see your good works and give glory to your Father in heaven. (Matthew 5:13-14, NRSV)

Mike: Jesus moves now to the role his followers are to play in human society. They are to be as salt and light.

Most Americans tend to think of salt as a seasoning. In the ancient world, salt was used primarily as a preservative. Those listening to Jesus speak might have heard him saying, "You are the preservative of the world." Translations generally fail to capture Jesus' intent when he speaks of salt losing its flavor. Jesus had contamination in mind. A good paraphrase would be, "But if salt has become adulterated with other materials, it loses its ability to preserve."

Verse 14 introduces the metaphor of light. Jesus provides two images: a city set on a hill and a lamp lit inside a dwelling. In order to appreciate the metaphor, most of us have to imagine a world in which nighttime was truly dark. Streetlights, office lights, traffic lights, light spilling through the windows of homes, light reflected from our great cities—it's hard to find genuine darkness these days. Ask amateur astronomers if you doubt me!

The first-century world, though, knew darkness. When the sun went down and clouds covered the sky and you were in the wilderness, pitch darkness engulfed you. Darkness was frightening precisely because it was thick, you could not see, and anything might be "out there." A traveler in the wild would have been grateful even for the dim, reflected light of a distant city. No one would have placed a bushel basket over a lit lamp, but instead would have hastened to place it on a lamp stand and so bring light to a small room.

Light and salt were vital to life in the first century. Jesus now places his followers in a similar category: well lived, their words and deeds and attitudes are crucial to others and to human society.

The preceding beatitudes provide the heart of what it means to live life well. Later in the sermon, Jesus will add depth and breadth to his teachings, but the core of the matter is the Beatitudes.

The Christian life, or the life of anyone who follows Jesus, cannot be solely private. In essence, Jesus commissions his followers to plunge into but not lose themselves in the life of society. Their mission is to preserve the way of God among humans by walking such a path themselves, to illumine the way of God by their lives.

Salt works quietly and unseen, and light lessens or banishes darkness without fanfare. Jesus does not draft an army, create a school of theology, tie his hopes to politics, or fashion an institution. Instead, he attempts to mold the hearts and minds of individuals, set them loose in culture, and inspire them to live true to his intentions. Jesus chooses to hope in the efficacy of such an approach.

Rami: You are right, of course, to pull us out of a twenty-first-century understanding of salt, so let me add a few more nuances to the salt reference of which Jesus' Jewish followers would certainly be aware.

In Exodus (30:35-38) we learn that salt is an essential ingredient in the incense God ordains to be placed in the tent of meeting, and in Leviticus (2:13) we are told that we are to include salt with our grain offerings to God. So salt reminds us of both the capacity to meet God and the gratitude that is our natural response to that meeting. But more than either of these references, when Bible-steeped Jews hear about salt, they immediately think of Lot's wife, who was turned into a pillar of salt (Gen 19:26).

The rabbinic commentary on Lot's wife extant in Jesus' time challenges the idea that being turned into a pillar of salt was a punishment. Lot's wife "sinned" because her love for her daughters overwhelmed her fear of God. Would God punish a mother because of motherly love? The ancient rabbis say "no." They tell us that by being turned into a pillar of salt, Lot's wife gave life to animals from miles around who came to lick her and live, for without the salt she provided they would die. By day's end she was totally consumed, and by dawn's light she was restored. Is this not a wonderful parallel to the sacrifice of Jesus and Communion?

I would suggest that being the "salt of the earth" means giving all we are for the well-being of others. This is in sync with Jesus saying, "For whoever would save his life will lose it, and whoever loses his life for my sake will find it" (Matt 16:25). This is also analogous to the Mahayana Buddhist ideal of the *Bodhisattva*, the enlightened sage who refuses to leave this world for *Nirvana* (the Buddhist "heaven") until the last and the least have preceded her there.

Regarding the rest of this text, I assume that Jesus' followers, the vast majority of whom were Jews, would hear his reference to hill and light and immediately think of the prophet Isaiah who said God's house shall be established on a mountain top "above all hills, and all nations shall come unto it" (Isa 2:2) and that Israel shall be "a light unto the nations" (42:6) opening the blind eye, and freeing those imprisoned in the dungeon and in darkness (42:7). This opening of the blind eye and freeing those entrapped in darkness may be the "good works" to which Jesus points in clear contradiction to those who claim that works have no place in Christianity.

While there are many substantial differences between Judaism and Christianity, there seem to be few between Judaism and Jesus.

This is all I have to offer regarding this text, but I cannot read your closing comment without hearing a voice of anguish. I may be projecting my own view of things, but when you say, "Jesus is not commissioning an army, creating a school of theology, tying his hopes to politics, or fashioning an institution," I cannot help letting out my own sigh of great sadness, for isn't this exactly what has happened to his teaching?

My only hope lies in those individual hearts and minds, those *Bodhisattvas* of every faith and none who, devoted to justice and compassion, are set loose upon the world to open blind eyes, soften hardened hearts, and free those imprisoned in fear and darkness. In doing so, they become the night beacons that show us the way to a new world.

Chapter 10

The Law

Do not think that I have come to abolish the law or the prophets; I have come not to abolish but to fulfill. For truly I tell you, until heaven and earth pass away, not one letter, not one stroke of a letter, will pass from the law until all is accomplished. Therefore, whoever breaks one of the least of these commandments, and teaches others to do the same, will be called least in the kingdom of heaven; but whoever does them and teaches them will be called great in the kingdom of heaven. For I tell you, unless your righteousness exceeds that of the scribes and Pharisees, you will never enter the kingdom of heaven. (Matthew 5:17-20, NRSV)

Mike: With these words, Jesus moves into the body of the Sermon on the Mount. He appears to stake out a position, possibly a claim. Most of the remainder of the chapter provides illustrations as he applies the claim to specific situations (see 5:21-47).

Jesus continues to deal with the kingdom of heaven. In this paragraph, he speaks of its connection to the law and the prophets. Whatever may be said (and people at different places on the Christian theological spectrum indeed have said many and varied things), Jesus did not intend to abolish the law and the prophets. Instead, he claims to "fulfill them."

That's interesting, if for no other reason than because few Christians since the late first or early second century CE have thought it necessary to observe dietary, ceremonial, or civil laws found in the Hebrew Bible. For the most part, they argue that all such laws were "fulfilled" in some way via Jesus. Most go on to teach that the "moral" law (personal behavior, etc.) remains in force. Personally, I'm not particularly enamored of this approach. It feels more like a slice-and-dice approach than a serious attempt to deal with Jesus' intent regarding the law and the prophets.

Both the law and the teachings of the prophets have to do with making a life pleasing to God and hence good for the individual, the community, and even the larger world. Perhaps the best way to read "but to fulfill" might be "but to enflesh" or "but to make clear in all their radicality." The remainder of the section and chapter makes clear that Jesus thought the law and prophets called for something more than most people (in his view) thought.

At the very least, Jesus raised the bar. While they have often gotten bad press among Christians, the Pharisees were well regarded by many first-century Jews. Many everyday Jews saw a Pharisee's brand of righteousness as something to be emulated or at least admired as a high standard. Verse 20, I think, came as a bit of a shock to Jesus' audience.

What might such righteousness look like in practice? Jesus will give particular examples in the succeeding paragraphs of Matthew 5.

Rami: This is a fascinating teaching of Jesus, and one that raises several questions for me.

First, why would Jesus have to defend himself against the slanderous claim that he came to abolish Torah (what the NRSV calls "the law and the prophets")? Could it be that his interpretation of Torah was that radical? I think it was.

The phrase "Torah and Prophets" in Jesus' day is equivalent to "God and country" in our own day. Both phrases refer to the political and religious status quo. Jesus challenged people to question the status quo, and those who would defend it would naturally claim that he was seeking to overthrow it.

Rather than defend himself, Jesus could have said something like, "Okay, you're right. If Torah and Prophets means what you say it means, then I am calling for their abolition." But to do so would be to abdicate the basic memes of his civilization, something Jesus refused to do. He insisted on using the very Torah his opponents used, but he interpreted it in new ways. This is why he says he has come to "fulfill" the Torah rather than abolish it. He has come to reveal its deeper meanings. In this, Jesus is a classic Pharisee, for interpreting Scripture and finding new meanings in ancient texts is at the heart of the Pharisaic experiment in Judaism.

This interpretation is bolstered by Jesus' next sentence: "For truly I tell you, until heaven and earth pass away, not one letter, not one stroke of a letter, will pass from the law until all is accomplished" (v. 18).

From similar phrases by other rabbis, we know that the letter Jesus refers to is the *yod*, the smallest letter of the Hebrew alphabet, and the stroke of a letter is the *dagesh*, the tiny dot placed in the center of certain letters to change their sound from soft to hard (the letter *bet/b* has the dot; drop it and you have the letter *vet/v*). Why mention these things? Because for the rabbis of his day (and ours), interpreting each letter and each stroke was one of the ways they found new meanings in the Torah. Jesus isn't denying Torah, only offering new interpretations of Torah.

Then Jesus says something even more mysterious: "Therefore, whoever breaks one of the least of these commandments, and teaches others to do the same, will be called least in the kingdom of heaven; but whoever does them and teaches them will be called great in the kingdom of heaven" (v. 19).

What is so wild in this saying is that both the breakers of the commandments and their keepers get into the kingdom of heaven! While their places differ, neither is denied entry. How painfully ironic that Jesus, unlike so many who claim him as Lord and Savior, rejects no one when it comes to the kingdom! And yet if this is so, what are we to make of the final teaching of our text: "For I tell you, unless your righteousness exceeds that of the scribes and Pharisees, you will never enter the kingdom of heaven" (v. 20)?

The confusion is removed when we realize that there is no equation between keeping the ritual commandments and righteousness. One can be mindful of ritual and totally thoughtless in one's dealings with other people and living things. Jesus is saying that entry into the kingdom of heaven is based on acts of righteousness rather than ritual or creedal purity. Once you're in, your place is then determined by how well you kept the commandments, but getting in has nothing to do with ritual and everything to do with ethics.

This again is totally in alignment with Pharisaic teaching. True, the Pharisees were rigorous in their keeping of the law, but it was just and compassionate dealings with one's neighbor that mattered most. Where Jesus and the Pharisees split is over their definitions of "neighbor." The Pharisees were not ready to accept the leper, the tax collector, the Samaritan, the Roman, or women at their table. Jesus was. This was his greatness and his genius.

It is a terrible shame that *Pharisee* and *Pharisaic* has become pejorative terms. The Pharisees were the liberals of their day, doing with Torah and the Prophets exactly what Jesus did: remaking them in their own image, according to their own understanding of what is good and just. I believe that Jesus, like Paul, was trained by Pharisees, though I suspect he was of the School of Hillel (liberal and focused on compassion), while Paul was of the competing School of Shammai (conservative and focused on rules). The fact that the Gospels show the Pharisees challenging Jesus only bolsters my argument: this is exactly what rabbis do with one another. Our entire educational system is based on argument, questioning, challenging, and dialogue. But we only do this with fellow Pharisees/rabbis. When the Pharisees challenge Jesus, they are acknowledging him as part of the Pharisaic community.

All Jews today are heirs to Pharisaic Judaism. Not that Judaism is unchanged since Jesus' time. Pharisaic or what we now call rabbinic Judaism is a method of reading, interpreting, and recasting Scripture that filters the ancient text through the imagination of the sages to reflect the zeitgeist of their age. This is what rabbis have done for thousands of years and why Judaism continues to be a living and therefore evolving religious civilization.

Okay, I have gone on quite long. Now back to you.

Mike: To summarize: you place Jesus squarely within the framework of the first-century Pharisaic movement.

A notable segment of Christian scholars has taken a similar approach over the past few decades. At first, they worked primarily with rabbinic materials from later centuries, a useful exercise though they sometimes fell into the trap of anachronism. If memory serves, Pauline scholars led the charge. Later, other scholars applied similar methods to Jesus studies. I think the approach has yielded good fruits, provided we keep in mind that first-century Pharisees cannot simply be equated with later rabbis.

I find myself in sympathy with the approach, not least because it redresses an old tendency among some Christians to insist on radical discontinuity between first-century Judaism and Jesus. The incarnation requires Christians to assume the full humanity of Jesus. To be human is to be immersed in one's birth culture. Whatever else might be said about Jesus, he was a first-century Jew.

Jesus used the available resources of his culture (Torah, methods, etc.) creatively. You point out that this has been the approach of the rabbis over the centuries, and I agree. From time to time, though, Jesus appears to have been criticized for not citing sources (i.e., other teachers, etc.). Christian commentators frequently note this and conclude that Jesus claimed a kind of autonomous authority that scandalized Pharisees. I would be interested in your take on the matter.

I agree strongly that one of the major dividing points between Jesus and most others had to do with "neighbor." The division carried over into the early Christian movement. In my opinion, it drove the late first-century divide between Judaism and emerging Christianity. Modern Christianity continues the debate within itself—just who can be considered a neighbor and treated accordingly.

The question of neighbor is the great issue of our time. How we view and treat one another is the filter through which all theology must be strained.

Rami: Actually, I can't recall a single instance where Jesus cites prior rabbinic sources. This doesn't mean he didn't do so, only that those who wrote the Gospels chose not to include those citations if in fact he made them— anything to separate Jesus from his Jewish heritage and promote him as a unique teacher and Son of God.

As for the Pharisees being scandalized, I would say it is, in a strange and intriguing way, the case of the pot calling the kettle black. While it became customary to honor one's teachers by citing their names, the rabbis cited in the Mishnah, the earliest codification of rabbinic teaching, did exactly what Jesus did, i.e., they espoused teachings without reference to earlier sources. Later rabbinic commentators on the Mishnah were careful to find links between the Mishnah and the much older Torah, but the Mishnaic teachers themselves claimed an authority separate from the Written Torah, asserting (without any outside corroboration) that God gave two Torahs on Mount Sinai. The Written Torah that was placed into the hands of the priests, and the Oral Torah, the key to understanding the Written Torah properly, was passed down through Joshua, the elders, and the prophets to the Pharisaic sages themselves.

The early rabbis believed that they embodied the Torah and that their teachings were Torah. Jesus did the same. The difference, and it is a huge one, is that the rabbis operated within a large community of scholar-saints who challenged one another's teachings in order to separate truth from mere opinion, while Jesus appears to make his teachings without the benefit of colleagues.

I can see how for many that bold assertion of his own authority was as scandalous to the Pharisees as their bold assertion of authority was to the Sadducees for whom only the Written Torah was authentic revelation.

Regarding the word "neighbor," I also think it is the great issue of our time. I'm not so sure it was the issue that drove the wedge between Jews and Jewish Christians in the late first century, however.

The battle between the Gentile Christianity of Paul and the Jewish Christianity of Peter and James could certainly be seen as a battle over "neighbor," but with regard to the larger Jewish world I suspect that the real divide came with the refusal of Jewish Christians to join with their fellow Jews in their war of liberation against Roman occupation.

Believing as they did that Jesus was to return within their lifetimes, entering into a bloody war with Rome made no sense to followers of Jesus. And it is not hard to imagine that early Christians who were being persecuted by Rome were more than happy to have the Romans preoccupied with some other people for a while. So I think it was more a matter of "you're with us or you're against us."

Yet Jesus' widening of the concept of "neighbor" was revolutionary. His was an open table fellowship that in our day needs to be broadened even more.

Controlling access to Jesus' table is part of the politics of religion, but broadening our understanding of "neighbor" to include not only all human beings but all beings in general is essential for the survival of our species.

If we understood that all life was our "neighbor," that the earth in all her diversity was our "neighbor," that the cosmos itself was our "neighbor," we would live on this planet in a way that honored the sacredness of life in all its forms. It is because we have defined "neighbor" too narrowly that we are on the brink of destroying the one table that sustains us.

Perhaps we should start a movement called "God's Table" that promotes a deep ecological neighborliness (using the word "ecological" in the sense that all beings are interdependent), and that would foster peace among people and between people and the planet. That is a table at which I would be honored to sit.

Mike: With regard to the two Torahs, I'm aware of the Oral Torah, which Christian commentators generally label the oral tradition or oral law. Most often they note it as a major point of difference between the Pharisees and Sadducees. I don't think I knew that the earliest versions of the Mishnah "espoused teachings without reference to earlier sources."

If I understand you correctly, you think a key difference between Jesus and the Pharisees was that "the rabbis operated within a large community of scholar-saints who challenged one another's teachings in order to separate truth from mere opinion, while Jesus appears to make his teachings without benefit of colleagues." Jesus, at the very least, may have seen himself as part of a prophetic tradition, the lone voice challenging the consensus of the community. From later Christian perspective, of course, he spoke a corrective word from God. On a personal note, given your qualms about the limits of community, I wonder how you feel about the contrast you've noted.

Let's turn back to "neighbor" and the first-century division between Judaism and Christianity. The division was well under way before the destruction of Jerusalem in the first century and an established fact well before the start of the second century. In the end, the core issue boiled down to something along the following lines. Could a Gentile become a full-fledged member of the community without becoming first a Jew (circumcision, food laws, etc.)?

Paul took the position that Gentiles could do so. Others within the broader community disagreed. Peter seems ultimately to have agreed with Paul in theory and occasional practice, even as he found it difficult to handle the resultant pressure. James, along with the leadership in the Jerusalem church, ultimately chose to pursue a moderate course, which in essence exempted Gentiles from most Jewish practices, though keeping in place certain food restrictions. In short, the three apostles had to contend with a culture war.

Nineteenth- and early twentieth-century scholarship posited sharp and clear divisions between two camps within Christianity. As it turns out, the situation was considerably more complicated. Tensions, though, were quite real. Toward the end of his life, Paul recognized the reality of the division. By the time Revelation was written (almost certainly in last decade of the first century), the division appears to have been deep and virtually complete.

All that is to say that I suspect the war of liberation against the Roman occupation may have put nails in the coffin, but little more.

"One table" or "God's Table" is the metaphor and reality with which we must come to grips. You state the matter well. The truth of the matter, I suspect, is that all of us already sit at that table. At the risk of understatement, I think table manners are the challenge. Somehow we must learn to believe and act as if it's a common table rather than one we can or dare to claim exclusively for ourselves (and others we may like).

Rami: At the risk of romanticizing the lone prophet, I do have qualms about community when it comes to spiritual breakthroughs and revolutions. To borrow from my teacher, the late Ellis Rivkin, one of the premier historians of Judaism, I can see how communities replicate past forms and innovate within them, but I don't see them mutating into new ones. Mutation or revolution comes from the genius (or madness) of the lone prophet or a small group of revolutionaries like the early scribes who ultimately morphed into the Pharisees.

Rabbinic or Pharisaic Judaism was a mutation. There is nothing in Judaism prior to the Pharisees that would lead one to imagine that God gave a second Torah to Moses on Mount Sinai. Once the mutation took hold and created a community, the community's job was to replicate the early teachings of the mutation and innovate from them.

The question now becomes, was Jesus a replication, an innovation, or a mutation? If we say he was a "corrective," then we can argue that he was an innovation, proving our point by citing Jesus' own teachings about the chief commandments in Matthew 22:37-39: "You shall love YHVH your God with all your heart, and with all your soul, and with all your mind," and "You shall love your neighbor as yourself." Jesus is simply quoting from Deuteronomy 6:5 and Leviticus 19:18, and while his understanding of these commandments may be innovative, he is not teaching anything radically new. Yet I cannot help thinking that there is more to Jesus' teaching than this.

I think that what makes Jesus a mutation rather than an innovation is his open table. The original Table of God was the altar on which the priests performed the sacrificial slaughter demanded by God. The Pharisees introduced a new table, the dinner table if you will, as an alternative place of meeting:

> Rabbi Shimon (ben Netanel) teaches, If three eat together and share no Torah, theirs is a feast for idols. Hence it [Scripture] says, "Without God, all tables are full of vomit and filth" [Isa 28:8]. But if three eat together and share Torah, theirs is a feast with God. Hence it says, "And he said to me, 'This is God's table'" [Ezek 41:22] (*Pirke Avot* 3:4).

Jesus didn't invent the idea of God's Table, but he did radically depart from the traditional guest list, and that was his mutation. But I may be quibbling over words, for I can certainly see how one might argue that this is innovative rather than mutative.

Your assertion that "all of us already sit at that table," however, is clearly a mutation. This is far more radical than saying that all of us are invited to sit at that table. Lady Wisdom in the Hebrew book of Proverbs (chapter 8) invites everyone to her table, and I can see how the Christian church in all its forms does the same, but to say that we are already at the table is to say something else entirely.

If we are all at the table, then creed, faith, religious preference, etc. neither preference nor prejudice one from sitting at God's Table. The notion that some are in and others are out, the core teaching of almost all religions, is dismissed as bigoted fantasy. We are all in.

I think you are clarifying the heart of Jesus' mutation: we are all already at God's Table. You don't have to earn a place at the table. You only have to realize that you are already there. So much for heaven and hell; so much for the saved and the damned; and so much for the chosen and the not chosen. There are only the full and the hungry, and being one or the other depends solely on one's capacity to stop and smell the pot roast.

Mike: I want to respond briefly to the idea that we're already at the table.

Thinking back, I believe the seed of the idea took root in me when I read C. S. Lewis's *The Last Battle* (London: Bodley Head, 1956). I do not have the book handy, so I'm going on memory. Late in the story, the children are cast into a dark stable. Some dwarfs, who have served the enemy and opposed Aslan, are also imprisoned there. As the world ends, the children see the stable vanish before their eyes, and they perceive that they are now in a wonderful place (Lewis's version of heaven).

The dwarfs are there as well, but they do not realize it. They no longer see the children, remain hunkered together as if hiding from the dark, and continue to "see" only their prison. Their bent minds deceive them and keep them bound in a prison of their own construction. No one can help them as long as they insist on clinging to their misapprehension.

This seems to me to be a fair description of the unreconstructed human condition.

In the next collection of sayings, Jesus starts to deal with "righteousness which exceeds that of the Pharisees." If you're ready, we'll start to deal with the passages.

Rami: I agree. We are already and always in "heaven"; we just lack the "eyes to see" and the "ears to hear." That is why I think that all authentic spirituality is about pulling the rug of illusion out from under us, and why most organized religion is about giving us an endless list of illusions to play with. Let's move on.

Part 3

On Righteousness
(Matthew 5:20-48)

Chapter 11

The First Example of Righteousness

You have heard that it was said to those of ancient times, "You shall not murder"; and "whoever murders shall be liable to judgment." But I say to you that if you are angry with a brother or sister, you will be liable to judgment; and if you insult a brother or sister, you will be liable to the council; and if you say, "You fool," you will be liable to the hell of fire. So when you are offering your gift at the altar, if you remember that your brother or sister has something against you, leave your gift there before the altar and go; first be reconciled to your brother or sister, and then come and offer your gift. Come to terms quickly with your accuser while you are on the way to court with him, or your accuser may hand you over to the judge, and the judge to the guard, and you will be thrown into prison. Truly I tell you, you will never get out until you have paid the last penny. (Matthew 5:21-26, NRSV)

Mike: Having called for a righteousness that exceeds that of the Pharisees, Jesus provides six examples (Matt 5:21-48). He takes a generally accepted version of a law or saying, insists that his followers go farther, and deals seriously with the sources and consequences of actions. The first of the six examples is Matthew 5:21-26.

Like any teacher of his day, Jesus accepts the prohibition against the act of murder. He goes on, though, to meddle with the human heart. Anger, says Jesus, is the breeding ground for murder. It can easily lead one to lash out with words, such as "fool" or "idiot." Left to fester, anger can incite murder.

Jesus does not forbid the feeling of anger. He knows very well that feelings simply happen. Instead, he teaches his followers to face the reality of the feeling, step away from whatever task is at hand (even the act of worship), and go seek reconciliation with their brothers or sisters.

Jesus extends the same principle to a less personal situation: if someone is taking you to court, deal with your anger by seeking reconciliation with that person.

Insofar as I can tell, Jesus calls for behavior consistent with the kingdom of heaven. One such indicator is a passion or commitment to reconciliation, to restored relationships. Interestingly enough, Jesus does not promise that the other person (the brother, the adversary, etc.) will respond in kind. His followers tend to chafe a bit at this point. For example, Peter will later ask how many times he must forgive someone who offends him. Jesus' classic answer is, "Seventy times seven," a proverbial saying that means "without limit."

Rami: The Sermon on the Mount is Jesus' articulation of how to live out the kingdom of God. As Jesus himself said, his teaching is not a repudiation of Torah but a highlighting of those aspects of Torah that he takes to be essential. This is certainly true in this section on anger and reconciliation. This is classic Jewish teaching.

For example, the book of Proverbs says, "A fool always loses his temper, but the wise man holds back" (Prov 29:11); and "A fool's wrath is known at once" (12:16). Proverbs also tells us that anger is the source of terrible strife (29:22; 30:33), and Psalm 37:8 urges us to "cease from anger" because it only causes harm.

Jesus' listeners, familiar with these and other Jewish teachings warning against anger, would not find Jesus' teaching surprising at all. Even Jesus' equating of anger with murder is part of Pharisaic teaching: "Whoever shames another in public is like one who sheds blood" (*Bava Metzia* 58b).

Of course even Jesus fails to live up to his idea. Jesus gets angry at the Pharisees' refusal to cure on the Sabbath (Mark 3:5), and he is certainly angry when he drives the moneychangers out of the temple (Matt 21:12). Both instances, however, are clearly in line with the righteous anger of the Hebrew Prophets, which only makes Jesus more Jewish rather than less. As for the notion that we shouldn't call each other names such as "fool," Jesus does this twice (Matt 23:17 and Luke 11:40). But I find these stories humanizing and endearing rather than troubling. Jesus is as human as the rest of us.

When elevating reconciliation over sacrifice, Jesus is drawing on Leviticus 6:1-7, where God says that if people have sinned against their neighbor, they must first make that right and then offer a sacrifice to God. The Pharisees even had procedures for what to do with a sacrifice that has to be postponed to allow time for one to return home and reconcile with one's neighbor.

Jesus' final teaching regarding the two plaintiffs going to court over some dispute is also standard Pharisaic teaching. Jesus directs these comments to the guilty party since he urges this person to "pay the last penny." In tractate *Sanhedrin* 95b of the Talmud, the rabbis make the same assumption and urge an out-of-court settlement. It is likely that both they and Jesus are drawing on an even older teaching in the book of Proverbs that, again speaking to the guilty, says, "Do not go hastily to court" (Prov 25:8).

The Hebrew Bible, the Pharisees, and Jesus are all saying the same thing: anger is dangerous, reconciliation with others takes precedent over prayer and sacrifice, and trying to avoid responsibility for one's actions by going to court is a bad idea. The Way of Jesus is the Way of Torah pared, in good prophetic style, to its ethical core.

Chapter 12

The Second Example of Righteousness

You have heard that it was said, "You shall not commit adultery." But I say to you that everyone who looks at a woman with lust has already committed adultery with her in his heart. If your right eye causes you to sin, tear it out and throw it away; it is better for you to lose one of your members than for your whole body to be thrown into hell. And if your right hand causes you to sin, cut it off and throw it away; it is better for you to lose one of your members than for your whole body to go into hell. (Matthew 5:27-30, NRSV)

Mike: Rami, would it be possible for you provide dates for some of the rabbinic sources you cite from time to time? Insofar as I know, the earliest date from the second and third centuries.

Jesus cites Exodus 20:14, prohibiting adultery. Most American Christians probably understand the commandment to mean all sex outside of marriage is forbidden. In its ancient setting, however, the commandment referred to sexual relations between a married man and the wife of another man. Adultery, therefore, had to do with property laws, in that a wife was considered to be her husband's possession. Officially, the offense required the death penalty, though in practice the penalty was seldom if ever exacted.

Whereas the commandment deals with a specific action, Jesus moves to deal with the heart (as in the imagination, will, desire, etc.). In effect, Jesus calls for a redefined relationship between men and women, one in which lust per se is taken off the table. Normal desire is not the issue here. Lust is. Lust is the feeling that reduces others to objects, even as it atrophies our own capacity for empathy.

Two things need to be said about the illustrations of eye and hand. First, they are a kind of hyperbole designed to drive home how seriously Jesus takes the matter. Second, they make a theological/existential point: in the end, lust reduces one to an utterly self-centered person, the kind of person who cannot experience the genuine, interactive presence of any other living being, even God. Such isolation is among the classic definitions of hell.

Rami: The issue of dating the early rabbinic material is complex. The literature was oral until the third century when Rabbi Judah haNasi, Rabbi the Prince or Head of the Rabbinic Court, wrote it down. This is the text we call the *Mishnah*. Some scholars say the material in the Mishnah stretches from 250 BCE to 250 CE.

After the writing of the Mishnah, oral debate resumed for another three centuries until that material was written down as the *Gemara* (the "conclusion"). Together Mishnah and Gemara comprise the *Talmud*, the authoritative collection of rabbinic teaching.

Alongside this material are collections of *midrash*, investigative (I would say imaginative) tales, some legal and others moral. These stories and teachings seem to date from before 200 BCE to around 200 CE, when the practice of writing them down began. Midrash continues to be created even today.

I assume you are asking about this to see if the texts and teachings I am referencing would have been available to Jesus. It is impossible to prove this one way or the other, but I was taught to back-date oral teachings generations prior to their becoming written teachings. So I am assuming that Jesus, trained as a Pharisee and recognized as rabbi, would have had access to these teachings.

Turning to our text, is Jesus extending the Jewish view of adultery? Probably not. He is conflating two biblical ideas of which we have already spoken in our examination of the Ten Commandments (see *Mount and Mountain*, vol. 1 [Macon GA: Smyth & Helwys Publishing, 2012]). We are prohibited from both committing adultery and coveting our neighbor's wife. The former deals with the act, and the latter deals with the heart or will. We also find a similar teaching in the Talmud: "Immoral thoughts are worse than immoral deeds" (*Yoma* 29a); and in the midrash: "Do not think that he is an adulterer who, by his single act, has sinned; he also is an adulterer who lusts with his eyes" (*Pesikta Rabbati* 124b).

It is true that, according to the Torah, adultery carried with it the death penalty. The rabbis, uncomfortable with capital punishment in any form, argued their way out of this by requiring that the adulterous couple be interrupted mid-coitus and warned about the consequences of their actions, and that without two witnesses to their sexual union no charge of adultery could be brought.

I am intrigued by your notion that Jesus calls for a new relationship between men and women. What is that relationship? Was the old relationship based on lust alone or even primarily? Was the old relationship to treat one another as objects, and the new one as equals? I would be hard pressed to see things that starkly. Yet women were certainly second-class citizens in biblical and rabbinic Judaism, and one could argue that inviting women to the table of Jesus changes all that. But then, most of Jesus' followers couldn't accept his radical egalitarianism, as the misogynist material attributed (falsely) to St. Paul (e.g., 1 Tim 2:11-15) and the anti-Mary Magdalene material in several of the Gnostic Gospels attest (e.g., Gos Mary 9:4-10; Gos Thomas 114:1-3). Once again, Jesus' message is lost on his followers and "his church."

I certainly agree that the talk of eye plucking is hyperbole and not to be taken literally. And I am interested in your notion of hell as self-isolation. I have heard this before: hell is being cut off from God. I would agree. For me, God is Reality—all that was, is, and will be. Being in touch with God is the realization of God as Reality and of our interconnectedness with all life, so it is only logical that being out of touch with God is being disconnected from all Reality, and that would be hell.

But, because I believe you need a self to be selfish and that the self dies when the body dies, hell is only in this world. When we die, the ego dies, and as it does it realizes the truth that all is God (*alles iz Gott*, as my Hasidic teachers put it is Yiddish), and so we all "go to heaven," just as every wave returns to the ocean from which and in which it lives, and moves, and has its being.

Mike: Thanks for the overview of the history of the rabbinic materials. Both of us draw heavily and easily on the accumulated "wisdom" of our traditions. Occasionally, it's good that we slow down long enough to share such information.

Turning back to the text and your remarks, I did not mean to suggest that lust was the primary or only ingredient in male/female relationships prior to Jesus. I think, though, that Jesus' words remove lust (as previously defined) from the list of acceptable components of the relationship. This is important. Historically, there's a rather large "disconnect" between the teachings of either of our traditions and the popular assumptions of large numbers of adherents. This is certainly true with regard to the relationship between men and women. The teaching and example of Jesus functions as a counter to the assumptions of many a male in many a society across the ages.

We agree as to the church's poor record with regard to women. Insofar as the church taught or supported the inferiority of women, it departed (and departs) from the intention of Jesus. At the same time, the church, operating within the context of various Western cultures, preserved the teachings of Jesus. Such teachings often furnished raw material for various forms of women's liberation. The "good news" (as we call it) keeps breaking through cultural constraints.

With regard to hell as a kind of self-isolation, the notion is really quite old. While we disagree as to what happens to the individual at death, I think we agree on the power of the paradigm of hell as self-isolation.

Rami: Let's go into the idea of "lust" a bit more deeply. Certainly lust that excuses treating an other as an object, what Martin Buber calls an "I-It relationship," is unhealthy and cannot be the foundation of any long-term holy relationship (defining holy as a treating one another as I-Thou, a manifestation of God equal to oneself). But, having said that, should we give up on the word altogether?

Is there such a thing as "holy lust"? This might be a level of desire/attraction that surpasses mere passion. I have no idea, really. I'm just thinking out loud. Yet I have a sense, perhaps a long-lost memory, of holy lust—a desire so great that it overwhelms the ego's sense of separateness (its intrinsic sense of hellish isolation), and pushes us beyond both I-It and I-Thou into the radical nonduality of I-I where self and other are united in a way that reveals something all embracing, all consuming—something the mystics of all traditions might call God—as the root and branch of all reality.

The intense sexual imagery that Jewish and Christian mystics use to speak of their relationships with God comes to mind, though I doubt they would use "holy lust" to describe it. I admit to a love of mixing words in odd ways to create controversy, but sometimes doing so also opens new windows and lets in some fresh thinking.

Chapter 13

The Third Example of Righteousness

It was also said, "Whoever divorces his wife, let him give her a certificate of divorce. But I say to you that anyone who divorces his wife, except on the ground of unchastity, causes her to commit adultery; and whoever marries a divorced woman commits adultery." (Matthew 5:31-32, NRSV)

Mike: Few New Testament passages provoke more conversation than Matthew 5:31-32. American Christians tend to treat it in one of several ways: make it a church law, apply it mostly to special groups (pastors, etc.), ignore it, restrict its application to the first century, interpret it in terms of leveling the playing field for women and men, or simply live uncomfortably with the knowledge that it exists within the canon. Individual Christians sometimes elevate the passage, treating it as a kind of supreme test of fellowship.

According to many a commentator, Jewish men in the first century could rather easily divorce their wives. Adultery, disobedience, and—at least in one often-cited list—burning the meal were considered ample cause for divorce. Insofar as I know, women had little if any recourse. My best guess is that divorce proved a little harder in practice, not because of legal restraints but because of the forces of family, economics, and compassion. Still, there seems little doubt that men held an enormous advantage with regard to power and that women were blamed for divorce.

Jesus seems to insist on at least two things.

First, he clearly takes marriage and divorce seriously. Kingdom life does not trivialize marriage. Ending a marriage is not a light matter. Even if we allow for the "exception clause" (and it may well have been added by editors), Jesus clearly teaches that divorce should be rare.

Second, he places enormous responsibility on the husband. The husband forces his former wife into a situation where she may well be compelled by economic necessity, family pressures, or other considerations to marry another male. In such a case, both men effectively force her to commit adultery. In the first-century world, a divorced woman had few economic options. If her birth family refused or was unable to care for her, she might be forced into prostitution or into another marriage in order to survive. All of the preceding can provoke endless discussion, but for me the key point is this: Jesus took the "get out of jail card" away from men.

In our time, roughly 50 percent of American Christians experience divorce. Most, in my experience, feel they had few options, yet they also tend to wrestle with considerable feelings of guilt. My personal position is that all the brokenness of human life (including divorce) is subject to the grace of God, through which we not only receive forgiveness but often find God fashioning an unexpected good thing. This does not eliminate personal responsibility and pain, but it does offer the possibility of an end to what we might call an "exile experience" coupled with some kind of restoration or rebirth.

Rami: This is a tough teaching. Is Jesus denying the option of divorce? It doesn't sound like it. If Jesus wanted to outlaw divorce he could have simply said, "But I say to you, you shall not divorce." He didn't say this but instead claims that a divorced woman is still bound to her husband so that she cannot remarry without committing adultery, which we know is a capital offense.

Two rival schools of Pharisees dominated rabbinic thought in Jesus' time: the conservative school of Shammai and the more liberal school of Hillel. More often than not, Jesus follows the position of Hillel, but in this case he sides with Shammai, who argues against divorce in all cases but that of sexual misconduct. The Pharisaic debate focuses on Deuteronomy 24:1, where divorce is allowed if a man finds "something objectionable" regarding his wife. The question is, *What is objectionable?* For Hillel it could be almost anything; for Shammai it refers only to sexual misconduct.

Jesus is drawn into this debate in Matthew 19:3, where the Pharisees ask him, "Is it lawful to divorce one's wife for any cause?" The key phrase is "for any cause." The Pharisees of Hillel's school hold that a man *can* divorce "for any cause," while the Pharisees of Shammai's school say there is only one cause for divorce: sexual misconduct. The Pharisees are asking Jesus to identify with one school or the other. Jesus sides with Shammai. The difference between these two teachings (Matthew 5 and 19) is that in the first he focuses on the woman and in the second on the man, saying that any man who divorces his wife (except in the case of sexual misconduct) and marries another woman is himself an adulterer.

The two teachings together are consistent and fair: both the woman and the man become adulterers if either remarries after divorce. But Jesus goes even further in his second teaching, arguing, "What therefore God has joined together, let no one separate" (Matt 19:6). Here Jesus sounds like he is opposed to divorce under any circumstances, perhaps taking up the teaching of God in Malachi, "For I hate divorce, says the LORD" (Mal 2:16). When the Pharisees ask him why, if divorce is to be outlawed completely, God allows it in the case of sexual misconduct, Jesus says God is bowing to human hard-heartedness (Matt 19:8).

Given that Jesus generally sides with the school of Hillel in matters of Jewish law, even his disciples are shocked by his pro-Shammai stringency. They say to him, "'If such is the case of man with his wife, it is better not to marry.' But he said to them, 'Not everyone can accept this teaching, but only those to whom it is given. For there are eunuchs who have been so from birth, and there are eunuchs who have been made eunuchs by others, and there are eunuchs who have made themselves eunuchs for the sake of the kingdom of heaven. Let anyone accept this who can'" (Matt 19:10-12).

Jesus is not anti-marriage, but he is uniquely pro-eunuch. In Leviticus 21:20 and Deuteronomy 23:1, we are told that eunuchs cannot marry or become priests or legislators. By holding up the eunuch as his ideal, Jesus is calling his followers to opt out of the social, religious, and legal systems that define the Judaism of his day. Jesus is calling to an elect that can achieve a status above householder, priest, and rabbi. This is an incredibly radical and new idea that reaches far beyond the issue of mere celibacy that troubled the apostles.

While I am intrigued by this hint of a higher state, and why Jesus chooses the term "eunuch" to reflect it, I admit to not knowing what to make of this call to become a eunuch for the kingdom of heaven. I would love to hear your take on this, Mike.

Mike: Thanks for the excellent overview of the Pharisaic debate and its possible application to Matthew 19:3ff. That being said, let's spend a little time on the matters of marriage, celibacy, and "eunuchs for the sake of the kingdom of heaven."

With regard to marriage, Jesus teaches that the dissolution of a marriage should never be taken lightly. I think we have to admit that the school of Hillel's position potentially lent itself to such an abuse. Whatever else we might conclude, Jesus' position brings a dose of sobriety to the matter.

In the first-century context, Jesus' teaching represents a large step forward for women in that he appears to treat both male and female as equals.

What about the exception clause? Some manuscripts do not include it, though the consensus of textual scholars appears to be that it belongs in the original text. Let's assume this to be the case. The followers of Jesus began to wrestle with the teaching within the first generation of the movement. We see that this is the response of the disciples. We also find Paul (1 Cor 7) suggesting that a believing spouse is not to be held accountable if an unbelieving spouse seeks divorce. In the past century or so, many Christians have concluded that spouse or child abuse should be added to the list of exception clauses. In the West, at least, most Christians recognize that when all efforts at reconciliation have been exhausted, divorce may become the only realistic option available. Here, I think, we see the living church and the Spirit of God working to interpret the teachings of Jesus in settings quite different from the first-century world.

To summarize, it seems to me that Jesus taught that marriage is meant to be an unbreakable union, that both partners bear responsibility for the success of the union, that it must not be lightly ended, and that divorce entails considerable consequences. At the same time, Jesus' teachings on the grace of God, coupled with the writings of Paul and subsequent developments in Christian thinking, make it clear that forgiveness and a new beginning are always possible.

Now, with regard to "eunuchs" for the kingdom of heaven, a small segment within the early church (second century and following) took the matter quite literally. Such has never been the interpretation of most Christians. Most ancient and modern commentators argue that Jesus taught that a minority of people might be gifted to embrace celibacy, so that they might focus solely on knowing and serving God. To put it another way, the strongly pro-marriage Jesus made space in his worldview for kingdom-dedicated singles.

Western Christianity, in my opinion, misapplied the teaching when it made celibacy a requirement for the priesthood and often devalued the spiritual possibilities within marriage. On the other hand, Protestant Christianity, in reaction to medieval excesses, went too far in the other direc-

THE THIRD EXAMPLE OF RIGHTEOUSNESS

tion, in effect creating a religious culture that is often uncomfortable with single and/or celibate Christians.

Jesus took a different tack. He taught that if we enter into marriage, we then are called to do all in our power to make it work well. In much the same manner, if we choose celibacy, we are to do so in order to devote ourselves to the kingdom of heaven.

One last thought: the account of Philip and the eunuch (Acts 8:26ff) demonstrates that the primitive church attempted to remove the stigma attached to eunuchs. With his baptism, the eunuch was admitted to the church with all the responsibilities and rights of any other person. At the very least, Jesus' teaching opened the door into the Christian community for such persons.

Rami: This is fascinating, Mike, even if only to the two of us.

Judaism, rooting itself in God's command to "be fruitful and multiply" (Gen 1:28), is decidedly pro-marriage. The *Shulchan Aruch*, the basic code of Jewish law, says, "Every person is obligated to marry in order to fulfill the duty of procreation, and whoever is not engaged in propagating the species is accounted as a murderer, diminishing the Divine Image and causing the presence of God to depart from Israel" (*Even ha-'Ezer* 1:1). The Talmud tells us that "One who has no spouse is less than human" (*Yevamot* 67a) and that "One who dwells without a spouse dwells without joy, without blessing, without good, and without happiness" (*Yevamot* 62b). And while the primary purpose of marriage was to have and raise children, the rabbis argued that sexual activity within marriage has its own value and should continue beyond the childbearing years.

The *Shulchan Aruch* also tells us that the ancient rabbis ruled that High Priests and judges presiding over capital crimes must be married (*Shulchan Aruch, Orah Hayyim* 53:9), though I can't tell if they ruled this way in order to make the judges more or less compassionate toward the accused.

Perhaps the most interesting teaching on marriage is that only a married man could study the deeper mysteries of the Torah (women were not allowed to study this at all until modern times). The rationale here was that these mysteries use sexual imagery, and one needed the grounding of a sexual partner to keep from being overwhelmed by the poetry of the teachings. We see that this is the case of many medieval Catholic mystics as well (especially nuns), who speak of their love of Jesus in very sexual terms. Sex may be so central to humanity that we cannot imagine the Divine without invoking the sexual.

While celibacy is not limited to Christianity (Hinduism too honors celibacy), and while I am pleased to hear that the early church removed the stigma Judaism placed on eunuchs, celibacy is still one of the clearest differences between our two traditions.

Chapter 14

The Fourth Example of Righteousness

Again, you have heard that it was said to those of ancient times, "You shall not swear falsely, but carry out the vows you have made to the Lord." But I say to you, Do not swear at all, either by heaven, for it is the throne of God, or by the earth, for it is his footstool, or by Jerusalem, for it is the city of the great King. And do not swear by your head, for you cannot make one hair white or black. Let your word be "Yes, Yes" or "No, No"; anything more than this comes from the evil one. (Matthew 5:33-37)

Mike: Jesus continues to illustrate kingdom life, turning to the matter of oaths.

Leviticus 19:2 and Numbers 30:2 prohibit swearing falsely, that is, purporting to tell the truth while in fact doing otherwise, whether by outright lying or shading the truth. In the time of Jesus, it appears many folk believed that oaths came in varying degrees of seriousness. For example, one might say, "Be it on my own head, if what I say is not true" or "As heaven is my witness, this is true." Such oaths were felt to be less binding than an oath sworn in the name of God.

Jesus says that kingdom people will not use such tactics for two reasons. First, anything we might call as witness to our oaths belongs to God. Invoking such things effectively involves God in our oath, and any attempt to act as if God is not involved is futile. Second, kingdom people should not need oaths. Living in the presence of God, they practice integrity. They do not need an oath to strengthen their own commitment to speak truth or keep their word.

Some attempt to restrict the teaching's application to formal settings, such as the courtroom. Like most Christian commentators, I think it applies to all arenas of life, but most especially to giving and keeping one's word and speaking truth in ways appropriate to a given setting.

I cannot help thinking of the passage when I listen to partisans "spin" the words of a political candidate. For example, I watched a debate between the presidential candidates. Each explained his particular approach to diplomatic conversations with leaders of rogue states. One used the term "precondition" to describe his own approach; the other chose the term "preparation." Try as I might, after listening to their explanations of their chosen terms, I could discern little difference in the mechanics of each candidate's approach (tone and style, perhaps, are different matters).

Immediately after the close of the debate, political pundits of various persuasions began to "spin the discussion." Most attempted to persuade me (and other viewers) that there was a considerable difference between the two candidates on this matter. To put it gently, the commentators had to shade the truth in order to make the attempt. Most of them, no doubt, have Christian or Jewish affiliations. I was struck, yet again, by how hard it is to take control of our tongues and speak with integrity rather than to use words to serve a particular ideology or party affiliation.

Lest I seem to pick only on political operatives, Baptist preachers have a mixed record at best. For example, the New Testament clearly records two approaches to baptism: one follows personal confession of Jesus as Savior and Lord, the other is administered to entire "families" (perhaps including household servants) when the head of a household becomes a Christian. Baptist preachers, for the most part, "spin" their discussion of the matter to make it sound as if the New Testament presents only one option, namely the one we practice. Again, it's awfully hard not to shade the truth to serve one's own position or felt needs.

One more word: Some Christians use the passage to argue that we must have a clear position on all matters or that we can never change our minds. In other words, they believe it is wrong to admit to gray areas or that one does not know the right answer, or to change one's position in light of new evidence. If ever you say "yes" to a position, it ought to remain your position, and so the argument goes. Nothing could be farther from the intention of Jesus. His call for radical truthfulness requires that we admit when we do not know, recognize the reality of ambiguity, and declare that we have changed our minds when we have done so.

Rami: I love this teaching of Jesus, and I too think it is central to the lives of "kingdom people" though, as an American I wish we could find a better term than "kingdom" to refer to those striving to live God's vision of a just and compassionate world. How about "the vision of God" rather than the "kingdom of God," and "vision people" rather than "kingdom people"?

And you are right to cite Leviticus 19:2 and Numbers 30:2. We should, given the nature of this dialogue, also mention the third commandment against taking God's name in vain (Exod 20:7) and the ninth commandment against swearing false witness against one's neighbor (Exod 20:16). It is clear, I think, that biblical Judaism has no problem with swearing oaths if done so with integrity. But by the time of Jesus, an anti-oath movement was well under way.

Here is a passage from the *Book of Enoch* written some decades before Matthew: "I promise you, my children, that I will not swear by a single oath; neither by heaven nor by earth, nor by anything else made by God. God said, 'There is no swearing in me, nor injustice, but truth.' If there is no truth in men, let them swear by a word—Yea, yea, or Nay, nay" (49:1-2).

Enoch seems to understand "yea, yea" and "nay, nay" as oaths, as do the rabbis in the Talmud (*Shavuot* 36a). Jesus' brother James may be trying to explain Jesus' teaching in light of the rabbinic notion that "yea yea" and "nay nay" are also oaths when he says, "But above all my brethren, do not swear, either by heaven or by earth or with any oath. But let your 'Yes' be 'Yes,' and your 'No' be 'No'" (Jas 5:12). In this rendering of the teaching, the double "yes" and "no" are not formulae as in the rabbis' thinking but simply a way of saying, "Say what you mean, and do what you say." If this is what Jesus meant, then there is no conflict with the rabbis of his day.

Philo, the Jewish sage of ancient Alexandria, also argued against taking oaths: "That being who is the most beautiful, and the most beneficial to human life, and suitable to rational nature, swears not, because truth on every point is so innate within him that his bare word is accounted an oath" (*On the Decalogue* 17, M. 2).

In *Ecclesiasticus* (the *Wisdom of Ben Sirach*), we find something similar, "Accustom not your mouth to swearing. Neither habituate yourself to using the name of the Holy One" (23:9-11). The Essenes, too, protested against the taking of oaths, claiming that their word was stronger than any oath and arguing that swearing an oath was worse than perjury (Josephus, *Jewish Wars*, 2.8, 6-7).

Given all of this, we can see that Jesus' position was not unique to him, and that he is simply taking sides in an ongoing Jewish debate on swearing oaths. But why is this so important? It could be that people were using the oaths and invoking the Name of God in support of lies, and Philo, Sirach, the Essenes, Jesus, and James are calling people to a higher level of integrity and honesty. This is important but somewhat prosaic.

Looking for something more challenging, we should note that in Jesus' day, swearing an oath of fidelity to Caesar was a major concern. Josephus in his *Antiquities* (15:368; 17:42) tells of two cases when the Jews refused to swear oaths to Rome. The first was a combined effort of both Pharisaic schools and the Essenes who refused to swear a loyalty oath to Herod, Rome's puppet king of the Jews. The second was a general Pharisaic refusal to swear an oath of loyalty to Caesar. Rome responded with uncharacteristic restraint, fining the offenders rather than killing them.

Maybe Jesus is using the oath issue with Rome in mind, making his teaching yet another act of nonviolent resistance to Roman occupation. By refusing to take oaths, one essentially denies the absolutist claims of the object of the oath, in this case Caesar. When Quakers refuse to pledge allegiance to the flag of the United States, they are resisting the temptation of many patriots to equate God and country. Since for most Romans Caesar was God, not taking oaths was a way of affirming political atheism.

The question for me is, how does this translate into living the "vision of God" today? Certainly being honest and avoiding spin is part of it, but there must be something more. I wonder if our money, with the phrase "In God We Trust" printed on it, is a kind of idol, and that participating in the American economic system is a betrayal of the vision of God. I really don't know, but I would love to hear from you on this.

Mike: Thanks for your overview of the "anti-oath" movement of Jesus' day. It's helpful. One of the guidelines I offer students of the New Testament goes like this: "Always remember, the words had to mean something to those who first heard them. Seek for that meaning. Find it, if possible. Build your interpretation and application of texts on such a base." Some listen, and some don't!

Turning to some of the matters you raise, like you I sometimes wish we could find a better term than "kingdom" for use in contemporary America. I'm not sure "the vision of God" and "vision people" suffice. In Christian theology, for the most part, "kingdom people" are those who live (or try to live) in constant awareness of the rule of God. There is a living God at work, both generally in all creation and specifically with individuals. I suspect that our different views on the nature of God are at work here.

Personally, I prefer to use "the way of Jesus." The phrase (for me) implies choosing a life direction centered in and guided by Jesus. All elements of life come into play: the mind, the emotions, self-care, caring for others, worship, daily "bread," work, play, rest, and the like. As you know well, "people of the way" probably was the earliest self-description Christians employed. I think they were on to something important.

With regard to swearing an oath of fidelity to Caesar, I think you've identified an often overlooked yet highly probable possibility. By the last decade of the first century, such an oath figured into persecution of Christians in Asia Minor. Insofar as I know, we do not have recorded incidents prior to that time. I am intrigued by your reference to "a general Pharisaic refusal to swear an oath of loyalty to Caesar" and would like to know more about the probable dating.

The larger issue, of course, is idolatry. When we place our ultimate trust in a system, a person, an ideology, or anything other than God, we divert from "the way." We may run off the road and into a ditch or wind up traveling another road if we stay fixated on the diversion. My hunch is that all economic systems (to stay with the matter you suggest) hold the potential to divert us. The same is true of recreation, the entertainment industry, or even our personal avocations.

Living on "the way" requires one's attention, to put it gently.

Rami: Whenever talk of idolatry comes up I always go back to the work of Erich Fromm, especially his book *To Have or To Be* (New York: Harper and Row, 1976). Fromm speaks of two ways of living: having and being. The former is all about living from a place of scarcity. The latter is about living with and in the abundance of the moment.

In the having mode, God becomes an idol, "something that we ourselves make and project our own powers into, thus impoverishing ourselves. We then submit to our creation and by our submission we are in touch with ourselves in an alienated form. While I can have the idol because it is a thing, by my submission to it, it, simultaneously, has me" (Fromm 40).

Having and being had is the great sin. The God of the prophets cannot be had, and therefore cannot have you. The God of the prophets is the opposite of an idol. From the second of the Ten Commandments to Jesus (whom

I understand to be among the greatest of prophets), any god that can be imaged is not the eternal God.[1]

The prophets' challenge is to accept the freedom of uncertainly, insecurity, and not knowing. Their way is the way of radical freedom, and they know that failure to be free can only result in enslavement to self and selfishness, and eventually exile from all that is meaningful and joyous in life.

A life of having is a life of being had. A life of being is a life of freedom. The "having life" is authoritarian and based on the false notion that you are other than the One Who Is. Alienated from God, you are forced to search for salvation, your sense of wholeness, by submitting yourself to externals. The "being life" is liberating and rooted in your unity with God as the One Who Is all things. Finding refuge in God, you are free from externals, and you lack nothing, need little, and fear no one. I think Jesus and the Way of Jesus is a life of being rather than having.

Note

1. Paraphrase from the opening line of the Chinese Tao te Ching: "the Tao that can be named is not the Eternal Tao" (Tao te Ching 1:1).

Chapter 15

The Fifth Example of Righteousness

You have heard that it was said, "An eye for an eye and a tooth for a tooth." But I say to you, Do not resist an evildoer. But if anyone strikes you on the right cheek, turn the other also; and if anyone wants to sue you and take your coat, give your cloak as well; and if anyone forces you to go one mile, go also the second mile. Give to everyone who begs from you, and do not refuse anyone who wants to borrow from you. (Matthew 5:38-42, NRSV)

Mike: Jesus starts by alluding to Deuteronomy 19:21 and 21:24. In its earliest context, "an eye for an eye and a tooth for a tooth" reined in revenge. It forbade exacting vengeance beyond the hurt one suffered. The concept continues to influence us today, being the core principle upon which most Western concepts of justice rest.

That being said, the saying also often lends a tone of legitimacy to those who want revenge. Left unchallenged or unmodified, "an eye for an eye and a tooth for a tooth" may (and does) fuel endless cycles of retaliation. It may restrict the scope of violence, but it cannot end violence.

Jesus calls for a kind of nonviolent resistance. His examples are drawn from his historical context. Striking someone on the right cheek with the back of one's right hand was a well-known way to insult another. It invited a similar response. Jesus called his followers to refuse to play the game. In similar fashion, an opponent might take advantage of his power or a corrupt justice system to take one's inner garment. If so, that person was to confound the opponent by giving up his outer cloak as well. A Roman soldier might legally compel one to carry his military equipment for a mile. Jesus instructed his followers to go an extra mile willingly.

His focus is on actions taken. Break the patterns of violence and resentment. Go beyond what the law or custom require. His words probably did not sit well with the majority of an occupied population.

The final injunction to give and lend to all who ask does not fit easily with the preceding verses. Had I been editing the materials that became Matthew's Gospel, I probably would have placed the verse in chapter 6, perhaps in the vicinity of verses 2 and 3. Still, I think it's fair to say that Matthew links the saying to the previous ones because of their shared extreme nature.

Following the way of Jesus is risky by normal standards. At best, your reputation may be called into question. You'll certainly frustrate friends and fellow "tribe" members when you refuse to respond to violence with violence. You may wind up broke (the nightmare of most Western Christians)! Your time may be consumed. Certainly, you might suffer physical harm and perhaps even death.

Jesus operates out of a vision: the cycle of violence and self-protectiveness can only be broken if we refuse to play by its rules. He clearly believes that he speaks for God in this matter.

I think it's best not to seek to explain away Jesus' radical position. His followers may choose other responses to violence, but when we do so we should acknowledge we have departed from the strict way of Jesus.

Rami: There is so much to say about this amazing teaching. Let me divide my response into two parts: "an eye for an eye" and "do not resist an evildoer," Jesus' program for nonviolent resistance to injustice. I will comment on each separately and invite your comments as we go along.

The phrase "an eye for an eye" originally comes from Exodus 21:23-27, where a person who has taken the eye of another in a fight is required to forfeit his own eye as compensation. This is called reciprocal justice, *lex talionis*, and can be traced back to the Code of Hammurabi. By the time of Jesus, *lex talionis* was understood in financial terms, with the guilty party paying a fine sufficient to cover damages, pain, medical expenses, incapacitation, and mental anguish.

Your reference to Deuteronomy 19:16-21 deals with a more direct form of *lex talionis* where conspirators testifying falsely in court are punished by having done to them what they planned to do to their intended victim. Deuteronomy also mentions the case of a woman coming to the aid of her husband in a fight by grabbing the genitals of her husband's opponent. The

Torah says, "you shall cut off her hand; show no mercy" (Deut 25:11-12). This severe reaction to "hitting below the belt" most likely reflects Iron Age fears about women touching men's genitalia, but by the time of Jesus this case was understood to refer to a woman who was going to kill her husband's attacker rather than incapacitate him. Cutting off her hand was thought to be a lesser punishment, taking into account her passion to save her husband, when she might have been liable to capital punishment as a would-be murderer.

In each of these cases, however, we are talking about official justice carried out by the courts, and not acts of individual violence or revenge. Even the one exception to this rule found in Numbers involves the courts.

In Numbers 35:9-30, a person charged with manslaughter is obligated by the court to flee to a "city of refuge" to await trial. No one can touch him as long as he remains in the city. If he leaves the city, however, and is killed by a relative of the original victim, no penalty is accrued because the accused is now considered an escapee in violation of the court order to remain in the city of refuge. The idea behind this ruling is, in a world without prisons, to scare the accused into staying in the city of refuge until his trial. Notice that this only applies to manslaughter, killing without forethought or intent. Murder, intentional killing, is punishable by death, and no city of refuge applies. But in every case the court must establish guilt and carry out the sentence.

In other words, even in biblical times, "an eye for an eye" was not about private revenge but about court-based justice. Private revenge was already outlawed in Leviticus 19:18, "You shall not take vengeance, nor bear any grudge against the children of your people; but you shall love your neighbor as yourself."

Given all of this, it is challenging to figure out what Jesus intends with his attack on "an eye for an eye." He cannot be referring to private revenge, because "an eye for an eye" doesn't refer to private revenge but to court-sanctioned punishment. So is he attacking the court system itself?

Maybe. Given the morally corrosive nature of Roman occupation, it is not hard to imagine that the justice system, like the high priesthood, was in the pocket of Rome. Justice may simply be for sale, and the people to whom Jesus addresses his message are not those with the wherewithal to buy it. I suggest that we are dealing with a call to abandon the corrupt courts and find a new way to "do justly, love mercy, and walk humbly with your God" (Mic 6:8).

Mike: Sometime back, I think, we briefly discussed how our respective traditions may incline us to approach interpreting texts differently. In a nutshell, my tradition tends to focus on the personal and a big picture, while your tradition encourages a greater focus on the corporate and particulars. To my mind, our differences enrich our conversation.

Given your focus on how an "eye for an eye" applied only to the courts, I wonder if you may underestimate the importance of "popular" interpretation and application. I suspect that any number of people absorbed the concept and went on to apply it to interpersonal relationships. From spouses to parents to clans to the world of commerce, my hunch is that individuals justified various forms of revenge on the basis of the maxim. Turning to politics, I cannot help thinking that the Zealots embraced the phrase as part of their justification for violent resistance to the Romans. Insofar as I determine, such sayings become not only law but also folklore, and their influence as folklore may or may not bear much relationship to their intended meaning.

I have no doubt that you are correct: the court system of the day was corrupt, and Jesus certainly called on his followers to take a different approach to justice. At the same time, though, I think Jesus sought to address and reform personal habits of the mind, heart, and hands.

Rami: I think your analysis of our differences is true to a great degree. Judaism is a corporate enterprise. It does not recognize the separation of religion and state. The Torah, both Written and Oral, is a legal and ethical code for both individuals and the state, addressing all aspects of personal and corporate life.

The Gospels, on the other hand, are not concerned with the details of politics or economics. Jesus is talking about a revolution of the individual. He may have thought that to change the whole, we must begin with the parts (I myself agree with this), or he may have believed that the end times were upon him and that history and the vehicles of history such as the state were coming to an end, so there was no need to speak to these entities. Or he may have felt that nothing could be or needed to be added to the Hebrew Prophets and their centuries-long call for social, political, and religious revolution. Whatever his reasoning, one is hard pressed to run a country or an economy or even a world religion based on the principles of the Sermon on the Mount.

This was probably not an issue until the conversion of Emperor Constantine and the eventual transformation of the Roman Empire into the no less oppressive Holy Roman Empire. The more power the Catholic Church accrued, the less Christian it became. Martin Luther's Reformation was a return to Jesus, but this simply resulted in a plethora of Jesuses each supporting the ideology of the state or group that worshiped him. When we go back to the original texts of the New Testament and try to understand Jesus as his original listeners may have understood him, we are engaged in a dangerous and revolutionary act, for what we find and hear is not the Jesus of this or that denomination or political party, shaped to sanction their policies, but the real Jesus demanding a revolution of the heart.

When George W. Bush said Jesus was the philosopher who influenced him the most, no one asked him where Jesus actually influences his policies. Bumper stickers asking "Who Would Jesus Bomb" show just how absurd it is to use Jesus to justify the brutality of the state. To put it bluntly, in a country driven by greed, addicted to oil, and so often trapped in the politics of hate, fear, and xenophobia, Jesus is a troubling role model. So we are offered a number of faux-Jesuses instead: the Jesus of the Prosperity Gospel, for example, who wants everyone to be rich (camels and needles be damned), and the Warrior Jesus where the Prince of Peace sanctions the ways of war, and the Jesus who hates homosexuals, Jews, blacks, and Democrats.

It seems to me that much of Christianity in the United States, like much of Islam in places like Saudi Arabia, Pakistan, and Iran and certain branches of Judaism in Israel, has been hijacked by those who use religion only to solidify their own power. This is why we need to go back to the prophets of justice and compassion in each of these traditions and reclaim the true revelation they all share: that we are to love God and to love our neighbor.

What I hope isn't getting lost in our conversation is just how radical the Ten Commandments and the Sermon on the Mount truly are.

Mike: Never underestimate the human capacity and willingness to make religion the servant and prop of power. If I understand you, we agree on this point.

Love God and love your neighbor is the heart of the matter and the goal of the Christian life. Unfortunately, the human heart is deceptive. We can go round and round about why this is so: original sin, cultural conditioning, genetics, and the like. I prefer simply to deal with the reality of the condition. Bound by our out-of-balance self-centeredness and self-protectiveness, we find it almost impossible to fully love (which is to trust) God. We, for the most part, also seem unable to love others in healthy ways or to extend such love beyond rather narrow groupings.

Jesus envisioned a revolution in human nature and behavior that is grounded in an individual response to his message and person. In fact, we can read Christian history as an ongoing series of mini-revolutions in which this vision of Jesus reemerges in counterpoint to institutional Christianity.

Jesus is too radical to be tamed by the church or the state, though both try mightily.

Rami: Yes, Jesus is too radical to be tamed! God is too radical to be tamed! I often think religion is about taming God, and that is what troubles me the most about it. So let's take a look at some of Jesus' radicalism.

If we are to understand Jesus' teachings on "turning the right cheek," "going the extra mile," and "giving one's cloak," we have to see them in the context of his situation.

Striking a person backhanded on the right cheek was the way Roman soldiers debased the Jews: striking them as one might strike a dog. Slapping a person openhanded on the left cheek, though a sign of anger, was also an affirmation of human equality. Jesus is saying, "Do not resist the evil of the backhanded slap, but dare the oppressor to strike you as an equal." This puts the Roman soldier in the morally awkward position of having to elevate your status from subhuman to human, walk away, or beat you senseless despite the fact that you did not threaten the soldier with bodily harm. In any of these three cases, the soldier loses, and the seeds of moral discontinuity are planted in both the soldier and those who witness or come to hear of the soldier's dilemma.

The same is true of carrying a soldier's gear the "extra mile." Roman law allowed soldiers to grab Jews off the street and treat them as pack animals for up to one mile. Jesus is saying, "Do not resist the insult of being treated as a pack animal. Rather, when your service is up, insist on carrying the gear as a free human being." This act of generosity again puts the soldier in a morally untenable situation. He cannot force you to carry his pack and has to force you to return it to him. Even if he again chooses to beat you senseless, the rationale for his actions—that you wished to help him carry his gear—makes his action and the system that supports it appear more and more immoral.

In both cases, the person following Jesus' challenge places himself or herself in danger of being beaten, but the beating is morally unjustifiable even by the soldier doing the beating. You are not endangering the soldier, so he cannot claim self-defense. You are simply refusing to accept his assumption that you are less than him. This is so important: Jesus is challenging us to resist our own dehumanization as well as to cease dehumanizing others. This challenge is no less relevant today than it was 2,000 years ago.

Jesus' reference to the cloak shifts his concern from Roman occupation to the corrupt courts run by the Roman-collaborating Jewish establishment. The courts are enforcing a system of injustice that keeps the majority of the population impoverished. The Bible speaks of everyone sitting unafraid under her vine and her fig tree (Mic 4:4), but in Jesus' day most people had been robbed of their ancestral lands and reduced to tenant farming on land owned by absentee landlords. Poverty and injustice were rampant. The system had lost its moral foundation, and greed rather than godliness was its watchword.

Jesus is saying, "If they take your outer garment because you cannot pay whatever monies the unjust system says you owe, give them your undergarment as well. Walk out of the courthouse naked." In a culture that finds nakedness more than a little troubling, this act of defiance makes a clear yet nonviolent statement about the corrupt nature of the legal system. "Look what the system is doing to us!" such an act says. "Look how we are violated!" The outrage such political theater would engender could lead to a revolution. Jesus didn't have to raise an army to frighten the Romans and their collaborators. He only had to revive the prophetic spirit.

All of this is glorious prophetic theater. Jesus knows, contra the Zealots, that the people cannot rise up and defeat the Romans militarily. (They will try a few decades later, resulting in an exile lasting for almost 2,000 years.) He also knows that collaboration, the preferred position of the Sadducees, is immoral. But he is equally unhappy with the passive withdrawal of the Essenes and limited cooperation of the Pharisees. Jesus wants to engage Rome, to take on the unjust system that oppresses his people, and to do so nonviolently. Jesus is a prophet speaking truth to power.

The sad thing for me, and it seems to be true for you as well, Mike, is that this legacy of prophetic nonviolence taught by Jesus has been largely abandoned (albeit with notable exceptions) since Constantine when the church was co-opted by Roman imperialism. And today, for so many self-proclaimed Christians, Jesus is the lord of hatred, fear, anti-intellectualism, anti-Semitism, and racism.

Of course, every religion has its extremists, and Christianity is not different from Judaism, Islam, and Hinduism in this regard. All of it sickens me, even as it breaks my heart. Religion is so easily co-opted by power. Wherever Judaism, Christianity, Islam, Hinduism, and even Buddhism become state religions, the prophetic call for justice fades and the clerics become puppets of politicians proclaiming holy what is solely in the interest of power—their power.

So what are we to make of Jesus' call to "resist not evil"? "Resist not evil" cannot mean that we are to ignore the commandment to "not stand idle while our neighbor bleeds" (Lev 19:16) and place our faith in some private afterlife salvation. Rather, he is urging us to find a nonviolent way to resist an unjust system of oppression. This is what Gandhi and the Reverend Martin Luther King, Jr., saw in the Sermon on the Mount. This is what we have to see ourselves. See, and then enact.

Mike: Your comments put me to thinking about guidelines for those who embrace a "nonviolent way to resist an unjust system of oppression." I think, as you might imagine, that one resists not only systems but also individuals. Here's a first draft of my list.

1. That which dehumanizes you or others is evil. No so-called necessity, philosophical or political difference, or vision of society can justify dehumanization.

2. Do not flirt with such evil or pretend it can be accommodated or tamed. Many have tried such approaches and failed. Inevitably, those who do so wind up supporting or ignoring evil for the sake of some supposed long-term good.

3. Never take up the weapons of evil to resist evil. Do no violence. Remember that the weapons we use may ultimately define or redefine us.

4. Accept the necessity of personal suffering. You may be hit, arrested, imprisoned, exiled, or killed. Suffering is the price you pay for nonviolent resistance to evil.

5. Embrace humility. Nothing is stranger than a pride-filled nonviolent prophet.

6. Do not presume to judge how others respond to evil; be content to live out your vision.

7. Do not, in your mind or deeds or words, dehumanize your oppressors—treat them as you wish they treated others.

8. Make nonviolent resistance to evil a life's work. Occasional nonviolence accomplishes little.

Well, it's a start. Do you have a list?

Rami: I don't have a complementary list, Mike, and I find yours helpful. So let me just work with that.

1. *That which dehumanizes you or others is evil.* This is a fine definition as far as it goes, but I would like to go beyond the anthropocentric and say that anything that debases life is evil. Now we can include human acts of animal cruelty and environmental degradation as acts of evil as well.

2. *Do not flirt with such evil or pretend it can be accommodated or tamed.* I love your choice of verb. To "flirt" has a sexual connotation that may indeed be apropos, though we would have to flesh it out (yes, pun intended).

3. *Never take up the weapons of evil to resist evil.* Are weapons used in defense of oneself and one's people's evil? I admit to not being a pacifist, so this idea is a difficult one for me to accept.

4. *Accept the necessity of personal suffering.* There is a cost for resisting evil. If we are not willing to pay it, we cannot succeed.

5. *Embrace humility.* Humility is the antidote to pride, and pride is the fuel of much evil. I love the prophet Micah's insight: "walk humbly with your God" (Mic 6:8). Why "your God" rather than just "God"? Because, so say the rabbis, each of us has our own idea of God and none of us has the whole of God, so Micah is telling us to be humble about our faith and our certainty.

6. *Do not presume to judge how others respond to evil; be content to live out your vision.* I have no problem with making judgments, and I believe that there are evil responses to evil (torturing of prisoners, even terrorists, being one example). So I would argue that if we have a standard for resisting evil, we should use it to measure the quality of other resistant movements as well.

7. *Do not, in your mind or deeds or words, dehumanize your oppressors—treat them as you wish they treated others.* This is one application of your first principle, and I wholeheartedly agree. There is an interesting documentary on the dehumanizing propaganda of the Japanese, Germans, and Americans during World War II. The Nazis dehumanized whole groups: Jews, Gypsies, Americans; the Americans did the same with its racist anti-Japanese cartoons; but the Japanese themselves limited their attacks to the Allied leadership and not all Americans or Europeans. Dehumanizing groups is the first step to annihilating them.

8. *Make nonviolent resistance to evil a life's work.* I agree. One who is only occasionally nonviolent is not nonviolent at all. Nonviolence isn't a tactic; it's a life strategy.

So we are in substantial agreement regarding your list, but let's not stop here. We are assuming that nonviolence is indeed the ideal, but why make that assumption? Especially when dealing with a sacred text that has God sanctioning the most horrendous acts of genocide.

God seems to have no problem with violence as long as it is done at his behest. God's destruction of all land-based life outside the ark (Gen 6–9); God's promise to drive out the Canaanites, Hittites, Hivites, Perizzites, Girgashites, Amorites, and Jebusites (Josh 3:10); God's sanctioning the murder of all the men, women, children, and animals of Jericho (Josh 6:21); God's command to commit genocide against the people of Amalek (1 Sam 15:1-3); and the murder of all nonbelievers in the book of Revelation make it clear that God is not a God of nonviolence. Can Jesus' single teaching that those who live by the sword shall die by the sword (Matt 26:52) turn the tide against the murderous God of the Bible?

Since I believe that the Bible is of human origin, reflecting the best and worst of what we humans are capable, I would argue (nonviolently of course) that violence is part of our DNA, and that seeking to impose nonviolence on instinctually violent creatures such as ourselves is itself an act of violence.

The question for me is this: Can we transform ourselves rather than simply control ourselves when it comes to violence? Can we literally change our minds and hence our responses? Can we, to use New Testament terminology, put on the mind of Christ (1 Cor 2:5; 2:16)?

I think we can. When we cultivate a capacity for contemplative self-observation—when we can look at our capacity for violence without reacting—then we can be free from this instinct and be in the world in a new way. Short of this truly revolutionary step, I think we can rely on the golden rule and refrain from doing unto others what is abhorrent to ourselves.

Mike: We, indeed, are in substantial agreement. As for your suggested additions and revisions, here's a brief response.

1. Agreed. Let's expand the maxim to include all creation.

2. I chose the term "flirt" with considerable intention. The sexual/relational connotations rest on insights from some of the prophets.

3. We differ a bit on the matter of pacifism. Insofar as I can tell, pacifism (which is a logical component of nonviolence) is the ideal of Jesus. When we take up weapons, we fall short of the ideal. I see no possibility of the ideal being realized at the corporate level, though individuals may on occasion

attain it. The ideal, though, pushes us to make violence a last resort rather than a preemptive or first response.

4. We agree.

5. We agree.

6. Upon reflection, I think you are correct! The one caution I would urge is that we be careful not to indulge in self-righteousness when evaluating others' responses to evil.

7. We agree.

8. We agree.

As for the remainder of your interesting post, as you know we hold different assumptions. From my perspective, all Scriptures must be read and evaluated in light of what we believe we know about Jesus. When it comes to the Hebrew Bible texts you mention, my assumption drives me to at least two conclusions. First, the teachings and actions of Jesus make it impossible for me to maintain that God sanctions such violence. Second, I tend to think that much of the Bible is a record of how humans apprehend or misapprehend God. God, to my way of thinking, gets a great deal of bad press, taking the blame for decisions made by humans, all of whom were conditioned by the culture(s) of their day.

Both of us, I think, argue that violence is part of the human heritage, ingrained in us by both genetics and culture. Controlling our violence is commendable. Transforming our natures, or from my perspective experiencing such transformation in partnership with God, remains a legitimate hope.

Rami: This is what makes our dialogue so much fun! We agree just enough to be able to speak meaningfully to one another, and disagree just enough to be able to learn constructively from one another. I agree with everything you said. So let's move on!

Chapter 16

The Sixth Example of Righteousness

You have heard that it was said, "You shall love your neighbor and hate your enemy." But I say to you, Love your enemies and pray for those who persecute you, so that you may be children of your Father in heaven; for he makes his sun rise on the evil and on the good, and sends rain on the righteous and on the unrighteous. For if you love those who love you, what reward do you have? Do not even the tax collectors do the same? And if you greet only your brothers and sisters, what more are you doing than others? Do not even the Gentiles do the same? Be perfect, therefore, as your heavenly Father is perfect. (Matthew 5:43-48, NRSV)

Mike: The test of true religion is how we act toward those who hate or harm us, or whom we have been taught to treat as enemies.

"You shall love your neighbor" is drawn from Leviticus 19:18. "Hate your enemy" presents a problem. To the best of my knowledge, this specific language is not found in the Hebrew Bible. On the other hand, a number of passages acknowledge the existence of such feelings. Going beyond texts, I think it is reasonable to conclude that many a parent taught their children to observe both maxims. Frankly, it's human nature.

Which, of course, is Jesus' point: "What more are you doing than others?" For someone of the Christian tradition, the injunction to love and pray for even enemies narrows our options. If we take Jesus seriously, we're forced to examine our typical reactions.

Rami, I took this matter seriously even as a child. The rural school I attended featured serious divisions among the students. To be frank, all students had friends and enemies. Your enemies could (and usually did) hurt you, not only in terms of shunning and teasing but sometimes to the point of physical violence. Naturally, we were tempted to buy into the system, choose a side, and go to war.

I wanted to do so, but each time I started down that road I stumbled over this teaching of Jesus. Sometimes I got up, shook the dust from my sneakers, and plunged into the fray. More often, though, I chose not to hurt "my enemies." Worse, I felt compelled to try to help at least some of them in the ways available to me: a kind word, a bit of help with homework, choosing them for a sports team, and the like. To put it mildly, such behavior was not well received by my "friends." I wish I could honestly say that all the teachings of Jesus took hold so strongly during my childhood!

Looking back, I now know that I was being granted a taste of the loneliness that comes to any of us who depart from the norm.

The Scripture passage teaches that those who follow Jesus' injunction may "be perfect" even as God is perfect. A better translation might be "mature" or perhaps even "complete." Love in action, without regard for the categories of friend and enemy, completes a follower of Jesus. In our better moments we remember this is so. Too often, we forget.

Rami: There is no doubt that this is a challenging teaching. Let me go into it slowly, beginning with the notion of "hate."

As you said, Mike, the Hebrew Bible doesn't enjoin us to hate our enemies, but I doubt Jesus has the Bible in mind here. He is living under brutal Roman oppression and may well be addressing the hatred Jews have of their Roman occupiers. Translating his teaching into our time would be as if Jesus were calling us to love the Taliban and Osama bin Laden.

And then there is the question of Luke 14:26, "Whoever comes to me and does not hate father and mother, wife and children, brothers and sisters, yes and even life itself, cannot be my disciple." And John 12:25, "Those who love their life, lose it, and those who hate their life in this world will keep it for eternal life." In these passages, Jesus seems to be obligating his followers to hatred. How are we to understand this?

Then there is the notion of "love." Is Jesus talking about feeling loving toward our enemies? Or, in good Jewish fashion, is he talking about acting lovingly toward them? For example, Exodus 23:4 commands that if you find your enemy's ox or donkey, you have to return the animal to him or her regardless of how you feel about the person. Since we cannot control our feelings—indeed by the time we recognize that we have feelings that might need controlling, we have already felt them—there is no point in command-ing certain feelings. But we can control our behavior. Hence Proverbs 25:21, "If your enemy is hungry, give him bread to eat; and if he is thirsty, give him water to drink."

But I may be too narrow in my thinking. Proverbs 24:17-18 does seem to speak to feelings: "Do not rejoice when your enemy falls, and do not let your heart be glad when he stumbles," so maybe there is a way to control our feelings even if I can't find one.

And then there is "pray for those who persecute you." This, too, is found in the Torah Jesus learned. Moses prays for Pharaoh five times (see Exod 8:24-27, for example); Job prayed for his enemies (Job 42:9); David prayed for Saul (1 Sam 24:12); and Jeremiah urges the Hebrew people to pray for the Babylonians (Jer 29:7).

My point here is simply that Jesus is not inventing a new way of living but rather gathering threads from his Jewish culture to weave a new Judaism bearing his special emphasis.

It is Jesus' last admonition—"Be perfect as your heavenly Father is per-fect"—that I find the most challenging. You are taking this to be "mature" or "complete," by which I guess you mean something like "be consistent in your loving actions toward your enemies, as God is consistent when He shines the sun upon the good and the evil alike."

If this is what Jesus means, then I think we can all work toward this level of moral consistency. But what if he does mean something more? What if, as you say, "perfect" means "complete," and "complete" means "whole," and "whole" means inclusive of opposites?

God seems to have a light and dark side. He can be loving and wrathful. The mere fact that there is a tree of knowledge of good and evil in the Garden of Eden suggests that there must be some evil to know. Where could that come from if not God? God is the source of all reality, and reality is composed of opposites: up and down, in and out, right and wrong, good and evil, mercy and judgment, etc. This is exactly what God says in Isaiah: "I form light, I create darkness; I create goodness and I create evil" (Isa 45:7).

Being made in the image and likeness of God, we, too, have these oppo-sites embedded in us. To be perfect, whole, complete, is to recognize what Judaism calls our *Yetzer haTov* and *Yetzer haRah*, our innate capacities for good and evil, respectively. According to the rabbis, both capacities are nec-essary for human life and flourishing. Evil, rooted in concern for the self, is the yeast that motivates us to marry, raise a family, and run a business. It is called "evil" because, if taken to extremes—that is, if left untempered by our capacity for good—it can turn to selfishness and lead to terrible abuses in marriage, family rearing, and business practices.

Similarly, the capacity for good is rooted in selflessness, and, unless balanced by the capacity for self-focus, leads to loss of self and failure to achieve anything of value regarding oneself or one's community. To be a successful human, we must yoke each inclination to the other. In effect, the *Yetzer haRah* is the energy for doing, and the *Yetzer haTov* is the direction that ensures our doing is for the good.

Maybe we can understand Jesus' command to be perfect to be a call to recognize our dual nature and place *rah* in service of *tov*, just as God softens His judgment with His compassion.

Mike: Interesting, isn't it, how we are driven toward certain questions, whether we're dealing with the Ten Commandments, the Beatitudes, or the body of the Sermon on the Mount. At least three resurface in your post: the matter of feelings, Jesus' creative use of existing themes in the Judaism of his time, and the light and dark sides of God.

Let's start with feelings. As I've noted at other times, I deeply appreciate the possible distinction between how we feel and how we act. We can choose to act lovingly toward enemies, regardless of our feelings. Doing so, though, still requires that we recognize and confront our feelings and judge hatred wanting. Over the long haul, I'm not convinced that we can maintain a separation between feelings and actions. Jesus recognized this reality. In "good Jewish fashion," he began with actions, but it seems clear from the tone and content of the Sermon of the Mount that he also dared to hope that feelings could be transformed as well.

Both of us probably could provide (or find) testimonies from those who have experienced such transformation. To my mind, such accounts matter. They strongly suggest that our feelings can change or be changed. Jesus' vision moves beyond the question of controlling our feelings. He seems to call us to yearn for new and better ones. This particular topic gets caught up in the larger Christian dream of a life made new by God.

As to Jesus' creative use of Jewish themes, I think we are in full agreement. The very idea makes some Christians uncomfortable. A few probably harbor a bit of anti-Semitism. Most, though, are guilty only of muddled thinking, the kind that insists that Jesus' perspective and teachings must stand alone, divorced from historical setting or precedent. Such thinking ignores the implications of the incarnation.

The light and dark sides of God: now there's a matter that has deep roots in Jewish history and interesting outbreaks in Christianity's story. We've played with *Yetzer haTov* and *Yetzer haRah* in previous posts. Christian scholars began to wrestle with the topic as they became better acquainted with rabbinic writings. Some Christians speak in terms of how light must always cast a shadow. Personally, I think the concept lies in back of the Apostle Paul's confession that he does not always do what he wills to do, not to mention his insistence that the "fleshly person" must die that the "spiritual person" might live.

We may be close to a functional agreement on what to do with our two natures. You write, "Maybe we can understand Jesus' command to be perfect to be a call to recognize our dual nature and place *rah* in the service of *tov*, just as God softens His judgment with His compassion." From my perspective, *rah* and *tov* both must die in favor of a "resurrected" and unified self, characterized by grace and strength and genuine wisdom, by a new life devoted to the worship and service of God.

These, of course, are deep matters. I am not certain I've yet found the language to express them well. Ah, yes . . . that's one of the purposes behind our conversation!

Rami: It looks that we will never agree on our capacity to separate feelings from actions. I suspect that you mean something far more profound than I do in this regard. Just imagine how much worse the world would be if people acted on every feeling that arose in their psyches. It is bad enough as it is. Nevertheless, I am very much in favor of "confronting our feelings" rather than controlling them. To confront our feelings inevitably leads to questioning them, and questioning them leaves open the possibility that we realize when it is inappropriate to act on our feelings. This requires a high level of self-awareness.

And with that level of awareness comes the opportunity for new feelings. When we operate from the reptilian brain, we are all about sex, fighting, and food. Regardless of what or whom we meet, we are going to mate with it, battle it, or eat it. But this is a low level of human functioning. The higher mammalian brain calls us to love, altruism, caring, and compassion. When this brain dominates our thinking, our feelings are elevated. And when we operate from the highest brain, justice and righteousness also come into play. As we move from lower to higher brain functioning, we expand our sense of "neighbor" and community.

I think there is an even higher "soul sense" that biologists cannot find that lifts us into the realization that all life is interdependent, and that to love my neighbor as myself is to realize that my neighbor includes all life, sentient and otherwise. I believe that Jesus and other God-realized prophets call us to this level of spiritual awakening.

Just a quick comment on Christian anti-Semitism: The Gospels, like all books sacred or otherwise, have an agenda, and, given the history of their time, part of that agenda was to paint the Jews as the enemies of Jesus even to the extent of blaming them rather than the Romans for his murder. The fact that this kind of thinking continues is an indictment of Christian education; a reluctance to read the Jews' sacred texts in the context of history. This is changing with the scholarship of people like Marcus Borg, Bishop Spong, and Dominic Crossan, but it is a slow process.

To be a Christian and an anti-Semite is to attack Jesus' mother, brothers, the apostles, and Jesus himself. But for too many Christians, the realization that Jesus was a Jew and that his religion was Judaism is a shock, and perhaps too much to bear.

The notion that God has a dark side is difficult for many people to understand, let alone accept. Even your reference to Paul sidesteps the issue, though I am in full agreement with your notion that both *rah* and *tov* must die in the resurrected self.

Few of us doubt that people have a dark side, but that is only half of what I am saying. God has a dark side. It comes out in the book of Job, in the flood story, in God's hardening of Pharaoh's heart in order to demonstrate God's power, and in all the acts of God-sanctioned murder and genocide in the Hebrew Bible and the book of Revelation.

In my classes at MTSU, when the subject of God's love comes up, students want to argue that God is love and that love is absolute. But then what do we do with the notion that if not for the sacrifice of Jesus on the cross God, would condemn all humankind once again? And what do we make of the notion of God condemning the vast majority of humanity (and most Christians by some accounts) to eternal damnation? I would never do such a thing. Can it be that I am more loving than God?

I doubt it. What I offer my students is the notion that God and theology are not the same thing. If God is love, religions are not. Religions and theologies reflect the agendas and biases of their all-too-human creators. I don't believe that Jesus called us to religion; he called us to God, and the God he spoke of in his parables is not the damning brutal God of so many theologians.

My opinion is this: we have too many priests, pastors, rabbis, imams, and swamis and not enough God.

Not long ago I joined with an imam and two Methodist ministers to write a short statement condemning violence in the name of God and religion. It was an easy task that took us just a few minutes. Then I asked if we could take this statement a bit farther and condemn violence in the name of God and religion perpetrated in the afterlife. It is one thing to say that God doesn't sanction the murder of people in this life, and another to say that God doesn't torture nonbelievers or differently believing believers in the next life. No one would sign on to this idea. They couldn't even imagine such a thing. Of course God wants to torture those who mis-believe. How could I imagine otherwise? But I could, and I do. And it bodes ill for humanity that my colleagues could not. I'm not going to put you on the spot regarding this, but I hope our readers stop and think about this for a moment.

Mike: I think we're nearly agreed about our capacity to separate feelings from actions. Confrontation versus controlling, raising questions, learning to see new possibilities, the opportunity for new feelings to develop, the realization that all life is interdependent—we're on the same page. We differ, I think, in that I harbor an additional hope: transformation by the power of God. The difference, of course, roots in our individual understanding of God.

Anti-Semitism is the core sin of the Christian movement. You're right. It's embedded in the background perspective of Christianity's Scriptures, and Christians (across the centuries) bear responsibility for failing to deal with the matter. Refreshingly, many Christian scholars now take the historical context of the New Testament's development seriously. The "Emergent Church" movement does as well. Over the next few decades, I expect such a perspective to become the majority viewpoint among American Christians.

Our discussion of "the dark side" of God seems to have two different threads. On the one hand, the Bible stories you mention depict God as the source of various evils, always in the service of some so-called larger purpose. If we read the Bible as a flat text, that is, with all parts having the same value and validity, we have no choice but to assign responsibility to God.

The alternative is to assign greater and corrective value to some texts. Many of us in Christianity insist on evaluating all biblical texts in light of what we think we know of God as revealed in Jesus. On that basis, we reject any theology that requires God to endorse genocide, murder, and the like.

All of which leads to another point, one you put well: ". . . God and theology are not the same thing." You're right.

We cannot rid ourselves of theology. As long as we think and feel, we will construct theologies. That being said, Christians would do well to focus on the stories of Jesus. When we do so, we find most classic theologies challenged at many points. The example you cite (the significance of the cross) is a prime example. When I take Jesus seriously, I see in the cross and resurrection a declaration of God's boundless love for all people, a love that cannot ultimately be defeated. When we see, admit, and accept this love, we are increasingly free to attempt to practice such love ourselves.

Rami: I was surprised to hear that you think we differ regarding "transformation by the power of God." This must be due to the way I word things, because I do indeed believe in this transformative power. Here is how I understand the matter.

Basing my understanding of God in Exodus 3:14, where God reveals the Name *Ehyeh asher Ehyeh*, "I shall be what I shall be," I take creativity to be an essential attribute of God. God is forever surprising Him/Her/Itself by manifesting new and unprecedented ways of being. I think this is why God uses the process of evolution: evolution is nothing if not the ongoing experiment with new and surprising life forms. I think the aim of evolution is the eventual manifestation of a level of consciousness that can be surprised, knows what surprises it, and sees it all around. On this planet at this time, that life form is us. We are the way God says, "Wow!"

We participate in the creativity of God when we step out of our conditioned selves to be in the world in new and unique ways. This is what I take transformation to be about: not a willed surrender to a fixed way of being, but a surrender of the will as a prelude to a new and unprecedented way of being more fully filled with God and godliness. This transformation cannot be an act of the conditioned will, and must be the result of grace—the surrender of the will to God by God.

I am certainly pleased to hear that anti-Semitism is on the wane in Christianity, and also intrigued by your notion that we can assign different values to different texts in the Bible. I agree with both points, and I find the second vital to salvaging biblical religion from God-sanctioned violence. The problem is that anyone can elevate any text at the expense of any other.

For example, I value those teachings of the Bible, Jewish and Christian, that speak to universal justice and compassion, and I devalue those that do not. But I know Christians who value the book of Revelation over the Sermon on the Mount and posit a violent Christianity that seems absolutely at odds with Jesus as I read him. And I know Jews who read the entire Torah in light of God's promise of the Holy Land and use that promise to excuse terrible injustice against Palestinians. And then there is the historical case of Baptists (for example) splitting over slavery in pre-Civil War times. Some cited Scripture to prove that slavery is God sanctioned, and others quoted different Scripture to prove it is not. So we are left with people using Scripture and God to promote their own agendas.

This is why, for me, the ultimate value in religion and theology is "humility." As I mentioned earlier, the classic Jewish commentary on Micah 6:8 ("walk humbly with your God") asks why Torah says "your God" rather than simply "God." The answer is that each of us has our own idea of "God" whose purpose is to serve our egoic desires. It is this "God" with whom we have to walk humbly, recognizing that "my god" isn't God; it is only my understanding of God. You are right that we "cannot rid ourselves of theology," but we can recognize it for what it is: me creating god in my own image for my own ends.

Last thought: focusing on the stories of Jesus. I couldn't agree more. The stories about Jesus and the stories/parables Jesus tells are timeless and vital to anyone seeking to explore the deepest/highest aspects of spiritual transformation. I would couple these with the Islamic stories of Mullah Nasrudin, Hasidic tales, the Taoist stories written by Chuang Tzu, and a few others to create a world story bible of universal wisdom.

Mike: Well, when you put it that way (nicely phrased, by the way), I do not think that we disagree on the outcome of transformation by God. You wrote, "This is what I take transformation to be about: not a willed surrender to a fixed way of being, but a surrender of the will as a prelude to a new and unprecedented way of being more fully filled with God and godliness. This transformation cannot be an act of the conditioned will, and must be the result of grace—the surrender of the will to God by God." We agree. Once again, we've bumped up against the limits of written conversation. Thanks for unpacking the matter.

As for Christians and anti-Semitism, I hope I did not overstate the case. The mindset the two of us bring to interpreting Scriptures remains a minority mindset at the present time. I dare hope it is growing in influence and that it will be the majority mindset in the near future.

Humility coupled with love is the ultimate value for a God-oriented person. It's a safeguard (not infallible, but useful) against using texts to coerce others to accept our own agendas.

Yes, if we accept the idea that we must assign different values to various portions of Scripture, we also must recognize that anyone can elevate a given text according to his or her personal perspective.

Classic convictions of our respective faith traditions may help guide us. For example, the earliest Christian confession of faith is "Jesus is Lord." That core confession draws us to pay attention first to the stories of Jesus, to try to understand and love and follow Jesus. This tends to lead us to judge other Scriptures on the basis of Jesus. Christians who start with Revelation, violence-supportive Hebrew Scriptures, or even the writings of Paul miss the mark. Jesus, from a Christian perspective, is the Great Corrective or Standard. It is possible to read Christian history as the story of how we Christians forget this is so, only to rediscover it.

Rami: Just a quick comment on "Jesus is Lord."

This came up in my comparative religion class at Middle Tennessee State. We were discussing the Koran, and a very devout and fundamentalist Christian student responded to the question, "How do we know which Holy Scripture is the true Holy Scripture?" with the following: "Since Jesus is Lord and Savior, the Old Testament is true because it predicts the coming of Jesus, and the New Testament is true because it affirms that Jesus is Lord, but the Koran is false because it does not affirm Jesus is Lord."

This is the kind of hubris that breaks my heart and feeds the darkest ignorance. I know for a fact that I could have gotten the same kind of response from Muslims and Jews, so this isn't about Christianity. It is about the way we approach religion and spirituality.

I am grateful to have a friend like you with whom to talk about these things.

Mike: The student's response is a classic example of circular reasoning, to put the most charitable interpretation on the matter. It is another example of the church's failure to teach people how to think well. Circular reasoning employed in the service of religious tribalism strengthens bigotry and fuels religious wars, both private and on a large scale.

"Jesus is Lord" is the earliest known Christian confession of faith. What we do with it matters. In the early church, the statement was not used as a weapon or to divide. Instead, the confession marked one's personal commitment to try to follow Jesus. Most also regarded it as descriptive of their experience of God through "the risen Christ." It was a declaration of identity and intention. To put it another way, the confession amounted to a person saying, "This is who I am—someone for whom Jesus is the center of my life."

Those who take such an approach usually find themselves walking a road that leads to deepening humility, appreciation for the image of God in all others, and sacrifice for the good of others. The way is narrow, though, and too few walk it.

Rami: Christianity has no monopoly on circular reasoning. Ask any Jew about the notion that we are the chosen people. How do we know God chose us? It is written in the Torah. Who wrote the Torah? We did. Even if your answer to the second question is "God wrote the Torah," the follow-up question, "Who says God wrote the Torah?" ends up in the same place. Jews say God wrote the Torah. Even Christians and Muslims who also claim that the Torah is divine revelation base their claims on the Jews.

One cannot escape the fact that in the end, it is the individual who decides what is true or false for herself or himself. Given the fact that we have no objective way of determining this, our conclusions should be drenched with humility.

Part 4

On Piety and Prayer
(Matthew 6:1-34)

Chapter 17

Motives

Beware of practicing your piety before others in order to be seen by them; for then you have no reward from your Father in heaven. So whenever you give alms, do not sound a trumpet before you, as the hypocrites do in the synagogues and in the streets, so that others may praise them. Truly I tell you, they have received their reward. But when you give alms, do not let your left hand know what your right hand is doing, so that your alms may be done in secret; and your Father who sees in secret will reward you. And whenever you pray, do not pray like the hypocrites; for they love to stand and pray in the synagogues and at the street corners, so that others may see them. Truly I tell you, they have received their reward. But whenever you pray, go into your room and shut the door and pray to your Father who is in secret; and your Father who sees in secret will reward you. (Matthew 6:1-6, NRSV)

Mike: Jesus focuses again on motivations. He uses two examples: almsgiving and prayer.

As I understand the matter, first-century Jews regarded giving alms to the poor, whether directly or as part of synagogue worship, as an act of piety. It was the right thing to do. Jesus accepts both the practice and its purpose. His quarrel does not lie with the poor or with those who use a well-established means to help them. Instead, Jesus takes issue with those who use the institution not to honor God or help others but to win applause for themselves.

In like fashion, Jesus does not have a problem with public prayers per se. He objects to those who use public prayers to win praise.

The hypocrisy in both cases lies in claiming to do something for the sake of others or in honor of God while actually giving or praying in order to enhance one's reputation.

Far better, Jesus maintains, to give alms and pray in private. The poor will receive aid and God will be honored. The giver/prayer will be insulated from the temptation to do the right thing for the wrong reason.

I've known many who misuse the passage to discourage public prayer, providing relief to the poor, or being held accountable in any way for what they do by way of prayer or almsgiving. Such applications abuse the passage and miss Jesus' point—namely, that we are to seek to become selfless, utterly unself-conscious, in all things, including prayer and almsgiving. Insomuch as we do so, we become more nearly like God.

Rami: I agree with your take on this passage, Mike, but I am troubled by Jesus' linking of piety (I think a better translation from the Greek would be "righteousness"), charity, and prayer to heavenly reward.

While the rabbis of Jesus' day did speak of heavenly rewards, they argued that the highest good was doing good for its own sake. The term they used (and that we continue to use) is *lishmah*, doing something for its own sake simply because it is right. I don't understand why Jesus would opt for a lesser standard than his contemporaries, especially when, as we have seen, he is not averse to demanding a higher standard than his rabbinic colleagues when he feels it necessary to do so.

I don't want to make more of this than we should, but I have often been surprised in discussions with devout Christians when the issue of *lishmah* is raised (by me) and dismissed (by them). I have been told on numerous occasions that it is the purpose of faith to ensure that the faithful escape eternal damnation in hell. "If there were no hell," I'm told, "there would be no reason to be a Christian."

If these were the random thoughts of a few uninformed laypeople, I would simply chalk it up to ignorance. Unfortunately, I hear this kind of thing over and over from supposedly educated clergy. It is hard to dismiss it as misinformation. The notion of doing good in order to earn a reward seems to be at the heart of Jesus' message here, and hence at the heart of contemporary Christianity as well (or at least a certain kind of contemporary Christianity).

Please don't get me wrong. I'm not claiming that Judaism is free of such thinking. It isn't. The essence of the Jewish relationship with God is covenantal, contractual: we will do "x" and God will do "y." But the rabbis of Jesus' day did try to lift the people beyond this quid pro quo level of theology with the idea of *lishmah*, doing right for its own sake.

So here are a couple of questions to which I would ask you to respond: (1) Do you think the need of many Christians to link piety to reward stems from this teaching of Jesus? (2) Why do you think Jesus didn't push for the higher rabbinic standard of *lishmah*?

On a separate matter, I am quite taken with Jesus' advice regarding prayer: that we shut ourselves in our room and pray to our Father "who is in secret." As you noted, it isn't hard to see how those who challenge the value of community worship would hold up this teaching to argue against such prayer, and, as I am sure you agree, it isn't a matter of either/or. There is a place for public worship as well as for private prayer and meditation.

But what intrigues me is the phrase "your Father who is in secret." I have no idea what this means. I would love some insight into this and would very much like to hear how you understand it.

Mike: Let's start by admitting that most Christians in any given era buy into the idea of rewards. Christians debate the nature, extent, and timing of such rewards. That being said, many Christians in any given era teach that the highest standard involves becoming the kind of person who practices righteousness without thought of reward. Fuzzy thinking, biblical illiteracy, unexamined religious traditions, and human nature often combine to complicate the picture.

I see the matter as follows.

(1) Jesus did not teach that heaven is a reward. Heaven is a condition, potentially experienced at any moment and potentially eternal. Heaven is to live in right relationship with God in each instant. Heaven is the kind of life God intended for humanity.

(2) It is incredibly difficult for any of us to undertake acts of righteousness without weighing the possible benefits to ourselves. Such benefits may include the approval of others. More subtly, we may fall into the trap of praising ourselves, of basing our sense of worth on the number or quality of our righteous works. Both approaches are highly self-conscious, and both push us to do good things for the sake of a reward.

(3) Jesus teaches his followers not to let one hand know what the other is doing. The core idea seems to be that his disciples are to be unselfconscious. In such a state, they may do good things without thought of any reward. They become so immersed in life with God that they no longer pay

attention to the response of others or even themselves to their good works. Ideally, they become selfless.

(4) Jesus adds a surprise: God rewards the selfless. Such people will not expect a reward. They will be surprised by it and are apt to try to give it away to someone else. They are like those who respond (paraphrased), "When did we see you in trouble, Jesus, and help you?" They do not serve for the sake of any reward but instead do so because such service is part and parcel of their identity, an identity shaped by their growing intimacy with God. If this is true, I do not think that Jesus abandoned the rabbinic standard of *lishmah* so much as he recast it.

With all of the above in mind, I tend to look upon the Christians you describe as people who have taken a first step. God has spoken to them, calling them to himself. Bound by culture (usually many layers of culture), they hear and interpret the call in terms of the life they know. There is no shame in starting from where one is, and God loves us more than enough to come and find us where we are. First steps, though, should never be last steps. As we follow Jesus, all of us should grow in our capacity for selflessness. Selflessness, of course, is only possible for those who depend on God for all they actually need.

Finally, I think I understand your interest in the phrase "your Father who is in secret." How could any mystic not focus on it? In the case of the passage, though, I think it wise not to read too much into the matter. The essential idea is "God knows." God knows what it is like to work quietly and unobserved, and God sees all that is done in secret, including quiet deeds of righteousness. The more deeply we move into relationship with such a God, the more we adopt God's mode of operation.

Rami: Wow! I love the idea that heaven is a condition rather than a reward. This places it outside of time: heaven is not a place we go to but a condition we awaken to here and now. This is what Jesus may have meant (and to my mind should have meant and must have meant) when he said, "the kingdom of God is within you" (Luke 17:21). This is comparable to the Pure Land of Shin Buddhism and Nirvana in Zen Buddhism. Both are states of mind, conditions of being, to which we awaken rather than places to which we go. Going implies time and distance; awakening is either there or it isn't. You can't be a little awake, at least not in this context.

As for selflessness, I agree that it is difficult to act without considering what's in it for me, but I would say that when we are totally present to the moment, when we are fully awake to the kingdom within and among us (to blend the King James and NRSV translations) we do in fact act without self.

We can get a glimpse of this in what Mihaly Csikszentmihalyi in his marvelous book *Flow: The Psychology of Optimal Experience* (New York: Harper & Row, 1990) calls the "flow state." In this state, time stops, self-consciousness fades, and we act effortlessly and joyously. Living the kingdom of heaven is living seamlessly with the now, acting in accord with the moment in such a way as to help manifest the potential for love present in each moment. I suspect that this is how Jesus is trying to teach us to live in the Sermon on the Mount. I wish organized religion devoted itself to teaching this as well, each using its own language and all pointing toward the same way of life.

You do mention some reward for selflessness, but to me selflessness is the reward, for with the ending of self arises the oneness of God, woman, man, and nature that is true Reality. If this is how Jesus recast the rabbinic ideal of *lishmah*, then *yasher koach*! May his power increase!

You also seem to pit selflessness against self-reliance, linking the former to those "who depend on God for all they truly need." I wonder if there isn't still a bit of self-hovering around those who depend on God. Indeed, the very fact that they posit a God over themselves suggests that they are not entirely selfless. True selflessness means that there is no egoic "I" at all: "Not I but Jesus in me," as Paul might put it. In a sense, when the self is gone, so is the Other, not that God is absent when the self is absent, but God is all there is and hence there is no room for any other.

My original question dealt with Jesus' phrase "your Father who is in secret." It is such an odd phrase (I assume the Greek says this as well) that it demands parsing, though you opted not to do so. So let me offer some ideas off the top of my head.

Try this: In Jesus' day the rabbis spoke of four levels of biblical interpretation: the literal, the allegorical, the homiletical, and the mystical. This last is called *sod*, which is the Hebrew word for "secret." While the first three levels are taught publicly, the fourth is hidden, only revealed by master to student, or by God. Could Jesus be referring to *sod*? Could he be saying something like, "your God who is revealed only in the secret teachings of Torah"?

Or this: A secret is unknown. Perhaps that is where God dwells: in and as the unknown. All that is known, all our ideas about God and godliness, are like a map that we mistake for the territory. The map is an approximation, not the thing itself. The religious worship the map, indeed insist that the map is God and do their best to keep themselves and others from seeing and walking the territory directly. Jesus is calling us to put the map aside and engage with God directly. Since God is the unknown and unknowable, God is found in secret, in mystery, outside the fixed notions and behaviors of the pious. Jesus may be saying that only when we step beyond the known and allow ourselves to confront the unknown do we discover the Unknowable One beyond all thought and theory.

Obviously I'm guessing here. Any thoughts?

Mike: Thanks for drawing attention to Csikszentmihalyi's description of the "flow state." His language captures the matter nicely!

Thinking back over the course of our ongoing conversation, we may differ in our visions for the self. You speak of a state in which "self is gone," and you view such an end as desirable. From my perspective, each "self" is a creation of God, made not to merge with God but to enjoy God and be enjoyed by God. The problem is that the "selves" tend to go rogue. That is, we focus on ourselves, enter into competition with other selves, seek power over others, and attempt to reduce or eliminate God. To put it another way, we try to take the place of God rather than the place we were created to occupy.

The ideal for the self, from my perspective, is to see, acknowledge, and willingly embrace what one was created to be. When we do so, we cease to compete with others. We start to "enjoy" ourselves, others, and God. We take up work for which we are suited. To borrow a New Testament image, we come home and find it the best of all possible states in which to live.

Interestingly, though, I think both our approaches may lead to the same kind of behavior toward ourselves and others.

Turning toward the phrase "your Father who is in secret," my only point was that I do not think the biblical text in question can support the weight of your inquiry. That being said, I'm all for a round of give and take over speculative matters!

For example, the four levels of biblical interpretation you mention remind me of the multiple levels of interpretation posited by some patristic and many medieval Christian bishops and scholars. I'll not go into detail at this point, other than to stress how most taught that one needed to be introduced to the perspectives and skills needed to move through the various levels. The Protestant Reformation tended to discount this approach.

Some Christian Gnostics appear to have taught that a secret knowledge necessary to fully understand the Scriptures was handed down from teacher to teacher. Gnosticism was a minority movement within broader ancient Christianity, though versions of it crop up throughout history.

The latter two possibilities you suggest find parallels in Christian mysticism. In all cases (I think), a given mystic would have acknowledged that even his or her own words were but a map, not the real God found in secret.

Rami: We often have slightly different takes on things, and our notion of "self" may be one of them.

You know that I spent ten years studying and practicing Zen Buddhism, and I admit that my understanding of "self" is colored by my experience in that setting. The "self" in the Buddhist context is a transient manifestation of equally transient conditions. It is often trapped in ignorance—literally ignoring the greater Reality of which it is a part, and insisting that it is separate and eternal in its own right. Maintaining the delusion of separation and permanence leads the "self" to live a life fueled by anger, greed, arrogance, and fear.

This idea of an eternal and separate self is essential to mainstream Judaism, Christianity, and Islam. Without it, there is no soul and no eternal reward and punishment. My experience with meditation and other contemplative practices, as well as my reading of the world's great mystics, leads me to deny the existence of individual selves and souls as well as eternal reward and punishment.

I like the analogy of the ocean and the wave. The "self" is like the foam on the peak of the wave. It is a natural phenomenon, part of what it is to be a wave, but it insists that it is other than the wave and even more other than the ocean. The foam is the ego so desperately clinging to the illusion of its own separateness that it lives a life of alienation and needless suffering.

The wave is the truer self, or soul if you like. It too can be deceived into imagining that it is other than the ocean, and when it does it feeds and is fed by the delusional fear of the foaming false self.

The ocean is Reality itself, God in my use of the term. It is not other than the wave or the foam, but it is infinitely greater than them.

The gift of enlightenment or salvation or awakening is the realization that foam, wave, and ocean are one. It isn't that we live without a self or ego, but that we live without the false notion that we are separate from the wave and the ocean. We don't merge with God; we realize that we are never other than God.

Regarding "your Father who is in secret," I was afraid that the Greek original might not support my take on the English translation, but your mentioning of the Protestant Reformation raises another question for me.

Part of Martin Luther's revolution rested on universal literacy and the technology of Guttenberg that allowed the average person to own her or his own Bible. I wonder if the miracle of literacy and the capacity to read what the Bible actually says rather than having to accept the interpretations offered by the church led Protestants to focus on the literal meaning of the text. Being able to read what the Bible actually says was so important, so new, and so revolutionary that they couldn't imagine needing anything else. Literacy and literalism may have gone hand in hand, and, at least in the beginning, necessarily so.

As for mystics and their maps—absolutely. All words are signs. The question is whether or not they point to something other than themselves. We all agree that the word "unicorn" points to a white horse with a spiral horn in the center of its forehead, but we might well disagree as to whether such a being actually exists or ever existed. For the mystic, all words are self-referential, referring only to themselves. Only silence—deep, transformative silence—takes us beyond the map of words to encounter the territory of the real as it is in and of itself.

Mike: For the most part, I think you have described the differences in the two viewpoints quite well. I want to explore the nuance of one or two items. First, from my perspective a self is a soul, a unity. Second, the concept of self/soul may be, and often is, linked to punishment and reward. Such linkage, though, is not a given. Finally, you write, "We don't merge with God; we realize that we are never other than God." I might write, "We don't merge with God but choose instead to love and serve God, without whom we are incomplete."

Turning to the matter of the Protestant Reformation, literacy and literalism, we need to be careful not to overstate the state of literacy in Luther's time. General literacy, of course, was not achieved for quite some time. Readers, though, were scattered throughout the population, and the easy availability of printed material enabled them to read aloud to large groups. Luther's translation of the Scriptures into German accelerated the growth of literacy.

You are correct: Protestants attempted to focus on the meaning of the text. "Literal" probably is not the best term to describe most of their efforts. They, instead, sought what many of them would have called the "plain" meaning of the text. To put it another way, they sought the simplest interpretation of any given text and thus produced interpretations ranging from the literal to the allegorical.

As literacy grew, individuals produced an often bewildering variety of interpretations. Some branches on the ever-growing Protestant tree succumbed to the "literal-only" approach.

I think you are on to something important with your suggestion that the availability of the Bible was so exciting that many could not imagine needing anything else. Most such persons became part of what historians usually call "The Radical Reformation." Over time, a majority of Protestants discovered the value of paying attention as well to interpretive tradition, experience, and the quiet voice of the Holy Spirit.

Rami: I admire your consistency, Mike. Your comment, "We don't merge with God but choose instead to love and serve God, without whom we are incomplete," reminds me of the Hindu saint Ramakrishna, who said, "I love sugar, I don't want to be sugar" when arguing for the fundamental otherness of God.

On the topic of literacy and interpretations of the Bible, it is fascinating that people continue to find new meanings in the text. For me there is no final meaning to the Bible. If there were it would be a dead text. It lives because I can allow my reading to reflect my life. We don't read the Bible as much as read our reflection in the Bible.

Chapter 18

The Lord's Prayer

When you are praying, do not heap up empty phrases as the Gentiles do; for they think that they will be heard because of their many words. Do not be like them, for your Father knows what you need before you ask him. Pray then in this way: Our Father in heaven, hallowed be your name. Your kingdom come, Your will be done, on earth as it is in heaven. Give us this day our daily bread. And forgive us our debts, as we also have forgiven our debtors. And do not bring us to the time of trial, but rescue us from the evil one. (Matthew 6:7-13, NRSV)

Mike: Fairly early in the church's history, a doxology was added to the above: "For the kingdom and the power and the glory are yours forever. Amen."

The prayer assumes that God desires to hear our prayers, that it is right and sane to pray, and that good prayer connects us with the great matters of God. God does not have to be persuaded to listen, nor do our prayers inform God. Instead, in ways roughly analogous to a human parent, God already knows our deepest needs. Prayer helps form us, freeing us from the illusion of false needs and teaching us to see clearly what we really need.

And what do we really need? We need to grow into a healthy relationship with this distant yet very near God. Our yearning must be reoriented so that we long for God's rule to become fully effective in us and the broader life of the world. We must be freed from all desire for more than we need and become content to have "daily bread." We need to acknowledge our debts (or trespasses) and ask forgiveness, even as we also become the kind of people who extend forgiveness to others. Pride must be subdued and humility put in its place as we increasingly recognize our limits and cease from boasting. All such developments come to pass over time as we embrace the practice of prayer.

Such prayer requires words and silence, action and waiting, speaking and listening. Ideally, it becomes our mode of life, so that all other things are subsumed in prayer. The Lord's Prayer may help both the individual and a congregation take steps in this direction.

Obviously, there is much to unpack in the phrases of the prayer, but I thought it best to start our discussion with a summary statement.

Rami: I am so excited about taking on the Lord's Prayer. It is perhaps the most Jewish piece of liturgy in the entire New Testament. But, as you said, it is wise for us to deal with more general issues first.

I agree that Jesus, along with the vast majority of his co-religionists, believed that God desires prayer and is ever ready to listen if not act. I pray daily, but I have to admit that I am not so sure about the assumptions behind the act of prayer.

I speak to God as if God were other, as if God were, as you say, "both distant and very near." For me God is the Source and Substance of all reality; God embraces and transcends the material world just as a word embraces and transcends the letters that comprise it. There is a level of meaning in the whole that the parts as parts lack.

For example, the letters "O," "E," "L," and "V" in and of themselves are meaningless, but the word "Love" is profoundly meaningful. When we look at the universe as a collection of discrete parts, we cannot find meaning in them, but when we see them as a wild yet integrated whole we do find meaning.

Of course there is no word without letters, so I am not discounting them. Indeed I see them as manifestations of God. So when I pray, it is God speaking to God in order to shift perspective from the part to the whole. This leads me to explore your position carefully. Does God desire prayer? Does God want to listen to us?

Certainly to the extent that I am God and I have desires, we can say that God has desires. But this is on the microcosmic level. What about the God as the whole and not simply the part? Does God as the Source (and not just the Substance) of Reality have desires?

I would say yes in this sense: God "desires" to manifest the universe the way an acorn "desires" to manifest an oak tree. Since the universe contains light and dark, good and evil, God "desires" this to be the case.

Could God desire otherwise? No more than an acorn could desire to be a fig tree.

Does God listen to my prayer? In my daily prayer walks I talk with God. Not simply to God or at God, but with God. I hear God's response. But I take this to be a lower spiritual experience filtered through my egoic consciousness. The way we humans meet is face to face, so the way God and I meet is Face to face. But this is a limitation of my ego rather than an accurate picture of the Divine-human relationship.

There are moments in my walking when the "distance" between God and myself vanishes. God is no longer "Other" but All. I sense God in me, as me. I feel God in and as all things around me. There is no talking at this point. God isn't listening to me, but rather I am listening—or more accurately sensing since all my senses seem to be engaged in this experience— to the universe and sensing not a voice but a presence felt as love. These are brief moments of ecstasy that often leave me twirling, dancing, hugging trees, laughing, singing, and engaged in other bizarre and thankfully unobserved behavior.

In this way I absolutely agree with you that "prayer helps form us, freeing us from the illusion of false needs and teaching us to see clearly what we really need." And what we really need is to realize God in all as all, and to allow that realization to transform us into vehicles for compassion and justice in the world.

I suspect that you are saying something similar, but the notion of "rule" troubles me. When you say "we long for God's rule to become fully effective in us and the broader life of the world" I cannot help thinking of those who claim to know what God's rule is and who seek to impose it on others. This Taliban-like quality exists in all three Abrahamic religions and is often the greatest source of evil perpetrated in their names.

In any case, I look forward to unpacking the Lord's Prayer line by line, and happily await your getting us into this.

Mike: Your understanding of the meaning of "God" sometimes reminds me of that shared by some ancient Greek philosophies and Christian theological systems heavily influenced by Greek philosophical thought. That being said, let's unpack the Lord's Prayer. It should be interesting to see where our understanding intersects or diverges.

The prayer opens with "Our Father in heaven, hallowed be your name" (v. 9). Prayer forms us, and the Lord's Prayer begins the ongoing process with its first term: "Our." The prayer does not begin with "My Father" but with "Our Father." Immediately, Jesus pushes us to step away from the rank individualism that characterizes much of modern American Christianity and discover (or rediscover) that we are one humanity before God.

Taken seriously, over time the insight may transform our perspective. It challenges our egoism, weakening our tendency to expect all the creation and

God to center on us. As time goes on and we become aware of the diversity of people praying the same words, we may begin to set aside divides fueled by racism, ideology, economics, culture, and nationalism. Eventually, we may realize that God is the parent of all persons, even those who do not acknowledge this is so. The term "our" is subversive of all typical human divisions, leading us to acknowledge our kinship.

"Father" presents problems for any number of modern Christians, mostly because of a heightened sensitivity to gender issues. The term "Father" plays a critical role in the prayer as the most apt translation of the Greek term *Abba,* which is the kind of intimate word a small child might use, the rough English equivalent being "Daddy." Praying the prayer encourages us to know the kind of God who is approachable, who loves us, and who wishes to nurture us.

Christian commentators of past generations often contrasted such an image of God with the supposed first-century Jewish notion of a distant, law-giving God. Commentators of the past half-century or so have demolished this viewpoint, noting that ancient Judaism held a position similar to that of Jesus.

"In heaven" nicely balances "our Father." We may know God as our loving parent, but we must not fall prey to the notion that we know all there is to know of God. The "God Who Can Be Experienced" is also the "God Beyond Knowing." Study and experience suggest that most of us are inclined toward one or the other pole. Jesus' prayer keeps both poles in healthy tension.

"Hallowed be your name" concludes the opening sentence. We might paraphrase it as, "May your name be treated as holy." Here, it seems to me, Jesus weaves the great commandment against using the Lord's name in vain into the practice of prayer, giving it a positive spin. More important, perhaps, Jesus makes adoration of God a crucial component of prayer, and so of the life formed by the practice of prayer. Learning to adore (worship, bow the knee, pick your favorite word or phrase) is the only lasting antidote to worshiping one's self or some piece of the creation.

I look forward both to your response and to what you have to say about the Jewishness of the phrase.

Rami: I remind you of Greek philosophers? Which ones? Plato? Aristotle? Or Arianna Huffington? Actually, I am taken with a number of Greek philosophers, especially Heraclites, Socrates, and Epicurus. Epicurus was so hated by the ancient rabbis that they used the Hebrew version of his name, *apikoros*, as a synonym for heretic. I am that to some. Proudly.

As we get into the Lord's Prayer, let me remind everyone that I come at this assuming Jesus was a Jew speaking primarily to Jews in the idiom they knew best. Given that, we should not be surprised that Jesus borrows from Jewish texts and teachings in fashioning his Way. The genius of Jesus is that he took the Judaism of his day and recast it for a new day.

I want to take up the Lord's Prayer section by section, sometimes line by line, to allow us time to go into this deeply. I will link the phrases (where applicable) to Jewish text and teaching, and then give my spin as to their meaning. Let's start with the text.

"Our Father in heaven." The metaphor of God as father is biblical— Psalm 103:13, Hosea 11:1, Isaiah 63:16, and Jeremiah 31:9, to cite just a few examples. So Jesus is again drawing on the prophetic tradition of Judaism.

In addition, referring to God as "our Father" was common in Jesus' time. The Hebrew prayer *Avinu Malkenu* (Our Father, Our King) dates from this period, and Rabbi Akiva who, like Jesus, was martyred by Rome taught the prayer, "Our Father, our King, we have no king beside You. Our Father, our King, have mercy on us for Your sake" (*Ta'anit* 25b). Having no king beside God is what got both Jesus and Akiva killed.

Linking "father" with "king" is the equivalent of Jesus balancing "father" with "heaven," and it means the same thing: God is both immanent and transcendent. The full phrase "Our Father in heaven" or, as Jesus would have said it, *Avinu sheh-ba-shemayim*, was an epithet much beloved by the rabbis of his day and earlier. In *Sotah* 9:15, for example, the rabbis say that true piety is doing the will of *Avinu sheh-ba-shamayim*.

"Hallowed be your name" is part of the opening line of the *Kaddish* prayer that ancient and contemporary rabbis use to close each teaching session: *Yitgadal, v'yitkadash, shemay rabbah*: "Make great and hallow Your great Name." It is also the prayer recited in honor of the dead, but this is a latter use of the prayer.

Without getting bogged down in textual history, I think it is safe to say that "Our Father in heaven, hallowed be your name" clearly reflects and draws on Jesus' Jewishness. But what does it mean?

One the one hand, it means just what it says: let us sanctify the One who is both as close to us as a father and as far beyond us as the heavens. But why refer to God's Name rather than directly to God? Why not say, "Our Father in heaven, be hallowed"? Why the reference to God's Name?

The Name to which Jesus refers is the *Shem haMiphorash*, the Ineffable Four-letter Name of God that Jews believed was revealed to Moses at the Burning Bush (Exod 3:14). God says to Moses that people used to know God as *El Shaddai*, the All Powerful, but now through Moses they will come to know God as *Ehyeh Asher Ehyeh*, the unconditional *I Will Be What I Will Be* that became the Four-letter Name, *YHVH*. Why the new Name? Because God is taking on a new role: God is not simply the transcendent Creator but also immanent Liberator. Our relationship to God is not simply one of thanksgiving and praise, but of active partnership in the liberation of the enslaved.

It isn't *El Shaddai* that sends Moses to Pharaoh, but *YHVH*, and it is this Name that Jesus wants us to hallow. It is this Name his rabbinic colleagues want us to make great. Why? Because it is the Name of liberation. What Jesus and the rabbis are calling for, albeit in highly coded language that only Jews would understand, are the end of tyranny and the establishment of God's kingdom on earth. The coding allows the message of liberation to spread without catching the attention of the Romans for whom the phrase "Your Name" is meaningless.

Thus as I read the Lord's Prayer, from the very first line Jesus is calling for revolution: "Our Father in heaven, let Your Name, let Your freedom, let Your liberation be hallowed, and not the name of Caesar and the tyranny that comes with it!"

As is common with us, Mike, we come at this from two different angles. I see Jesus the revolutionary, and you see Jesus the Christ. I hear a call for resistance, and you hear a call for transformation. But I don't think either of us is wrong. On the contrary, I think Jesus, like every authentic prophet of any religion, is a catalyst for both social revolution and personal transformation. You cannot have one without the other, at least not if you expect either to be fully authentic. In fact, by hearing each other's understanding of Jesus' words, I suspect we each broaden our own perspectives and understandings of Jesus as well. At least that is my hope and my experience so far.

Mike: I think you are right. We come at the matter from different angles, both of which have their own merits, and our perspectives complement one another.

Personal transformation, if authentic, must lead one to face and address social/political matters, especially with regard to liberation and equality. A prophetic stand against tyranny and a subsequent social revolution minus personal transformation may well lead to another kind of tyranny in the long run.

That being said, I want to move to the next phrase of the prayer: "Your kingdom come. Your will be done on earth as it is in heaven" (v. 10). Jesus refers to the kingdom of God, the core of his message and vision. He calls us to pray that the way of heaven might become the way of earth.

What does the way of heaven (the kingdom of heaven) look like? We know from the other teachings of Jesus, such as those we've been unpacking from the Sermon on the Mount or the declaration of his ministry as found in Luke 4:18-19. It's the kind of world in which the blind see and the captives are set free, both by the rightful presence and rule of God and through our cooperation. The worship of God and the welfare of others unite to become the primary value around which life is structured.

Jesus' words assume that his followers will want, or learn to want, such a world. The prayer itself may reshape us into such persons. Of course, the more we learn to yearn for God's kingdom to shape the world in which we live, the more open we become to changes in our personal lives and the broader life of society.

Rami: We call what you are talking about *teshuvah*/return and *tikkun*/repair. The two operate together: you return to God and repair the world with godliness: doing justly, loving mercy, and walking humbly with God and God's creation (Mic 6:8). Some people are more prone to begin with *teshuvah* and the life of prayer, study, and contemplation that is the way of return. Others are more comfortable beginning with *tikkun*, becoming socially active and working for justice for both persons and planet. Wherever one starts, the other is always bound to kick in at some point. My understanding is that when one lives *teshuvah* and *tikkun*, one lives in *Malchut Shamayim*, the kingdom of God.

Jesus' reference to God's kingdom is itself very Jewish. In the Talmud, tractate *Berachot* 40b (published centuries after Jesus, but containing the teachings of his rabbinic predecessors and colleagues), the rabbis taught that for a prayer to be valid it must mention both the Name of God and the kingdom of God. In practice this has become the classic opening of almost every Jewish blessing: "Blessed are You, YHVH our God, King of the universe."

Judaism speaks of two opposing kingdoms, *Malchut Zadon*, the kingdom of the proud, and *Malchut Shamayim*, the kingdom of heaven. Pride, along with anger, arrogance, greed, and ignorance, is what keeps God's kingdom from manifesting on earth. The way we will know God's kingdom has come is that justice and peace will reign around the globe. Because we believe only the Messiah (or messianic consciousness) can bring this global transformation, and because we believe that this will be a this-worldly socio-economic-political-spiritual transformation, we believe that the Messiah has yet to come. When Jesus says, "My kingdom is not of this world" (John 18:36), we Jews lose interest. This is where the kingdom is needed, not in some heavenly realm.

Judaism is a profoundly this-worldly faith. We have little to say about life after death and pay scant attention to heaven and hell. We believe that behavior alone determines your fate after death and that a person whose good deeds outweigh her bad deeds by even a feather's weight will have a place in heaven. Our hope is articulated in Jeremiah 23:5: "The days are surely coming, says YHVH, when I will raise up for David a righteous Branch, and he shall reign as king and deal wisely, and shall execute justice and righteousness in the land." The "land" refers not only to Israel but to the whole world—this world.

I understand that for many Christians this Branch is Jesus and that the second coming will accomplish what we Jews expect from the first. Numbers aside, the goal is the same: global peace and justice.

I am struck by Jesus' prayer that "Your will be done on earth as it is in heaven." What keeps God's will from operating on earth? Again, I would point to pride, anger, arrogance, greed, and ignorance. If we want to see the kingdom of God, our prayers must be, to borrow from Rabbi Abraham Joshua, "subversive" and thus overthrow *Malchut Zadon*, the kingdom of pride. Unfortunately most of us are so invested in *Malchut Zadon* that we rarely if ever pray subversively. On the contrary, our prayers reinforce our own will and pretend that God wills what we desire.

True prayer is humbling, subversive, and transformative. It reveals the holiness at the heart of humanity and liberates us from fear that we might refashion the world in love. It manifests as *teshuvah* and *tikkun*, returning us to God that we might remake the world with godliness.

Mike: "Give us this day our daily bread" (v. 11). The petition was and is countercultural.

In the first-century context, it spoke directly to the daily reality faced by the poor. Daily bread did not come easily. Day workers, such as those depicted in the parable of the owner and the workers for hire, lived from day to day. Taking one day at a time was not a maxim but instead a harsh reality.

By contrast, upper classes with property, prosperous businesses, government connections, and the like lived in a long-range world. Holding on to what they had and adding to it preoccupied many of them. They did not have to worry about bread for the day, but they no doubt invested considerable energy in trying to build their holdings and pass them along to their children.

At the risk of oversimplification, the two classes felt different needs. The poor might well have prayed, "Give me bread for today." Those better off might well have prayed, "Prosper my investments." The first is a prayer of acknowledged dependence, while the latter is an invitation to God to help grow the family business.

Jesus' choice of phrase is congruent with his contention that God loved the poor and that riches make it difficult to choose to depend on God.

The term "us" is important. It challenges the tendency of poor and rich alike to settle for self-centeredness. Positively, it pushes us to care not only that we and our loved ones (or "folks like us") have enough to eat (and, by extension, have enough of the basics of life) but that others do as well. Personal acts of charity and sacrifice ensue. The more we grapple with the matter, we realize social, legal, business, and government structures must also be addressed.

Let's not forget the question of "enough." With rare exceptions, humans act out of insecurity, both real and imagined. We find it hard to know and admit when we have enough of anything. The prayer calls us to scale back expectations, to recognize that each day is all we have, and to live accordingly. Obviously, when we do so, there's more to go around. Less obviously, we begin to free ourselves from slavery to pointless anxiety about the future. We start to become people more nearly able to live in the present moment.

Rami: Let me just tack a few things on to your fine comments, Mike.

In addition to what you said about the economics of the time, a first-century Jew listening to Rabbi Jesus could not hear him speak of "daily bread" without immediately thinking of Exodus 16 and the manna given to the Jews during their wandering in the Sinai desert. God provides the Jews with manna each day and instructs them to take no more than a single day's portion (with an exception made for Friday, when they are to take two day's portion so as not to have to gather manna on the Sabbath).

As is always the case, someone has to test the rule. Someone gathers a double portion, hoping to secure enough by taking more than enough. In the morning, however, his leftover manna is teeming with worms. The Torah's message, carried by Jesus into his prayer, is that it is tough to live with enough.

The Lord's Prayer calls the Jews back to Sinai. Jesus is challenging them to surrender to God once again and to trust that God will lead us to where we need to be and sustain us as we journey there. He is saying, "The treasures we store up for ourselves cannot sustain us. Tomorrow they will be as rotten as the illicit portion of manna. God provided for us in Sinai and God will provide for us now, but only if we learn to live within the confines of enough."

There is enough for all if each takes only enough. Most of us, however, take more than enough, or at least desire to do so. We imagine (wrongly) that life is a zero-sum game where my abundance depends on another's lack, so we pursue more than enough, fearful that if we don't do so, someone else will take our portion as well as their own. It is grasping for more than enough that is at the root of most if not all the world's suffering. And it is here that Jesus' use of "us" comes in.

First, we should remember that Jewish liturgy is intrinsically communal. We almost always speak in the first person plural rather than the first person singular. Second, Jesus is again reminding us of Sinai, where there was enough for all of us as long as each of us took no more than we needed.

The challenge of course is to trust that this is so. Few of us do. We are always seeking that extra portion of manna, expecting that this time it will not rot. As the economy has recently reminded us, there is no security in stored-up treasure.

Mike: Thanks for pointing to the imaginative connection between the prayer and the manna stories. You point is true and enriches our appreciation for the prayer. Let's turn attention to the prayer's next phrase.

"And forgive us our debts, as we also have forgiven our debtors" (v. 12). I think it best to view this petition against the backdrop of the Jubilee Year (see Lev 25:8-17). The Jubilee Year ideal called for the forgiveness of all debts and the restoration of all property to its original owners every fifty years. Insofar as I know, the ideal was never put into full practice, but it certainly gripped the imagination of many. Such a practice would have the practical effect of placing everyone on an equal footing once per generation. In addition, the practice probably would loosen attachment to and dependence on property, turning followers into stewards rather than owners. Applied on an empire-wide basis, it would have involved the Romans leaving the region (though surely disputes would have arisen over the question of who originally owned the property!). In short, the petition carried economic and political implications.

That being said, we ought not to neglect the personal dimensions of the prayer. Jesus places responsibility to start the process of forgiveness on us. We pray to be forgiven our debts in accordance with how we have forgiven the debts owed us. At this point, I think the petition extends its reach beyond economics and politics to the realm of personal relationships.

For example, Jesus seems to be saying to his first-century Jewish listener that he or she must practice preemptive forgiveness, whether of an offending fellow Jew or even a Roman. He calls for breaking the all-too-common human cycle of revenge and what we might call "compensated forgiveness" in favor of something more radical. Much to our consternation, Jesus never implies that such forgiveness on our part guarantees a like response from others. On the other hand, if we take his way, we at least drop the terrible burden of holding mortgages (of all kinds) on others.

Does the petition mean we cannot be forgiven by God until we learn to forgive others consistently? I would not put it so. Rather, it seems to me that we cannot experience (recognize, absorb, be changed by) forgiveness and live knowingly in God's kingdom without practicing forgiveness. I suspect learning to practice forgiveness of all kinds is an integral part of growing from infancy to maturity in the kingdom of God.

Rami: Your reading of this passage is close to my own, and since you blend both the communal Jubilee Year with the personal aspect of forgiveness, I am free to focus on other matters.

First, let me offer some comfort to those who may be troubled about the different versions of this teaching in Matthew and Luke. In Matthew Jesus speaks of "debts" while in Luke he speaks of "sin." Both may be correct. The Gospels are written in Greek, but Jesus most likely preached in Aramaic, the vernacular of his listeners. In Aramaic the word *choba* means both debt and sin, and it is this word Jesus spoke and that Matthew and Luke both translated rightly even as they translated differently.

Second and more important, I am struck (and, if I were a Christian, troubled) by Jesus' teaching on forgiveness. Jesus says nothing about praying in his name or believing in him as the Son of God as a condition for forgiveness. Rather, he links the forgiving of others to God's forgiving of us. This is very much in line with Jewish thinking then and now.

In the second century BCE text the *Wisdom of Ben Sirach*, we are instructed, "Forgive your neighbor the wrong he has done, and then your sins will be pardoned when you pray" (*Ben Sirach* 28:2, NRSV). In the Talmud God says, "I forgive your sins against Me, but go to those against whom you have sinned and ask their pardon also" (*Rosh HaShanah* 17b). In the older text, God's forgiveness requires us to get the forgiveness of others. In the later text, God's forgiveness comes before human pardon and is an impetus for it.

Jesus differs from Sirach and the Talmud by focusing on giving forgiveness to others rather than asking them to forgive us, though this too can be found in rabbinic teaching: "All those who are forbearing and forgiving of others and who do not insist on their rights will be forgiven their sins" (*Yoma* 23a). This last text may be the source of Jesus' teaching in Mark, "Whenever you stand praying, forgive, if you have anything against anyone; so that your Father in heaven may also forgive you your trespasses" (Mark 11:25).

In all these cases, however, it is clear that belief in Jesus has nothing to do with securing God's forgiveness. Forgiveness is ours to bestow, and when we do so God does likewise unto us. This a variation on the golden rule: do unto others as you would have God do unto you.

I am neither a theologian nor a scholar of Christian history, so I am wondering why and when Christianity shifts from the Jewish teaching of Jesus about forgiveness to the Christian teaching of forgiveness through Jesus. Not that you need more work to do, Mike, but I look forward to hearing your answer and insight into this.

Mike: See if I ever again leave you "free to focus on other matters"! That being said, you raise a good question with regard to the Christian teaching of forgiveness through Jesus. I do not pretend to be a scholar on the subject (either the particular example you raise or the larger matter of Christology). Still, I harbor strong impressions, which I hope are based primarily on reflection on biblical texts, Christian history, and experience.

Christians view Jesus through the lens of the resurrection. All his words and actions take on additional meaning for us as a result. To the best of my knowledge, early Christians interpreted the resurrection as God's validation of the life and teachings of Jesus. Almost immediately, they concluded that Jesus must be the Christ. Some tended to view him as a man whom God elevated to the status. Others soon began to see Jesus as the incarnation of the Word (to borrow John's language from his Gospel). We see a bit of both tendencies in Paul's letters. Ultimately, the Christian doctrine of the Trinity evolved from such considerations. With regard to your question, Christians felt it natural to pray in the name of such a Jesus or to ask forgiveness in his name.

The practice also derived from early Christian reflection on other sayings of Jesus. For example, Jesus told his disciples that whatever they asked in his name would be granted, that no one came to the Father but through him, and the like. You and I live in a time when sets of scholars debate which sayings should be regarded as authentic. The first followers seem to have accepted and worked with whatever sayings were available. That being the case, they soon began to pray in his name and seek forgiveness through him.

Experience played a role as well, I think. The first generation of Christians clearly believed that the Holy Spirit was active in and among them to comfort, bring to memory the teachings of Jesus, guide them in ministry, and instruct them. My personal hunch is that if we could interview early Christian leaders, they would tell us they believed that the Holy Spirit led them to pray in the name of Jesus and seek forgiveness through him.

All of the above begs the question of Jesus' intentions. How we deal with the matter seems largely determined by whether we factor genuine resurrection into the equation. By that, I mean we're either dealing with a life and its attendant perceptions/intentions, which ended with death, or with someone who lived bound within the limitations of genuine incarnation and then lived again with expanded perceptions/intentions via resurrection. The early Christians went with the second option.

Rami: This certainly helps with an understanding of how the idea of forgiveness through Jesus as Christ evolved, Mike. Thanks. From the Jewish perspective, the issue is still problematic, though over the centuries many Jews have adopted somewhat similar practices such as praying at the burial sites of great rabbis and sages in hopes of invoking their help in convincing God to do whatever it is they wish to have done.

My own position is that God neither rewards nor punishes, and that forgiveness only makes sense in the human sphere. For me God is Reality—all that was, is, and ever will be, and that which transcends this as well. My experience of God is not one of forgiveness but of infinite compassion. God, and I am speaking metaphorically here, simply mirrors back to me the complete fabric of my life and how my actions affect others, and does so in such a way that I cannot avoid feeling the suffering I cause. It is this realization that motivates me to make amends and ask for forgiveness from those I have hurt or harmed.

When I say that God is love, the love I imagine isn't sweet but searing. This love burns away all the nonsense and lies that poison my life and keep me from fully experiencing the depths of suffering and joy that life contains. When I die, I don't expect God to forgive me or condemn me. I expect God to embrace me the way an ocean embraces the river that flows into it or the wave that arises from it. I am not concerned with heaven and hell except as they play out here on earth. I am passionate about the "kingdom of God" among us and between us and within us, but I have no interest in such a kingdom above or a horror show below. In this I am quintessentially Jewish.

I suspect it is the Jewish focus on this world that makes the validation of Jesus as Christ through the resurrection irrelevant. It doesn't matter that Jesus returned to his Father in heaven. What matters is that we are still making a mess of things here on earth. To say with Jesus that his kingdom is not of this world is, from a Jewish perspective, to say that his teaching is irrelevant to the world. Neither you nor I believe that, of course.

I think the teachings of Jesus, which I see as profoundly Jewish drawing from and expanding both the prophetic and rabbinic traditions (as opposed to the teachings about Jesus that form the basis of Christianity), are as vital today as ever—perhaps more so. The power of the Sermon on the Mount is that it is a deeply spiritual and transformative way of living here and now. Nothing can diminish or add to that—not the resurrection or the denial of the resurrection. It is Jesus' teaching that matters, and I don't want to limit the validity of that teaching to a supernatural understanding of the teacher.

Mike: Let's move on to the next passage: "And do not bring us to the time of trial, but rescue us from the evil one" (v. 13). Many of us memorized the KJV version: "And lead us not into temptation, but deliver us from evil." The NIV splits the difference: "And lead us not into temptation, but deliver us from the evil one." Translation is a bit of art. Each version represents a faithful attempt to render the Greek in English.

That being said, what might Jesus have in mind? Start with "the time of trial." I interpret the petition in terms of proper humility. A follower of Jesus recognizes his or her limits. We do not seek tests of faithfulness, mostly because we admit that our strength is inadequate to ensure that we will make the right choices.

In the Gospels, Peter serves as the model of a follower who long failed to recognize his own weakness. Peter rashly declares that he will be faithful to Jesus regardless of circumstances, only to betray Jesus three times before the dawn of the next day. In the setting of the last supper, Peter seems to crave to be tested. He is convinced of his unbreakable integrity. Peter's humiliating defeat by the fireside is traumatic, not least because it destroys his inflated sense of his own invincibility. Lesson one: Do not seek to be tested.

The petition, however, suggests that God indeed may test us, even as Jesus was tested in the wilderness. A wise person asks God not to do so, even as she or he recognizes that God is free to impose such testing for God's own reasons. The Gospel model of this approach is the prayer of Jesus in the garden: "Let this cup pass from my lips; nonetheless, not my will but your will be done" (Matt 26:39). The petition holds the potential to renovate our mindset so that we increasingly trust that the loving God will not place us in any situation beyond his power to see us through (even if we should die in the process).

"Rescue us from the evil one" is a perfectly fine translation, but I rather prefer the KJV: "And deliver us from evil." We speak such a petition because we increasingly sense the scope of the opposition, the weight of that which would separate us from God. Evil as embodied in human institutions, ways of thinking, unwritten codes, and daily practice wields enormous power. By the time most of us become able to think abstractly, we are so entangled by such evil as to make it practically impossible to escape on our own. Through the petition, we ask for God's ongoing intervention on our behalf.

Keep in mind, of course, that all of the above applies not only to the individual but to groups as well. In the case of Christians, we pray the petition on behalf not only of ourselves but of the entire Body of Christ. Personally, I pray the petition on behalf of all humanity.

We pray the petition continually, recognizing that even the light we are given today burns only through that portion of the darkness nearest us. We shall need yet more light if we are to walk very far.

Rami: Two things strike me in this passage, Mike. First is its affinity with Jewish liturgy, and second its departure from Jewish psychology.

The similarity is found in the morning liturgy of the Authorized Jewish Prayer Book:

> *And may it be thy will, O Lord our God and God of our fathers, to make us familiar with thy Law, and to make us cleave to thy commandments. O lead us not into the power of sin, or of transgression or iniquity, or of temptation, or of scorn: let not the evil inclination have sway over us: keep us far from a bad man and a bad companion: make us cleave to the good inclination and to good works: subdue our inclination so that it may submit itself unto thee; and let us obtain this day, and every day, grace, favor and mercy in your eyes, and in the eyes of all who behold us; and bestow loving-kindnesses upon us. Blessed art thou, O Lord, who bestows loving-kindnesses upon thy people Israel.*

Both Jesus and Jewish liturgy worry that God might lead us to sin or to times of moral testing. I take this metaphorically. When I say that God is testing me, I mean that life is presenting me with challenges that force me to make difficult choices. I don't imagine that God is consciously doing this. This is simply the nature of reality, and, since for me God is reality, it is the will of God.

What is more interesting to me is Jesus' use of "the evil one" verses the rabbis' use of the "evil inclination." If my memory is correct, the Greek for "evil one" is masculine, suggesting that Jesus is talking about Satan or the devil. Jesus uses the same term in the parable of the sower, where "the evil one" steals what has been sown (Matt 13:19).

It seems that Jesus believes in an independent devil working in opposition to kingdom people, while the rabbis saw evil more as an aspect of human psychology: "the imagination of the human heart is evil from its youth" (Gen 8:21), and "every imagination of the thought of the human heart is only evil" (Gen 6:5). "Imagination" here means selfish fantasies that excuse exploitative and harmful behavior. The rabbis believed that the human capacity for such thinking develops around puberty (youth).

Satan is nearly absent from the Hebrew Bible, and by the time of Jesus most rabbis understand Satan to be a metaphor for the evil inclination. In this way, they reject any independent source of evil at war with God. This is probably one of the major differences between Judaism and many forms of Christianity.

The mainstream Christian position as I have encountered it here in Middle Tennessee posits Satan as the prince of this world, and in this way mimics Zoroastrianism and its pitting of *Ahura Mazda*, the Lord of Light, against *Angra Mainyu*, the Lord of Darkness. While Ahura Mazda is destined to triumph, humans must choose sides. Substitute Jesus for Ahura Mazda and Satan for Angra Mainyu, and I know lots of Christians who would assent to this belief.

Judaism is too monotheistic for this. We prefer Isaiah 45:7, where God admits that good and evil are both of God. For us, evil is a psychological phenomenon fully within our power to control: "sin lurks at the door, and desires you, and you shall rule over it" (Gen 4:7). Or, as rabbi Simon Ben Zoma taught, "Who is strong? One who controls the evil inclination" (*Pirke Avot* 4:2).

I find it odd that the Jewish writers of the Gospels would have opted for Persian dualism over Isaiah's biblically normative monotheism. Their decision had huge consequences for Christian belief through the centuries. As far as I know, no other religious tradition is as concerned with the devil as is Christianity, at least in its Western forms.

Thoughts on this?

Mike: Thank you for pointing to the affinity between the morning liturgy of the Authorized Jewish Prayer Book and the Lord's Prayer passage. Like you, I find it rather striking.

That being said, let's take up your various comments relative to Jesus and Christianity's understanding of the devil, evil, and the like.

The Greek term in question may be translated either as "the evil one" or "evil." Even in the other passage you mention (Matt 13:19), the Greek term might be rendered either as "the evil one" or "the enemy."

More important, any account of Jesus' concept of the devil or evil should take the rest of his teachings into account. For example, Jesus made it clear that he thought our greatest danger came from within ourselves. Even the classic accounts of the temptations in the wilderness do not require us to posit a literal devil with a capital "D." The account itself leaves it to the reader to decide if the conflict takes place between two individuals facing each other in the desert, or within the mind and heart of Jesus. Given the teaching I mentioned first, I believe the latter is most likely. If this is the case, I tend to think that Jesus' concept fits within the broad scope of first-century Jewish thought, even as we've found considerable continuity between Jesus and first-century Jewish teachers with regard to other matters.

You're quite correct that Satan plays a relatively minor role in the Hebrew Bible, though Job does take up a good bit of space, and the story itself certainly exercised considerable influence on both Jewish and Christian imagination. The influence of Persian Zoroastrianism, insofar as I can tell, found its way into Jewish thought during the exile. Quite a few years had passed, of course, and Judaism (for the most part) had resolved the matter along the lines you suggest. Again, it seems to me that Jesus' concept is congruent with this resolution.

I see little evidence that the writers of the Gospels opted for Persian dualism. They used the language of the day, language that later readers took either literally or as metaphor. Such are the limits of language.

Certainly, formal Christian thought rather consistently rejected the dualism you posit, insisting on the unity of God and the role of God as creator of all. Evil, sin, and even a literal Satan (in those cases where a writer so believed) were the consequences of free will abused. Even so, evil is not free of God in Christian thought; God shall take even its worst consequences and bring forth something new and good that otherwise would not have been.

Having said all of the above, like you I know any number of American Christians who function as dualists. The reasons, I think, lie within American history and culture, ranging from the influence of revivalism as developed since the Second Great Awakening, premillennial dispensational teachings, and popular fiction. Dualism is one of the great temptations that beset each generation of Christians. Properly understood, though, neither the New Testament nor historical Christian thought endorses it.

Rami: This was very helpful. Let me clarify my thoughts a bit, and then I want to go more deeply into the issue of the nondual.

I didn't mean to say that the dualism of God versus the devil that seems to haunt much of Christianity came directly from Zoroastrianism. You are right that Zoroastrian ideas entered Judaism during the Babylonian exile in the latter decades of the sixth century BCE. I just meant that there seems to be a parallel view between Christian and Zoroastrian dualism.

Dualism is the great error of the Western religious traditions. The pitting of God against some form of personified evil lends itself to identifying one's enemies as being against God. The terms we use for those we oppose make this all too clear: heretics, infidels, unbelievers, etc. If God is battling with the devil, and we are on the side of God, it stands to reason that those who stand against us stand against God.

The idea of unbelief is so ingrained in our culture that even President Obama used it in his inaugural address when speaking of Jews, Christians,

Muslims, Hindus, and "unbelievers." There are no unbelievers, only people who believe differently.

We might sum up the entire history of Abrahamic religion as "Our God is bigger/truer than your God, and we can prove it by killing more of you than you can kill of us." Body count as religious proof text is a horrible legacy. I'm exaggerating of course, but not by much.

The solution, though, is not less religion but better religion. And by better I mean religion rooted in a nondual understanding of reality. Nondualism as I would define it here is the belief that all things are manifestations of a singular reality I call God. This is not the same as saying there is one God, for one only makes sense in opposition to many. The One and the many are subsumed into the larger whole that is the nondual singularity.

When Jesus says, "I am the vine, you are the branches. The one who abides in me while I abide in him bears much fruit" (John 15:5), he is speaking in nondual metaphor. There is a clear distinction between vine and branches, and yet both are part of a single living system. We are in God and God is in us, just as the wave is in the ocean and the ocean in the wave. Similarly, the Christian mystic Meister Eckhart (1260–1328) says, "the eye with which I see God is the eye with which God sees me," again speaking to a nondual understanding of reality. Every religion has this insight, though in the West it is most often limited to mystics.

In nondualism, good and evil are both aspects of the singular reality, God. To limit God to the good alone is to define God down from the all to the less than all. Seen this way, temptation and resisting temptation is all a part of God.

Chapter 19

Fasting

And whenever you fast, do not look dismal, like the hypocrites, for they disfigure their faces so as to show others that they are fasting. Truly I tell you, they have received their reward. But when you fast, put oil on your head and wash your face, so that your fasting may be seen not by others but by your heavenly Father who is in secret; and your Father who sees in secret will reward you. (Matthew 6:16-18, NRSV)

Mike: We move into a series of sayings on fasting, treasure, and allegiance. Let's take up fasting first.

Fasting was an acceptable act of piety in Jesus' day. To the best of my knowledge, he had no issue with fasting per se. He was less enthralled with what he felt to be a self-defeating form of public fasting. Perhaps with a bit of exaggeration, Jesus paints a picture of someone who alerts others that he or she is fasting by assuming a gloomy look or decorating the face with ashes, paint, or such. I don't believe Jesus cared one way or the other about the use of ashes or other facial decoration. His question was, "For whom or for what reason are you fasting?"

His targets fasted in order to get public credit for the act. More subtly, they fasted in order to gain a kind of power over those who observed them. In such cases, fasting became not a tool for spiritual liberation but a means of binding oneself even more tightly to the "normal" human game of social manipulation.

Jesus opted for private fasting. While one might well go out in public while fasting, one's appearance and behavior ought to give no clue that one was fasting. To Jesus' way of thinking, fasting was meant to be a tool that might free us to better experience or focus on God.

That's the point of the language about God seeing what is done in secret and rewarding us. The reward is not something postponed until some judgment day, but instead comes in bits and pieces and occasional transcendent moments as we experience liberation from preoccupation with self, coupled with a sharp awareness of the reality/presence of God.

Rami: As you said, Mike, fasting was common in Jesus' day, but Jesus' teaching is a bit confusing to me.

First of all, who are the "hypocrites"? The Pharisees fasted on Mondays and Thursdays, the weekdays when the Torah is read in the synagogue, but there is no outward sign for these fasts. If the disfigured face Jesus is referring to means a face unwashed accompanied by hair unoiled, the prohibition against washing and anointing is only found in regard to Yom Kippur, the most holy day of the Jewish year, and one on which all Jews fast. Could Jesus be downplaying Yom Kippur? And since the prohibition of washing and oiling one's hair was applicable to everyone, are all Jews hypocrites?

It may be that Jesus is attacking fasting in general, though he himself fasted for forty days (Matt 4:1-2). In the Gospel according to Mark (2:18-20, NRSV), Jesus abolishes all fasting for his followers as long as he is alive: "The wedding guests cannot fast while the bridegroom is with them, can they? . . . The days will come when the bridegroom is taken away from them, and then they will fast on that day." It sounds like Jesus is abolishing fasting as a practice with the exception of a fast on the day of his death. It is possible to read the text as meaning an annual fast on Good Friday or just a fast for his followers on the first Good Friday. According to the *Didache* (8:1), the early Christians followed the Pharisaic custom of fasting twice weekly, but did so on Wednesday and Friday to avoid being mistaken for Jews, but I don't know of any text telling Christians to fast on Good Friday.[1]

Your understanding of fasting as a means of shifting one's focus from self to God makes sense, though the rabbis frowned on private fasting (*Taanit* 11a) as a way of repentance, and focused the meaning of fast days on the needs of the poor. Those who fast are obligated to give charity to the poor so that the poor will have enough money to eat well when the fast is over (*Sanhedrin* 35a).

It seems to me that Jesus is balancing his political teachings regarding justice to the poor with inward-focused practices that bring one closer to God. If so, Jesus' take on this particular practice is a departure from the rabbis, who taught that fasting is not about getting right with God but about doing right by the poor: "The merit of the fast day is in the amount of charity given to the poor" (*Berachot* 6b).

Mike: Interesting insights, Rami!

I am particularly taken with the rabbinic insistence that fasting be tied to providing food for the poor. Quite a number of Christians now make the same connection. For example, a number of Christians of my acquaintance fast on Fridays throughout Lent and donate the money they would have spent on food to help feed the hungry.

Such practices make sense to me. At the very least, they actually feed someone who needs food. They also help the one fasting to remember that all spiritual practices have something more than personal benefit or even transformation in view. In the end, spiritual disciplines must strengthen not only our bond with God but also with our "neighbor."

I like your question: ". . . who are the hypocrites?" Traditional Christian interpretation often assumes that Jesus meant some of the Pharisees. Personally, though, I think both of us may be tempted to make a mistake when we ask the question—the mistake of assuming that first-century documents ever tell the whole story. My guess is that Jesus had in mind people he knew whose personal practice departed from the norm of first-century Jewish life with regard to fasting.

I don't know that I would say fasting's primary purpose is to help one "get right with God." Fasting, like any spiritual discipline, may clear or refocus one's mind, freeing it from many distractions, so that it may better apprehend the truth about one's self and the presence of God. As I've noted, this should always lead the individual to better align with the purposes of God, not the least of which is to minister to others. Like any spiritual discipline, fasting is not an end in itself but a means toward a desirable end.

Rami: No argument from me, Mike. Oh, I take it back. Of course there is an argument from me. What would a rabbi be without an argument?

I'm just wondering about the idea that spiritual discipline is a means toward a desirable end. I used to think that my meditation and chanting practices would get me something or take me somewhere. But I no longer think that. There is nowhere to go and nothing to be gotten. God is in, with, and as all things, so where is there to go and what is there to get? Now I meditate and chant for the sheer pleasure of doing so.

As we have discussed earlier, in Judaism we call this *lishmah*, practice for its own sake. This is considered the highest form of practice: no aim, no reward, no expectations, just rejoicing in the presence of God, the *Shekhina*, through study, prayer, contemplation, and chanting. Works for me.

On to the next verses?

Note

1. *Didache* means "the Teaching" and is perhaps the oldest catechism, laying out the teachings and practices of the first- or second-century church.

Chapter 20

Treasure, Allegiance, and Faith

Do not store up for yourselves treasures on earth, where moth and rust consume and where thieves break in and steal, but store up for yourselves treasures in heaven, where neither moth nor rust consumes and where thieves do not break in and steal. For where your treasure is, there your heart will be also. The eye is the lamp of the body. So, if your eye is healthy, your whole body will be full of light, but if your eye is unhealthy, your whole body will be full of darkness. If then the light in you is darkness, how great is the darkness! No one can serve two masters; for a slave will either hate the one and love the other, or be devoted to the one and despise the other. You cannot serve God and wealth. Therefore I tell you, do not worry about your life, what you will eat or what you will drink, or about your body, what you will wear. Is not life more than food, and the body more than clothing? Look at the birds of the air; they neither sow nor reap nor gather into barns, and yet your heavenly Father feeds them. Are you not of more value than they? And can any of you by worrying add a single hour to your span of life? And why do you worry about clothing? Consider the lilies of the field, how they grow; they neither toil nor spin, yet I tell you, even Solomon in all his glory was not clothed like one of these. But if God so clothes the grass of the field, which is alive today and tomorrow is thrown into the oven, will he not much more clothe you—you of little faith? Therefore, do not worry, saying, "What will we eat?" or "What will we drink?" or

"What will we wear?" For it is the Gentiles who strive for all these things; and indeed your heavenly Father knows that you need all these things. But strive first for the kingdom of God and his righteousness, and all these things will be given to you as well. So do not worry about tomorrow, for tomorrow will bring worries of its own. Today's trouble is enough for today. (Matthew 6:19-34, NRSV)

Mike: While most commentators divide Matthew 6:19-34 into at least four sections (vv. 19-21, 22-23, 24, 25-34), I tend to think the passage should be treated as a whole.

The core thesis comes late in the passage: "But strive first for the kingdom of God and his righteousness, and all these things will be given to you as well." To be frank, this is the central thrust of the entire Sermon on the Mount. Paraphrased, it might go something like this: "Devote yourself solely to God; all other things will then find their proper place."

Such a perspective clears one's vision. We see the source of our life (God), our family (all others), our home (the creation), and our direction (love). Any lesser perspective clouds our vision and leaves us to walk in gathering darkness.

In such darkness, we fixate on trying to secure our security (storing up treasures, whether of gold, expertise, reputation, etc.). We fail to see how all such treasures are prone to decay or loss, indeed that loss is inevitable. In effect, we wind up trying to walk two paths and serve two very different masters at the same time—God or our anxieties. As Jesus says, such a double-vision approach to life does not work. In the end, we opt for one option or the other.

Like any good teacher or preacher, Jesus illustrates his point with particular examples, hence his injunctions not to worry about food, drink, clothing, and the like. Such worry turns out to be futile and betrays a nagging tendency to trust in ourselves (or other providers) rather than in God. More important, indulging such worries pulls us toward dependence on "wealth." We find the allure of its promise of independence from God or others too much to resist, and we give it our worship. Both of us know what our traditions have to say about idolatry!

Rami: I admire your synthesis of these passages, Mike, but I'm going to take the more traditional approach and comment on various teachings as they come up.

"Do not store up for yourselves treasures on earth, where moth and rust consume." This reminds me, as it would Jesus' audience, of Ecclesiastes. who teaches that everything "under the sun" (Jesus' "on earth") is *hevel*, transient as morning dew (a much more accurate translation than the conventional "vanity" or "futility"). Ecclesiastes says, "The lover of money will not be satisfied with money; nor the lover of wealth, with gain. This also is impermanent" (Eccl 5:10). Everything on earth is in the process of dying. Nothing is permanent, and so trying to overcome our fear of mortality with things always fails.

I especially like the line, "For where your treasure is, there your heart will be also." We treasure that which we imagine will save us from the fate of all life—death. Some of us imagine that this treasure is on earth, others that it is in heaven. I am not much of a believer in heavens and hells, nor do I think there is any way to escape my own transience. Jesus, unlike Ecclesiastes, seems to hold out hope for a better world in heaven. I tend to side with Ecclesiastes, taking comfort in living life as best I can without clinging to anything or anyone.

"If then the light in you is darkness, how great is the darkness." To me Jesus is saying this: Use your eyes to pierce the façade of permanence; see, as Ecclesiastes saw, that all is *hevel havalim*, transient and insubstantial as breath. Then you will be free from clinging, from storing up treasure. But do not think treasure is material only. Ideas, too, can blind the eye and leave us in darkness. Wrong thinking is subtler than material wealth, for it leads to mistaking error for truth and darkness for light. Take no refuge in thoughts or things, but only in the unknowable God alone. Taking refuge in the Unknowable, you hold to nothing. When you are free of material and spiritual clinging, you are at last in the kingdom of God.

"You cannot serve God and wealth." It didn't take long for the followers of Jesus to forget this teaching. By equating wealth with God, they deftly finessed Jesus and established a church whose wealth is the envy of even the super rich. But this is not unique to any one religion. I read all sacred texts and teaching and ask, "Whom does this teaching benefit?" Jesus' teachings, like those of the other Hebrew prophets, most often benefit the poor and powerless, and because they do I believe they are from God. Texts and teachings that sanction the accumulation of wealth and power in the hands of the few are most likely the product of those hands as well.

"Therefore I tell you, do not worry about your life." Or as the immortal Alfred E. Newman says, "What? Me worry?" Worry adds nothing to life. On the contrary, it distracts us from living it. Living without worry isn't living with the bliss of ignorance, for as Jesus says, "tomorrow will bring worries of its own. Today's trouble is enough for today." Trouble and suffering are as natural to life as tranquility and joy. When we worry about these things (having too much of the former and not enough of the latter), we distract ourselves from dealing with the troubles and enjoying the pleasantness that are before us right now. Worry takes us out of the present, and Jesus, like Ecclesiastes, is challenging us to live in the present (though not for it).

Living without worry allows us to engage life fully and righteously, doing what is right because it is right and not because we imagine it will earn us some reward in the great by and by. The kingdom of God, as I understand it, is not in heaven but on earth—it is this very life lived with justice, compassion, and humility (Mic 6:8).

Jesus, I believe, anticipated the coming of God's kingdom on earth in the lifetime of his followers. When it failed to come, these same followers put it off into the future. When the future too proved too soon, they projected it into the afterlife, where it can never be too early or too late. Unfortunately, removing the kingdom from this world allowed the teachers of the kingdom to store up treasures in this world, deliberately misrepresenting darkness as light and exploiting the fears of people in the name of God.

For me, the challenge of Jesus is not faith but action. Striving "first for the kingdom of God and his righteousness" means living this moment with an open mind, an open heart, and an open hand. This I believe is what Jesus modeled, and this is what we must try to do in our own lives as well.

Part 5

On Judgment
(Matthew 7:1-5)

Chapter 21

Against Judgmentalism

Do not judge, so that you may not be judged. For with the judgment you make you will be judged, and the measure you give will be the measure you get. Why do you see the speck in your neighbor's eye, but do not notice the log in your own eye? Or how can you say to your neighbor, "Let me take the speck out of your eye," while the log is in your own eye? You hypocrite, first take the log out of your own eye, and then you will see clearly to take the speck out of your neighbor's eye. (Matthew 7:1-5, NRSV)

Mike: What kind of judgment does Jesus have in mind? Our answer determines our response to the passage. For example, when we say that someone has good judgment, we usually mean he or she possesses discernment, whether when dealing with decisions or with others. That person makes wise decisions. If Jesus is calling us to refrain from discernment and decision-making, we have a problem.

Insofar as I can tell, that's not what Jesus has in mind. Instead, he speaks of the all-too-human tendency to label others negatively. We too often think we can categorize others as wrong or right, good or bad, and the like. Frankly, we may subject ourselves to the same kind of self-evaluation. Theologically speaking, the Christian tradition generally teaches that only God can rightly judge the heart of a human and that only God has the "right" and wisdom to do so. When we judge, we in effect try to take God's place. We cannot bear such a burden well, so inevitably we wind up hurting others and ourselves.

More subtly, such judgment may mask our desire and need to control our environment. We want to keep others "in their place," deprive them of power, or eliminate them as "players." We're afraid of certain aspects of ourselves, so we project our dark side onto others and attack it. We judge because it makes us feel safe, though in reality the practice puts us in grave danger of alienation from God, others, and even ourselves.

Discernment generally engenders humility and compassion. Judgment, on the other hand, breeds pride, disdain, and violence.

How might we remove the log in our own eye? We need help. In my religious tradition, we believe that the Holy Spirit undertakes to help us see the log and remove it. As you might expect, this is not a one-time event but an ongoing process. Personally, I've found it helpful to meditate on Scriptures such as Matthew 7:1-5, read how others have identified and dealt with the matter, and listen to a handful of close friends who sometimes know me better than I know myself.

I must say that the reward of pursuing discernment while dropping judgment is considerable. Our need to determine who is in or out diminishes. We indeed become able to be more honest about our own dark side, which in turn enables us to more readily accept and enjoy our gifts. As humility grows, we relax. After all, we're no longer out to remake the world and others into our own image! Instead, we learn to appreciate the individuality of others. Our task is redefined. Now we seek to discern and nurture the gifts of others. We also learn how to enjoy others and be enriched by what they bring to the table.

Rami: I agree that we should not take Jesus' blanket prohibition against making judgments literally. Otherwise Jesus is being illogical, for simply to place not judging above judging is a judgment. So I understand Jesus to be arguing against becoming judgmental.

Jesus' teaching should be compared to those of his rabbinic colleagues. The rabbis taught, "Judge all people by their deeds" (*Pirke Avot* I:6). Judging a people according to the quality of their actions provides a sound foundation for good judgment and avoids playing God and trying to judge a person's heart. The rabbis also taught, "Those who judge according to deeds will in turn be judged according to deeds" (*Shabbat*, 127b). While the rabbis believe "God desires the heart" (*Sefer Hasidim*, 5-6), it is the quality of one's actions that determines one's fate because actions are controllable while feelings or thoughts arise of their own accord. Last, we can see parallels to Jesus' log and speck analogy in the rabbinic teaching, "Those who condemn others see in them their own faults" (*Kiddushin*, 70a).

One question I would raise regarding these teachings of Jesus is whether or not he himself lived up to them. Clearly he did not. Jesus not only judges but is often judgmental. To cite only one example, Jesus regularly calls people hypocrites. The word occurs only once in the entire Hebrew Bible (Ps 26:4, NRSV) and twelve times in the Gospel according to Matthew (6:2; 6:5; 6:16; 15:7; 22:18; 23:13; 23:15; 23:23; 23:25; 23:27; 23:29; and 24:51, NRSV)! I have no problem forgiving Jesus his log, and in fact it makes him all the more human and accessible, but it is still important to note that he himself had work to do.

Regarding personal log removal, I think I understand what you are saying about the Holy Spirit, though I prefer to place my faith in trusted friends and a good therapist. When it comes to helping me see the log in my own eye, I suspect that the Holy Spirit is often my ego in Holy Spirit clothing excusing the log and exaggerating the other person's speck.

My last comment speaks to your notion that "we're no longer out to remake the world and others into our own image." I know what you mean, and I don't disagree, but in the interest of creative dialogue let me suggest that when we realize our true image, meaning God in whose image we are made, we are indeed out to remake the world in our/God's image. The entire Jewish enterprise is one of *tikkun hanefesh* and *tikkun haolam*, reclaiming the image of God in our souls that we might remake the world in that image as well, applying justice and compassion as best we can on every level of human interaction (personal, interpersonal, and transpersonal), as well as in our interactions with other species and nature as a whole.

Chapter 22

Toward Self-awareness and Humility

First take the log out of your own eye.... (Matthew 7:5, NRSV)

Mike: We're in agreement that Jesus argued against our being judgmental. Still, I want to address the nuances of the point by focusing on the passage above. In the passage, Jesus calls us to healthy self-awareness and humility. The more we become aware of our own sin (or whatever you prefer to call it), the better the chance that we may not rush to pass judgment on others. We might even develop empathy and its companion virtue, compassion.

As for the role of the Holy Spirit in "log removal," I appreciate your point. From my perspective, Holy Spirit (Spirit of God, etc.) most often works through others to help us see the log in our own eye. Such a community of friends and advisors keeps us honest. If we listen only to the voice within ourselves, it's all too easy to deceive ourselves. In fact, we have to move beyond our circle of friends and learn to listen well to those with whom we disagree. This provides a safeguard against the kind of "group think" that often characterizes human communities.

Regarding Jesus, I suspect that our faith perspectives place us on different pages. Seeing Jesus through the eyes of the Christian faith, I believe him uniquely qualified to judge others on the basis of their deeds. It seems to me that he consistently does so. If I accept the premise of the incarnation and all it implies, then Jesus has the right and wisdom to judge, forgive sins, and all the rest. In short, Rami, I doubt that we will come to agreement on this particular point.

Thanks for the way in which you elaborated on my statement: "we're no longer out to remake the world and others in our own image." I strongly agree with you. That being said, I want to clarify my own point. When we live without awareness of the log in our own eye or in denial of the image of God within us, we tend to try to shrink the world to fit us comfortably. A racist wants to remake the world into a racist world, and so it goes. The greatest danger we pose to the world and one another rises from this kind of tendency. Your comments point to the opposite side of the coin: the hope we may offer the world insofar as we reclaim the image of God and live accordingly.

Rami: I'd like to take a moment and explore a bit more the place of our most fundamental disagreement: that Jesus is God. Actually, I have no problem affirming that Jesus is God. Where we differ is that I would add to the affirmation "and so are you."

Jesus is God, and so are you.

God, for me, is reality in all its manifestations. When Jesus says, "I and the Father are one," I say, "*Mazal tov*! Congratulations! You get it! You and God are one, and so is everything else." If God is infinite, there cannot be anything that is not God. I have no problem accepting Jesus as a fully awake and God-realized manifestation of the Divine, far beyond my meager knowing. I just take him as paradigmatic of what all humans can achieve and not, as Christians do, the one and only such manifestation.

Okay, so much for my theological stance. My question is, why do you believe what you believe?

My own conviction comes from an initial experience I had at age sixteen. Meditating on a lakeshore in Cape Cod, Massachusetts, during the summer of 1967, I suddenly knew the absolute nonduality of all things in, with, and as God. I was everything and everything was me, and there was only this One Thing which I call God. Subsequent experiences have reinforced this knowing, and I cannot deny it.

So, if you don't mind, please tell me a bit more about your experience of Christ. Where does your faith conviction come from? Did you have (and do you continue to have) a deep encounter with Jesus Christ? What was it like? In what way is Jesus a living presence for you?

Mike: You know my love for classic science fiction, so you'll not be surprised that your take on God inevitably jogs my memory and calls to mind Robert Heinlein's *Stranger in a Strange Land* (New York: Putnam, 1961). Heinlein probably did more than anyone else to introduce to mainstream American culture the idea of "Thou art God" and so is everyone and everything else. (And, yes, as you know I'm aware of the ancient roots of the perspective!)

If I were not Christian, I suspect that I would adopt such a view.

That being said, I want to turn to your specific question: why I believe what I believe. You phrase my belief as "Jesus is God." That's good shorthand, but of course what I believe is a little more complicated. With that acknowledgment, let's turn to your question.

Experience drives my belief. For example, during my childhood the stories of Jesus that I read caught my imagination. I experienced God through Jesus. Looking back, I regard such experience as preparation.

An intense experience during my sophomore year in college strengthened my conviction. While minding my own business in my room, in fact while working on a paper, I suddenly felt myself in the presence of something far greater than myself. At first it felt as if a great weight lay over the entire room, including me. Then the weight lessened. I felt small, unworthy, more than a little frightened (think Isa 6:1ff). Then something changed. I felt known yet loved. I had never before felt that anyone knew me to my depths, and I had always believed that no one could love me if they actually knew the real me. Now I found myself known and loved without condition, though all the help I might ever need to become more fully me was offered freely. I relaxed, I let down my guard, and I surrendered to the embrace of the presence. Subsequent experiences have not been as dramatic, but they have been real to me, reinforcing and informing the initial experience.

Afterward, as I reflected on the experience, I found my mind returning to the stories of Jesus, and I realized that I saw in him the presence I had experienced. I think that's when I decided firmly and for myself that the incarnation had happened, that it was real. Obviously, all this can be written off as a typical young adulthood matter or as being solely conditioned by religious culture. In my own case, I think not. My inner skeptic is alive and well and always has been.

Jesus has proven to be the focal point or lens through which I continue to experience the presence, love, and guidance of God. It's fair to say that experience drives my belief. The stories of Jesus help shape my response to experience, both in terms of my private life and my life in community.

Rami: Thank you so much for sharing this, Mike. You raise at least two issues on which I would like to comment.

First is your assertion that "If I were not Christian, I suspect I would adopt such a view." The view in question is my understanding of God as the source and substance of all reality, and Jesus as paradigmatic of the God-realized human that each us can become.

If I were to say this in the context of my own life, I would say, "Were I not Jewish, I suspect I would adopt such a view." But I am Jewish, and I do affirm this view! I do not affirm it because I am a Jew. I affirm it because every fiber of my being tells me it is true. If Judaism insisted on something different, I would have to be something different. I manage to stay within the Jewish fold for two reasons. First, because being a Jew is a matter of birth and/or tribal membership, and there is no one theology that defines us as a people. And second, because the Jewish mystics do allow for just such a theology.

I place truth, as best as I can perceive it, above theology. That is to say, a thing is true for me not because the Bible says it is true but because my experience and reason tell me so. The Bible may affirm what I know to be true, but it isn't the source of that truth. For example, I believe it is true that we should love our neighbors as ourselves. I believe it not because God says it (Lev 19:18), but because when tested against my experience I find it to be true. God also says that we should avoid mixing linen and flax in our clothing, but I do not find this compelling at all and do not worry about it. But God says both things. If one is true because God said it, the other can be no less true, seeing as how it comes from the same source. The fact that I pick and choose among God's teachings makes it clear that I place my own sense of right and wrong above God's as presented in the Hebrew Bible.

Regarding your experience in college, I have no doubt that you were both working on a paper and touched by the presence of God. What is interesting to me is that this Presence wasn't identified as Jesus until later. This, I think, is the norm among most of us who have had similar experiences. This Presence is Nameless, beyond religion and theological niceties. This Presence crushes (Muhammad, too, felt the Presence of Allah as a crushing weight) and loves. But it isn't Jesus, or Yahweh, or Allah, or Krishna, or any of the thousands of names we humans invent for the Ineffable. It just is.

When the experience passes and we try to make sense of it, we draw from the language with which we are most comfortable. For you that language is Christianity. For me it is Judaism. For others the language might be Buddhism, or Islam, or art, literature, or science. The key is to distinguish the ineffable experience from the words we use to describe it.

Religion goes wrong when it mistakes the word for the event. Religion is vital when it preserves the event story as a reminder of what each of us can discover for ourselves.

Mike: I think we understand one another, at least insofar as is possible via words on a screen or page. That being said, I want to add a few more words to our conversation.

First, I appreciate your points about what it means to be Jewish and the room afforded you within the tradition. For what it may be worth, Christian mystics often make room for a wide range of ways in which to experience God and articulate the experience. Thomas Merton, for example, comes to mind. Systematic theologians have more trouble doing so, not least because they (as a group) major on precision and distinctions. Experience does not lend itself to such treatment.

Second, you speak of testing matters in light of experience and reason. We're on common ground here. Within the limits of a single entry, it sounds as if you refer only to your personal experience and reason. I'm fairly certain that is not the case, but that's for you to say. As for me, I try to pay attention to a mix of things: personal experience and reason, the experience and reason of others as found in their stories and in general human history, the experience and reflection of the church over the centuries (this includes but is not limited to the Scriptures), modern science, the arts, and the like. Again, my hunch is that our approaches are similar, though we might weigh various elements differently.

Third, naturally we try to make sense of such experiences by calling on the language(s) we know. You say this is Judaism for you. Actually, though, wouldn't it be more accurate to say that it is Judaism, one or more other world religions (or philosophies), modern science, and the arts? You are multilingual, so to speak. So am I. In both our cases, we try to distinguish between the language(s) we use and the reality we're attempting to describe. What I have learned for myself is that Jesus best describes the presence and its implications for me.

One quibble. I appreciate your perspective when you write, "Religion is vital when it preserves the event story as a reminder of what each of us can discover for ourselves." We agree, I think, that we can discover a good bit for ourselves. In the case of the particular experience I described, though, I have no sense that I had set out to find or discover anything. Instead, I should say it was given me.

Rami: You refined my thoughts quite nicely, Mike. Thanks.

I am multilingual to be sure. Sometimes I wonder if I am not my own private Tower of Babel. I think we are able to find such richness in our conversations because we share so many languages. While this may not be rare among peoples of faith, admitting it seems to be. So many people find being bilingual dangerous, let alone multilingual. I find that the more languages of faith I know, the richer my understanding of Reality becomes.

I also agree with your final comment that the experience of God's Presence is a gift. Contemplative practices can prime the pump and help make us receptive to the gifts of the Spirit, but in the end it is always a matter of grace.

Part 6

On Holiness
(Matthew 7:6-29)

Chapter 23

Regarding Dogs and Swine

Do not give what is holy to dogs; and do not throw pearls before swine, or they will trample them under foot and turn and maul you. (Matthew 7:6, NRSV)

Mike: What might we make of this neglected brief statement, sandwiched as it is between Matthew 7:1-5 and Matthew 7:7-11, which are classic, oft-cited passages?

The passage sounds like a proverb, and it certainly is structured like one. If so, I think it best to treat it as a kind of wisdom saying. The sayings found in the book of Proverbs often sound jarring to Christian ears. For the most part, they lay out tactics for a stable, productive life. There is little "high sounding" about a proverb. Some proverbs, in fact, come across as harsh. In the context of first-century Judaism, I suspect the terms "dog" and "swine" did so.

When I treat Matthew 7:6 as a kind of proverb, I interpret it as a necessary corrective to a tendency often found in Christians. I call it the "argue with a fence post mentality." It's characterized by an inability or unwillingness to recognize when someone simply is not open to the Christian way. Wise Christians drop the subject and move on. Many Christians, though, insist on force-feeding their version of the gospel to the reluctant, closed, or openly hostile person. The results are never good, either for the Christians or the person they've cornered.

In like fashion, Jesus counsels his followers to be gentle as a dove and wise as a fox. He tells them not to spend their time with villagers immune to his message but to move on to another village.

Put positively, Jesus' point is this: invest your time and message with those who will receive it—that is, who will listen carefully and respond. Note that he does not promise such people will always accept what you have to offer, but they will display a willingness to listen and interact.

This kind of wisdom finds its way into pastoral ministry. Many years ago, a well-known pastor often told young ministers, "Don't allow 5 percent of the people to take up 95 percent of your time." He meant that we were to focus our time and energy on those receptive to our ministry rather than burn up time trying to help those who refuse help. For the most part, I've found his insight on target.

Rami: I agree, Mike, that Matthew 7:6 is a proverb, but that only begs the question, who were the dogs and the swine? Nobody literally tosses holy objects to dogs or throws pearls to pigs, so Jesus doesn't mean for us to take him literally. It seems to me that the "dogs" and "swine" are either Jews who reject Jesus and his teaching, or Gentiles in general. So much for "do not judge" (Matt 7:1).

The first reading is on par with Jesus calling his rabbinic opponents "hypocrites" and "children of hell" (Matt 23:13-15). It might not be much of a stretch to imagine Jesus calling them dogs and pigs as well.

If we don't want to stretch at all, we can look to Matthew 15:26, where Jesus uses similar language to refer to Canaanites. The Canaanite woman beseeches Jesus to heal her daughter, but Jesus at first refuses. His rationale is that he has come to teach the lost sheep of Israel, and that "it is not fair to take the children's food and throw it to the dogs" (Matt 15:26). Here the "children" refer to the Jews, the food is the teaching of Jesus, and the dogs are the Canaanites.

The Canaanite woman understands that Jesus is talking about her and her people and says, "even dogs eat the crumbs that fall from their master's plates" (Matt 15:27). Jesus is impressed with her faith (and her *chutzpah*?) and heals her daughter. This does not spark a change of heart in Jesus, however, and he instructs his apostles to refrain from entering Gentile cities (Matt 10:5), again suggesting that Jesus' mission is to the Jews and the Jews alone.

Jesus' reference to "swine" is more problematic. He never calls anyone "swine" or uses pigs in a parable. He does cast demons into swine (Matt 8:32), but I doubt Jesus is admonishing us from casting his teachings to the demon possessed. So "swine" escapes me.

In any case, I understand the need to clean this up a bit, but I don't think Jesus was talking about the 5 percent of the people who take up 95 percent of a pastor's time. Jesus wasn't always polite, and I think we have to allow him his biases and judgments. Just imagine how much pressure that would take off those who try to live up to his example.

Mike: You're good! I especially appreciate the way in which you pull together several Scripture passages that present similar challenges. Let's stipulate that you clearly cover one of the standard interpretations. As you know well, it's an option articulated by a number of Christian interpreters.

Jesus certainly was not always polite. He could be, and often was, blunt. In addition, I would add that he strikes me as having been a realist with regard to human nature. Some will listen and accept, and others will not— so what's a disciple to do? We've already discussed our differences over judgment/discernment and being judgmental.

Both of us know that "dogs" and "swine" are not to be taken literally but instead as powerful metaphors. Whatever Jesus might have in mind, neither term was complimentary in his culture. Both of us are aware of the debates over the place of "the Gentile mission" in Jesus' mind. We differ over how this passage might apply to the matter. You focus on the question of Jesus' attitude toward Gentiles; I focus on the passage's possible application to the work of those who took Christianity to the Gentiles and some first-century Jews. Strange and interesting, isn't it, how the two of us look at the same words yet ask different questions of them.

Several factors seem to me to be in play and to fuel our different responses to the passage. The first relates to how each of us chooses to deal with the "rough" aspect of the passage. Let's face it. I sometimes take understatement past all reasonable limits. When I briefly wrote of the passage's harshness and the like, I automatically "felt" as if I had said a great deal. What you took to be an effort to "clean up" the passage did not feel that way to me. That's a mistake on my part, by the way. I assumed too much on the part of potential readers and should have taken more space to unpack the terms.

Second, it's probably impossible for me not to interpret a Scripture passage without taking into account most of twenty centuries of interpretive work in the Christian community. The long tradition no doubt affects me in ways of which I am both aware and unaware. One feature of that tradition is a tendency to apply Scripture passages to one's own slice of life—hence, the pastoral life story.

Third, it seems to me that both of us may be reacting to the Christian stereotypes of Jesus that we encounter. We've discussed one or more of these in recent posts. In this particular case, I deal often with people who believe that Jesus (or a disciple of Jesus) could never "move on" from anyone in order to deal with someone else more open to Jesus' teachings or potential lordship—hence my tendency to read and apply the proverb the way I did in my entry.

Reading back over the preceding paragraphs, plus your comments, I have no difficulty understanding why so many trees have had to die so that endless commentaries might be written!

Rami: I am good! And the advantage I have over you is ignorance. You have spent your life studying these teachings and 2,000 years' worth of Christian commentary on them, while I once read a book about it. But this is America, and here ignorance trumps scholarship almost every time, so on to the next text.

Chapter 24

Ask, and It Will Be Given

Ask, and it will be given to you; search, and you will find; knock, and the door will be opened for you. For everyone who asks receives, and everyone who searches finds, and for everyone who knocks, the door will be opened. Is there anyone among you who, if your child asks for bread, will give a stone? Or if the child asks for a fish, will give a snake? If you then, who are evil, know how to give good gifts to your children, how much more will your Father in heaven give good things to those who ask him! (Matthew 7:7-11, NRSV)

Mike: Let's start with the literary context. Jesus has challenged his followers on many fronts throughout the sermon. Even a partial list is daunting: the Beatitudes, taming the heart as well as behavior, loving enemies, meaningful prayer, laying aside materialism, discernment versus being judgmental, and the like. It seems to me that any sane person might have asked himself or herself, "Where will I find strength and wisdom enough to begin and follow such a life's path?"

Matthew 7:7-11 addresses the matter. Jesus once again calls his followers to rely on God. He uses active language: ask, seek, and knock. One may ask, seek, and knock via prayer but also through study, reflection, and conversation. Seeking God's way is not a passive affair!

Lots of nonsense has been written over the years regarding the phrase "and it will be given to you." Given that Jesus did not always receive what he prayed for, we cannot accept the idea that we shall receive whatever we request. I prefer to link the phrases "will be given," "will find," and "opened to you." Here I think Jesus practiced parallelism, stacking similar phrases atop one another in order to drive home his point: God is prepared to give you what you most or really need.

That's the point of Jesus' language about human parents and their children. If a human parent (assuming a "normal" relationship) can be trusted to try to give good things to his or her children, then surely God can be trusted to do so and to get it right.

My experience (and that of others) is of a God who often does not answer the question I ask but instead another question. God frequently does not give me what I seek but something else instead. As for doors, God most often does not open the one I want opened but instead leads me through another. It can be quite frustrating. Here's the thing, though: such experiences reshape us, given time and acceptance, from self-centered urchins into adults more willing and able to flex, give of ourselves, appreciate others, and walk in faith.

Rami: This teaching of Jesus is right out of the Hebrew Scriptures. The idea of "asking" hearkens back to Deuteronomy 32:7, "Ask your father, and he will show you"; and Psalm 2:8, "Ask of me, and I will give you." Seeking suggests Proverbs 8:17, "And those who seek me diligently shall find me"; and Jeremiah 29:13, "And you shall seek me and find me." Knocking may be unique to Jesus, though he may have in mind the passage in Song of Songs that says, "It is the voice of my beloved that knocks saying, open to me" (5:2). So there is nothing in the teaching itself that is startling to Jewish ears.

Your notion that Jesus offers us this teaching to calm our fears that the program of action prescribed in the sermon is impossible to live up to, however, is intriguing.

First, I'm struck by how Pauline it sounds. Paul saw the Torah (or Law as he insists on mistranslating the Hebrew for "instruction") as an impossible burden designed to condemn rather than save. For him faith in Jesus was the antidote to damnation under the law. Now I hear you saying that asking, seeking, and knocking are the antidote to the impossibility of living up to Jesus' Way set forth in the Sermon on the Mount. This may not be what you meant, but before you correct my misunderstanding, consider for a moment that you may be on to something.

My reading of Jesus suggests that he is imagining people on the edge of total despair who frantically cry out, grasp, and tear rather than respectfully ask, calmly search, or politely knock. I think that Jesus, like other spiritual geniuses, sets forth a plan of salvation (enlightenment, God-realization, etc.) that is designed to fail. Why? Because we cannot transform ourselves. The very ego that needs transforming is the ego that is asked to make the transformation. It can't be done. The ego must be surrendered by our failure so that God can transform us through grace.

Paul was right about the commandments—they are designed to condemn, for only the condemned are ready to be transformed by God. His mistake was to offer the condemned another escape from the reality of condemnation.

Just as you cannot meditate yourself into enlightenment or earn your way into heaven through the *mitzvot* (commandments) of the Torah, so you cannot get to heaven through the Sermon on the Mount. What you can do in all of these systems is exhaust your ego and bring yourself to the point of absolute despair. Here you have no choice but to cry, grasp, and claw at heaven's door just as a drowning man cries, grasps, and flails. And then God changes everything. To me Jesus is saying, "When you finally realize you can't walk the path to heaven, storm the gate! God will let you in. He doesn't care how you get to Him; just come home, come in!"

This is similar to Kafka's parable of the Law. A man spends his entire life waiting to be invited into the Gate of the Law (salvation) only to find at the moment of his death that there is no invitation, that this gate was for him alone to walk through. He just lacked the desperation needed for him to do it.

Your second point is also interesting, but no less troubling for me. To say that God always responds to our beseeching, but not in the way we like, seems like a cop-out to me. All I hear is that life happens regardless of what I want and don't want. I have no problem with the theology. I believe God when he says he creates light and dark, good and evil (Isa 45:7). But if I ask for a bike and God sends me cancer, what's the point? If I didn't ask for the bike, would God not have sent me cancer? Did my asking for what I want trigger God to send me what I need?

Ascribing reality to God's will adds nothing to my experience, unless I assume that God always acts for my good, something that Job and I cannot accept.

This is not a problem unique to Christianity, of course. The ancient rabbis also believed in that "whatever God does is entirely good" (*Berachot* 60b); and that "God never deals harshly with his creatures" (*Avodah Zarah* 3a). So you are in good company, but I'm not among them. I find Job's God more accurate and comforting: God does what God wants, and human ideas of good and evil have nothing to do with it. What I have to learn is how to live gracefully without knowing which is coming my way next.

Mike: Taking up your first observation, I am not sure if the passage sounds Pauline or if we hear it as Pauline because we know Paul. I think, for example, that Augustine read the Gospels through the lens of Paul. I am certain that Martin Luther and Calvin did so, along with many of their theological descendants. I prefer to try to reverse the order and read Paul in light of the Gospel accounts. All of this is only slightly related to the main thrust of your point! I simply could not resist taking the detour.

As to your idea that Jesus, like other spiritual geniuses, sets out a plan of salvation designed to fail so that we might be driven or led to surrender the ego, etc., it parallels a long-standing approach adopted by Christians of various stripes. In the tradition I refer to, the core idea is that, taken seriously, both the Commandments and the Sermon on the Mount teach us that we cannot achieve God's standard of perfection. Ideally, the realization delivers us from pride (i.e., ego gone amuck, ego in charge, etc.), and we turn to God to do the transformative work only God can do.

I tend to adopt the insight, but I think to stop there is a mistake. Once we begin to surrender our ego (or self-righteousness, to use Pauline and Christian language) and depend on God, we find that God has loved us all along. The way to God and life with God has been blocked by our own ego. Freed of "the need to transform ourselves," as you put it, we become free to live into transformation. Changing metaphors, we become free to be as children for whom watching, learning from, and imitating a parent is both natural and a form of healthy play. For us, the Commandments and the Sermon on the Mount become not an end but the ethos of our home, an ethos we take with us into any external environment.

With regard to the second point, I did not mean to imply that God always responds but never in the way we like. Even if that were my position, I'm not sure it would amount to a cop-out, but it surely would be bleak, akin to the Norse resignation to fate. That is not my position.

Instead, I believe that God may grant or deny what we request in accordance with his wisdom and within "the rules" of the created world. Children ask for many things, all of which they want in a given moment. Being the parent of two, I know this is so, not simply in theory but in practice. That's why the analogy Jesus uses speaks so strongly to me. My intentional responses to such requests have included silence, explanation, denial of the request, granting the request, granting a modified version of the request, requiring something of the child he or she did not expect or especially want, explaining why the request was impossible to fulfill, and delaying the request. In each case, though, I responded as I thought best and possible.

Let's face it: I had a much larger frame of reference than my child and a greater responsibility as well. I tend to think God plays a similar role with regard to us.

The story of Job can be interpreted along the lines outlined in the preceding paragraph. In that case, both Job and his "friends" have much to learn although Job is farther along than any of his friends and asks much tougher questions. His questions are so good that they provoke a divine answer! We, of course, are starting to grapple with theodicy. My hunch is that the subject would require a book of its own.

A minor point of clarification before I end: the "nonsense" I had in mind is any version of "name it and claim it" theology. This particular passage is one of the classic proof texts for what I can only regard as theological nonsense.

Rami: I was pleasantly surprised to hear that you agree with my notion that spiritual practices are designed to lead us to surrender. I don't believe we can surrender, for that is still an act of will, but I do believe that we can be surrendered, and this is the great goal of authentic spiritual practice.

I also appreciate your taking this even further. The great discovery one experiences when surrendered to God is that we are loved just as we are. This is the parable of the prodigal son. The fallacy of religion is to think that we need to bring the kingdom of God in the future, when in fact all we need do is live it here and now.

I still have trouble with God granting or denying my requests, however. First of all, if God agrees that what I desire is good, why doesn't God just give it to me in the first place? And if what I desire is wrong, why entertain the request at all? And then there is the problem of God playing the role of parent or potentate. In the first case we are reduced to children, in the second to serfs. I'm not happy with either.

As I have said many times, God for me is Reality: all that was, is, and will be. Reality is creative and open to change, indeed Reality is change, and so I am not fated to do one thing or another. I don't ask Reality for anything (though I can and do thank it for everything). Rather, I engage what is to the best of my ability and then move on to engage what is next. The quality of my interaction in this moment will influence (though not control) the quality of the next moment, and religion at its best teaches me how to live out of the highest qualities—justice, compassion, and humility.

On to the golden rule?

Chapter 25

The Golden Rule

In everything do to others as you would have them do to you;
for this is the law and the prophets. (Matthew 7:12, NRSV)

Mike: Versions of the golden rule abound. No doubt you can share examples from several cultures. Jesus offers a positive version.

Negative versions of the rule seem to me to be akin to the old medical dictum: "Do no harm." That is, they call us to avoid hurting others. The rule of thumb becomes, "Don't do anything to someone else you would not want them to do to you." I admire the insight into human nature that lies in back of such formulations. Most of us, I suspect, have little trouble envisioning what others might do to harm us. Identifying and refraining from such actions provides the makings of a workable social order (assuming, of course, that we are healthy people in most respects).

Such a dictum finds particular expressions in the Ten Commandments ("Don't murder," etc.) and the prophets (don't misuse the justice system to steal from the poor, etc.).

In short, the negative formulations of the golden rule, if applied, serve to regulate destructive human behavior.

Looking back, I find that I've made use of the negative formulation in my personal life. To make a long story short, I grew up in a home dominated by an alcoholic father. A good bit of the first three decades of my life was shaped by a core idea: "Don't do to anyone else what my father did to me." Frankly, the commitment sufficed for a long time, but I must confess that it was not sufficient for the long run.

Which leads me back to the positive, or as I prefer proactive, formulation Jesus offered. Taken seriously, it forces us to ask a hard question: "Just what would I really want others to do for me?" Some of us may be inclined to say, "Nothing." In more nearly sane moments, though, I think we realize that's not so.

Assuming we are reasonably healthy persons, and taking into account "the law and the prophets" plus Jesus, I suggest that most of us want at least the following from others:

- to be taken seriously, to be treated as if we matter;
- to be "kept company" when life crashes in;
- to be accorded opportunities to discover and use our gifts;
- to be given opportunities to help others;
- to be treated with dignity regardless of economics, health, race, gender, or age;
- to be offered friendship.

Obviously, the list may be applied at the personal level. I think it provides a reasonable guideline at the societal level as well.

I do not regard the list as complete, and I'm keenly aware that such a list is conditioned by our living in relative economic security. A person in dire circumstances might make a different list and include items such as food, clothing, shelter, and the like. Still, I think the first list captures some of our deepest yearnings.

Jesus' formulation pushes his followers to be proactive toward others, to intentionally offer such gifts to one another. In his worldview, behavior restrictions are fine but not enough. From my perspective, he has much in common with several of the prophets at this point.

Rami: Mike, you covered this well, so let me take a few detours.

Regarding the positive and negative versions of the text, Judaism has both. While Hillel states the golden rule in the negative, Leviticus 19:18 is positive, "Love your neighbor as yourself," as is Rabbi Elazar ben Arach's teaching that you should "Let your neighbor's honor be as dear to you as your own" (*Pirke Avot* 2:15). These are just two examples, but the idea is simple enough. Those who make much of the positive and negative forms of the commandment are probably making too much of them.

We have been following the Gospel according to Matthew, in which Jesus concludes his version of the golden rule with "for this is the law and the prophets." It is interesting to me that Luke's version drops any reference to the Law and the Prophets. Since Matthew is the older Gospel, I assume that Luke was aware of the original but left it off since his largely Gentile audience had no connection to Torah and Prophets.

From a Jewish perspective, it is the older version that is more compelling and challenging. Matthew's version parallels the older saying of Rabbi Hillel, "That which is hateful to you do not do to another. This is the whole of the Torah. Go and study it" (*Shabbat* 31a). What interests me is not so much the positive or negative articulations of the golden rule as the claim that both Hillel and Jesus make that ethics is the whole of the Torah and the Prophets.

Given the overwhelming amount of text devoted to ritual, holy days, and other non-ethical material in the Hebrew Bible, it is quite radical to argue, as these two great sages do, that God's instruction (the proper translation of *torah*) can be encapsulated in this single call for justice and compassion. And yet that is what they have done, and rightly so.

This is what matters: doing justly, loving mercy, walking humbly with God (Mic 6:8). Hillel and Jesus are affirming this prophetic challenge to priests and priestcraft ancient and modern. How did the religion of Hillel and Jesus get hijacked by legalists and theologians? What would it take to reclaim the true message of Torah and Prophets? What would Judaism and Christianity be like if Jews and Christians actually followed the teachings of these sages rather than the myriad rabbis and theologians who try to complicate matters?

Chapter 26

The Narrow Gate

Enter through the narrow gate; for the gate is wide and the road is easy that leads to destruction, and there are many who take it. For the gate is narrow and the road is hard that leads to life, and there are few who find it. (Matthew 7:13-14, NRSV)

Mike: Let's clear away one matter upfront. This passage is often used in American evangelical and fundamentalist circles to argue that Christianity is the only way to salvation. Matthew 7:13-14, taken in context, is not concerned with such a question. Instead, the passage fits neatly into a strand of Jewish tradition and also serves as the opening volley in a concluding challenge.

For example, when I read the passage I am reminded of Psalm 1: "Happy are those who do not follow the advice of the wicked, or take the path that sinners tread, or sit in the seat of scoffers; but their delight is in the law of the LORD, and on his law they meditate day and night." The idea of two ways, one leading to life and the other to destruction, has deep, old roots. The Christian tradition absorbed the image, first from Jesus then through various reformulations, ranging from the *Didache* to John Bunyan's *Pilgrim's Progress* (1678). It even crops up in J. R. R. Tolkien's *The Lord of the Rings* (1954–1955), when Galadriel warns Frodo that the quest walks on the sharp edge of a knife, in other words on a very narrow road.

The tradition assumes human choice. We decide which way to take. In my view, this is not so much a single decision as a series of decisions. We choose whom to take seriously, whom to believe, and so set the course of our lives. Our choices shape us. Over time we become more nearly like that on which we focus. That being so, Jesus' warning and promise is on target.

A related question arises: if our lives are shaped by the road we choose to walk, by that to which we pay attention, what is it we're called to take seriously? Context helps answer the question. The two of us have covered much of the content. It's summarized to a great extent in the golden rule. The Beatitudes and the Lord's Prayer contribute additional particulars. If I had to sum it up in a sentence, it would go something like this: "The way of life is to love God, neighbor, and self well and take the consequences!" Based on our past interaction, I would guess you might prefer a phrase that employs terms such as "justice" and "compassion."

Jesus challenges his listeners to take the matter seriously, as something of transcending importance. In subsequent verses, he will illustrate some of the challenges faced by those who do so: false teachers, false self-perceptions, and the like.

Rami: The first thing that strikes me in this teaching is its parallel in Luke. Replying to the question, "Lord, will only a few be saved?" Jesus says, "Strive to enter through the narrow door, for many, I tell you, will try to enter and will not be able" (Luke 13:23-24). While you are right to preempt any notion that Jesus is saying only Christians can be saved (after all, there was no Christianity when Jesus taught), he does seem to be saying that most of humanity will be damned.

Why is salvation so difficult? When I ponder this question, I cannot come up with a satisfactory answer; at least not as long as I posit a God who consciously set up a system of salvation. Why would God make it so hard to find Him? Why not make the gate to God as wide as possible? Doesn't God want us to come to Him? This would be the message of the prodigal son, at least as I read the parable. Has Jesus changed his mind?

I can imagine a system of salvation in which people can opt out. If someone decides that they prefer hell to heaven, fine. But why set it up so that most who desire heaven are denied entry?

In Pure Land Buddhism, Amida Buddha, the Buddha of Infinite Light, puts off his own salvation until he has facilitated the salvation of all sentient beings. All you have to do to get his help is call his name. Sure, most people try to make it on their own, but when they finally realize they can't succeed, they sincerely call for help, and Amida is there. This seems much more Christ-like than Jesus' notion that "the owner of the house [whom I assume is God] has got up and shut the door" (Luke 13:25), leaving millions clamoring to get in. Where is the love and compassion in that?

It seems to me that a loving God would make finding Him easy, and that it is only we humans that imagine the way to be hard. Which leads me again to Franz Kafka's parable of the Law. In this parable, Kafka imagines a man who finds the gate to the Law (God) but fears to enter because the gate is guarded by a giant. The man spends his entire life trying to bribe the giant to let him in, but the giant never grants him entry. At the end of his life he asks the giant to explain why no one else has ever come to the gate. The giant explains that this gate was for him alone. No permission to enter was ever needed. All he had to do was walk through it.

In other words, the narrow gate is the gate made just for you. It is narrow because only you can fit through it. It isn't narrow to keep people out, for each person has her own gate. The challenge is to find our gate and walk through it. What is our gate? It is this very moment; it is whatever life asks of us here and now. If we engage this moment loving God, neighbor, self, and stranger, then we enter the gate. If we engage the moment with something other than love (and I would say compassion and justice are the two ways of love), then we do not enter the gate. The choice is ours.

In this way of understanding salvation, the way to God is universal. Each person has her or his own gate. There is no attempt to keep people out. True, you have to find your gate and walk through it, but it is right there in front of you. Walk on!

Mike: Interesting, isn't it, how our minds see different connections between the biblical passage in question and other Scriptures or traditions. I regard such differences as a benefit derived from our ongoing conversation.

I am not at all sure that saying "the way is narrow" (etc.) is the same as saying God makes salvation difficult. Rather, I read such language as descriptive of the reality of human life. We seem to have a remarkable capacity to select self-defeating ways intentionally or by default. You write, "It seems to me that a loving God would make finding Him easy," and I agree. We humans do not so much imagine that finding God is hard as we make it hard for ourselves. From my perspective, Jesus may suggest that most of humanity will fail to find their way, but if this is so, it is by the choices we make.

Certainly, God wants us to come to him. You're right. That's the major point of the parable of the loving father (or prodigal son). Still, the son has to come to his senses and choose to take the path home to his father and trust his father with his life. As for your point about Luke 13:25 (the owner shutting the door), don't you think you might be pushing the metaphor a little far? It seems to me that all Jesus is saying is that we should choose and act as if all opportunities may come to an end.

I've always loved the Kafka parable! It's written, partly, in reaction to the Christianity Kafka knows, but the point about walking through the gate seems apt. The parable's injunction against bribery is correct. Bribery is but one of the false solutions to the quest for "salvation." It's on a par with fleeing to a far city to find one's freedom and self, when all the time real freedom and the real self could only be realized in the presence of the loving Father.

We agree, of course, that if we engage the given moment loving God, neighbor, and self, we enter the gate, walk through the door, or find our way. My hunch is that we differ in our estimate of human wisdom and strength.

Rami: Before we move on, Mike, I want to revisit the narrow way issue. My intent with the Kafka connection was to suggest that the Way itself isn't narrow, only that we imagine it to be so. Reality is just wide enough for each of us to pass through—alone. This is what "narrow" suggests to me: that we must each find our way in and enter alone, and that no two people can share the same point of entry.

The radical individualism of the Way makes it difficult for us to follow. We humans are social creatures, pack animals if you like, and we follow the herd. We imagine that if most people are flocking to something, it must be something worth flocking to. Our entire civilization and culture rests on this herd instinct. Kafka and Jesus are telling us something else.

The Way is narrow. It is your way only. Judaism teaches that each of us is a unique expression of God and that imitating the ways of others is a kind of idolatry. This is why, or so the rabbis teach, Jews always pray to the "God of Abraham, the God of Isaac, and the God of Jacob" rather than to the more succinct "God of Abraham, Isaac, and Jacob." The repetition of the phrase "the God of" reminds us that each of us comes to God in our own way just as Abraham, Isaac, and Jacob each came to God in his own way.

This works well with the parable of the prodigal son. He came to God (his father) in his own way. Had he not left home, had he not squandered his fortune, had he not hit rock bottom, he would never have been ready to accept the radical nature of his father's love. It was only when he realized he was unworthy of that love that he could accept it as the freely given gift it was (and still is).

If I am on the right track, what then should we make of Jesus' call to "Follow me"? In this I would say that Jesus isn't referring to himself as a person but to his actions. In other words, to follow Jesus is to do what Jesus did: to live the kingdom in the face of oppression. Jesus is revealing a paradigm to be lived rather than a creed to be believed. When we make Jesus an object of worship, we excuse ourselves from having to live the kingdom—all we have to do is believe in it. *Metanoia* isn't really repentance but getting beyond the egoic mind and putting on the mind of Christ—seeing the world as Jesus saw it, living in the world as Jesus lived in it, and dying for the kingdom as Jesus died for it.

The narrow Way is the way of living the kingdom. The wide way is the way of conforming to beliefs about the kingdom. I realize, of course, that such a view runs counter to everything many Christians believe Christianity stands for, but then, not being a Christian, this may not be surprising. I imagine you have much to say on this point, and I look forward to hearing from you.

Mike: I find your take quite interesting. At the same time, I am not at all certain that we are very far apart. In fact, I suspect each of us has hold of a piece of a single garment. That being said (and meant), I want to respond to a few matters.

Like you, and the majority of modern Western thinkers, I resist herd mentality in favor of radical individualism, by which I tend to mean a kind of lonely and responsible individualism. We always enter the narrow way alone, if we enter it at all.

Once on that way, though, I think we may well find others walking it as well. This is a new community in the making, made up of individuals who share the experience of entering through the narrow door and walking the narrow way. At this point it is not so much that we are coming to God as that we are walking with God. Strangely enough, there's room on the way for all those who choose to walk there.

Walking is a key term. Those who find and walk this way may not share a language, culture, or era. They may have quite different concepts of God and very different belief structures as well. But they find themselves walking the same road, and over time they find that they share a deepening commitment to continuing to walk, helping one another, and even coming to care for one another.

Strangely, and sometimes to our aggravation, the narrow way combines radical individualism with community.

Now for some particulars. Your take on the prodigal son is apt, insofar as it goes. The beauty of a story, even a parable, is that it offers many sides for our inspection. I certainly agree that your take is real and powerful. If we start with the end of the story, it makes sense. Does it grasp all the possibilities in the story? I do not think so. It seems to me that the prodigal could have found his way without leaving home, but he did not choose to do so. Had he stayed at home, his personal story would have played out differently, and his way to God would have been easier, at least with regard to physical, economic, and emotional suffering. Either way required that he accept his father's love as a free gift.

Repentance or *metanoia* has never been about a creed or set of beliefs, though at any time strands within Christianity act as if it were so. *Metanoia* means to turn around and look a different way, walk a different direction, put on a different mind, and the like. Paul, in his better moments, saw this rather clearly. When we do so, we increasingly see life with the perspective of Jesus and live accordingly. What that means for each follower must be discovered and fashioned as an individual. Again, though, as we do so we often find a community of others who share the perspective and the journey.

Rami: It's true that I like to think of myself as an individualist, but I admit that I belong to the individualist club and conform as much to the conditioning of that community as anyone else conforms to the conditioning of her or his own communities. And I agree that the journey of the alone to the Alone is never really traveled alone. In fact, there is no alone for we are always in the community of the One.

The other day I was asked why the Hebrew name for God as Creator, *Elohim*, is written in the plural. It is clear that the name is meant to be understood as singular since all verbs and adjectives attached to it are in the singular, but this only begs the question, why use the plural. My answer at that moment (all my answers are limited only to the moment in which they are given) was that the confusion of singular and plural points to the fact that the creativity that is God is plural, giving rise to many life forms, some lasting but moments, all of which are expressions of the One Divine Reality. God creates the community of living and dying, and we are residents of it.

I think the idea is less about being alone and more about not imitating others. We honor God when we are true to our own uniqueness. Otherwise we are denying God's creativity and rendering ourselves redundant. Just as each snowflake is unique yet all snowflakes are nothing but snow, so you and I and all living things are unique and yet nothing other than God.

I think walking is such a central term because the act of walking is intrinsically capable of awakening us to this truth and the reality of God in, with, and as all things. I have been leading walking meditation workshops both locally and across the country, and integrating walking meditation (using labyrinths wherever possible) into my other workshops. Walking with God, in God, and as God is the gift that such a practice offers us. And as we so walk, we discover that we never walk alone.

I appreciate your deepening of my understanding of the prodigal son parable. I have nothing to add, so let's walk on.

Chapter 27

Discerning False Prophets

Beware of false prophets, who come to you in sheep's clothing but inwardly are ravenous wolves. You will know them by their fruits. Are grapes gathered from thorns, or figs from thistles? In the same way, every good tree bears good fruit, but the bad tree bears bad fruit. A good tree cannot bear bad fruit, nor can a bad tree bear good fruit. Every tree that does not bear good fruit is cut down and thrown into the fire. Thus you will know them by their fruits.

Not everyone who says to me, "Lord, Lord," will enter the kingdom of heaven, but only the one who does the will of my Father in heaven. On that day many will say to me, "Lord, Lord did we not prophesy in your name, and cast out demons in your name, and do many deeds of power in your power?" Then I will declare to them, "I never knew you; go away from me, you evil-doers." (Matthew 7:15-23, NRSV)

Mike: What are we to make of these two related yet distinct Scripture paragraphs? Both look ahead in time to a movement or community after Jesus. While well-respected scholars often ascribe such passages to the early church rather than Jesus, I think it reasonable to assign Matthew 7:15-23 to him. With due respect to those who prefer to restrict Jesus' perspective to the apocalyptic, I find him to have been more complex. In particular, he often seems to have anticipated that a community would develop in his aftermath. Such a community, while informed by his teachings and life, would be subject to the dangers of deception and self-deception. It seems to me that Matthew 7:15-23 addresses these matters.

Many a modern tale and animated feature has drawn on the image of the wolf in sheep's clothing. In the passage, the core message is to beware of would-be leaders who claim to follow the Good Shepherd but who actually aim to ravage and fleece the flock! I can't speak to Jewish history, but Christian history provides numerous examples of sheepskin-wearing wolves. Some sought to divorce Christianity from its Jewish roots by discarding the Hebrew Bible (or the Hebrew Bible as mediated through the LXX). Others pushed forms of antinomianism, gnosticism (no matter how ill defined the term), expanded membership requirements, and the like. In recent centuries, false teachers have tried to lead the Christian movement to endorse slavery, racism, discrimination, sexism, greed, preemptive war, and torture. Both of us could cite numerous specific examples. The results (the fruits) are division, pain, suffering, and death for many—a fracturing of the community of the human race and the subversion of the church.

Jesus indicates that we need never let matters go so far. If the church will practice a kind of tough vigilance, it may discern the fruits of false leaders and move to stem the damage. Jesus assigns the community and those within it the responsibility for discernment. We are to tend our own fruit grove!

Self-deception also poses an ongoing threat. Verses 21-22 speak of the all-too-human tendency to confuse lip service with reality. "Lord," of course, became part of the earliest Christian confession, by which one not only signaled one's commitment to follow Jesus but also one's entry into the Christian community. Here Jesus gives clear warning against reliance on confessional or other religious language. Such language, while useful, must line up with one's inner orientation, or it means nothing.

In like fashion, good deeds, such as the two examples of inspired preaching and exorcism, may or may not reveal a genuine commitment to God. Something more is needed: alignment with God. The Sermon on the Mount captures much of what that might be. I suspect 1 Corinthians 13 does as well.

Rami: There is so much in this section, Mike, and it is one of my favorite passages of the Bible, but it is also one of the most troubling.

"Beware of false prophets, who come to you in sheep's clothing but inwardly are ravenous wolves" (v. 15).

Who are the false prophets? I have heard preachers claim that Jesus is referring to the Pharisees, but this is hardly convincing. When denouncing the Pharisees, Jesus and the Gospel writers always refer to them as Pharisees not prophets. And the Pharisees would never refer to themselves as prophets. So who is Jesus talking about?

Some scholars suggest that this reference to prophets was added long after Jesus' death and refers to Paul and his followers, but I don't think we have to stretch so far. And I heard a fellow on the radio today insist that "false prophets" refers to Muhammad (Peace be upon him), Buddha, and other great saints. Personally, it isn't difficult for me to read this passage as Jesus imagining the future of his teaching when teachers use him and his words to further their own ends. How can we protect ourselves against being fooled? "You will know them by their fruits" (v. 16).

This sounds right on the surface, but it is far more difficult than it seems. Take the preachers of the "prosperity gospel," for example—those who use the teachings of Jesus to line their own pockets with gold. Their fruits are their own riches, yet their followers see those fruits as proof of the authenticity of the teaching. In other words, when bad fruit is defined as good fruit, it is impossible to tell one from the other.

This is true in every religion. The people are convinced, as George Orwell taught us in the Newspeak of *Nineteen Eighty-Four* (New York: Harcourt Brace, 1949), that war is peace, slavery is freedom, and falsehood is truth. And once they are, the wolf can abandon the sheep's clothing and no one will know the difference.

Jesus is warning us against placing our faith in human beings and human institutions. Jesus is warning us against the seduction of words and miracles. He tells us to look at the fruits. But what if we no longer know good fruit from bad fruit?

"Not everyone who says to me, 'Lord, Lord,' will enter the kingdom of heaven, but only the one who does the will of my Father in heaven." But what is that will? Every religion claims to be doing God's will. The rampant rape and abuse of thousands of innocent children in Ireland's Catholic orphanages was no doubt done under the aegis of God's will. The murder of the doctor in Kansas, the slaughter of Shias by Sunnis and Sunnis by Shias, the assassination of Yitzhak Rabin, and the oppression of Palestinians in Israel's occupied territories are all excused as God's will.

False prophets are not without power. They "prophesy in your name, and cast out demons in your name, and do many deeds of power in your power." So, again, how are we to tell the true prophet from the false when the works of both are identical?

I agree, Mike, that we must remain vigilant, but according to what standard? Jesus may be able to say, "I never knew you; go away from me, you evil-doers," but the rest of us cannot be so sure. When the church (synagogue, mosque, temple, etc.) itself is the source of so much evil, in a world where church, state, and marketplace have educated us to the point where we can no longer distinguish grapes from thorns and figs from thistles, the only option we have is radical doubt. Trust no one. Not even yourself.

Five centuries before Jesus, the Buddha warned us against listening to teachers simply because they are called wise or following books simply because they are old. He admonished us to test every idea against our own experience: to see for ourselves what is wise and true, to trust our capacity to find enlightenment for ourselves. He may have had too much faith in humanity, but the idea that we must test teachings against reality rather than accept them on faith and insist that reality conform to ideology is a sound one.

The problem today, however, is that ideology is reality. There is no objective standard against which to make a sound judgment. I always come back to Micah 6:8, "You know what God requires, Do justly, love mercy, and walk humbly," but the truth is that justice, mercy, and humility are so open to interpretation that this text, too, is no longer sufficient.

Bottom line: I don't know how we can protect ourselves against false prophets. In fact, the very label "false" may no longer be meaningful. There are prophets of one faith or sect who argue against those of another faith or sect, but there is no way to tell which is the truer.

Mike: Your take on the difficulties associated with false prophets, "fruits," God's will, and vigilance strikes a chord with me. At times I rather despair of our being able to discern false prophets. We have trouble enough sorting through our own self-deceptions! Your closing lament (if you will grant me the term) captures the contemporary challenge: "I don't know how we can protect ourselves against false prophets . . . there are prophets of one faith or sect who argue against those of another faith or sect, but there is no way to tell which is the truer."

Your words remind me of an episode in Tolkien's novel *The Two Towers* (1954). Aragorn encounters a young nobleman who is confused and frightened by the competing claims of the time. The nobleman (I'm paraphrasing, not having the novel at hand) cries out, "How is a man to choose in such times as these?" Aragorn's reply (again, paraphrased from memory) braces him: "As he has ever chosen. Good and evil have not changed in a day."

The key point is that nothing absolves us from the burden or responsibility of choosing. When it comes to false prophets, truth, right, wrong, and the like, I may be confused but still I must choose, either deliberately or by default.

Given that cheery thought, here are the guidelines I follow. I draw on the Christian tradition, mix in a dash of what I hope is wisdom gleaned from experience, and leaven the whole thing with intentional humility (i.e., acknowledging that I will make mistakes and resolving to try to admit mistakes when they happen and rectify them as I can). Here are my guidelines:

1. Does the "prophet," teaching, or proposed action square with persons being created in the image of God? If I follow up, will I find myself according others the freedom and responsibility and dignity inherent in their being made in the image of God? It's surprising how many times this simple guideline leads me to choose not to enlist in a given "prophet's" agenda.

2. Would I want to be on the receiving end of a given prophet's agenda? If not, I become cautious about embracing such agendas.

3. Will the agenda, teaching, or action contribute to the enhancement of human community or instead fracture it further? If division seems to be the likely result, I grow cautious.

4. Does the agenda, teaching, or action require some genuine sacrifice on my part, or does it mostly serve to protect my interests (economic, career, comfort zone, etc.)? I tend to be suspicious of anything that essentially promises to help me "keep what's mine."

My decision making is more complicated than such a simple list implies, but still I find that the four guidelines help challenge me to take seriously the matter of choice.

Obviously, I've not answered the common question: "But how can you know what is true and take actions accordingly?" I'm not sure that's the best question, frankly, even if it does appeal to folk reared in the scientific era. Instead, I think aspiring to guide my actions on the basis of seeing God in others, putting myself in the other person's shoes, building community, and embracing sacrifice for the sake of others offers a more productive approach. Mind you, my approach does not provide surety of any kind! But it does preserve me from paralysis.

Rami: I agree with you, Mike, that we must choose. And we always choose the good and the right. Regardless of which side of an argument we are on, which policy we back, or which side of a war we choose to fight, we always assume that we are on the side of the good. Slavery, oppression, genocide, and torture are rarely done in the name of evil and most often done in the name of good. The argument continues on CNN and Fox right up to this morning. Those who support torture do not do so because it is evil but because, in their minds, it serves the greater good.

Given the ambiguity of goodness, let me respond to your guidelines, holding your second question for last.

1. *Does the "prophet," teaching, or proposed action square with persons being created in the image of God?* The challenge here is to hold on to the idea that our enemies are in fact created in the image of God. The first stage of evil is always to dehumanize those we wish to abuse. Once that is done, once we are convinced that the other is in fact not human, then we are willing to do unto others any horror we can imagine.

2. *Would I want to be on the receiving end of a given prophet's agenda?* This is the golden rule, and it makes sense to me. At the risk of sounding Pollyannaish, I think this is the only guideline that might work. Would I like to be slaughtered? Would I like to be tortured? Would I like to be abused or enslaved? At least on the level of personal ethics, this works. And if people would hold to such an ethic, our communal ethics might come to reflect this rule as well.

3. *Will the agenda, teaching, or action contribute to the enhancement of human community or instead fracture it further?* Again the issue is our definition of "human community." Once we define "us" as human and "them" as gooks, huns, nips, kikes, niggers, baby-killers, white devils, and the like, we can excuse incredible evil perpetrated against them. And then there is the argument current during the days of American enslavement of Africans that it was in the best interest of the enslaved to be slaves. Better a Christian slave in America, the argument went, than a free pagan in Africa. There is no end to the human capacity to rationalize evil.

4. *Does the agenda, teaching, or action require some genuine sacrifice on my part, or does it mostly serve to protect my interests (economic, career, comfort zone, etc.)?* This works for you and thoughtful people like you, but most of us put "keeping what's mine" at the top of our agenda. American foreign policy, regardless of the party in power, is about keeping what is ours and expanding what is ours often at the expense of others. This may bother you, but not the majority.

Mike: I agree with all you say about the ambiguity of goodness, the ways in which we justify evil by appealing to a greater good, our tendency to develop narrow definitions of human community, and our bent toward selfishness. I even agree with your take on the golden rule.

Metaphors are always risky, but here's one I find useful. Think of the human story as a piece of music. All of the horrible themes we've identified comprise a major movement within the piece. At times the movement dominates, sometimes it recedes into the background, but it is always there. Still, it is not the only movement. There is another one, a second one, and it plays the great themes of an all-inclusive humanity, humility, sacrifice, and deeply shared interests. The two movements play, contend, rise, and fall, but they go on playing. Some of us hear one movement more clearly than the other; some of us hear only one theme. We often think we've mastered the music, though no one ever really does. Still the music plays on, and neither theme is eliminated.

Now, in my view there is a Conductor who never ceases to try to bring the second movement to the forefront. This may be the core difference between us. I don't know. In any case, though, I believe that the Conductor is involved, though he operates within the limits set by the role he has assumed.

I choose to pay attention to the second movement, to allow its cadences and runs and pace and tone to become the music that is my life. I may mishear a note, sing off key, get out of beat—but as long as the second movement plays and as long as I try to listen, I ultimately will be drawn back into the movement.

So I dare to sing or play or simply beat time to the second movement. As long as the second movement plays, I will not lose hope.

Rami: You are right, Mike—metaphors are always risky. Especially when shared between friends who delight in tweaking each other's metaphors. So, with all due respect, let the tweaking begin.

First, I love the symphonic metaphor. Second, I agree that there are various movements that flow through the piece to create the dramatic point/counter point essential to the quality of the music.

I'm not so sure about the conductor. Who would this be? God, I assume, is the composer, and while the composer could also be the conductor, I assume that since you didn't say that, you didn't mean that. So maybe Jesus is the conductor. But Jesus, having left the symphony in the hands of the Holy Spirit at Pentecost, makes for a poor conductor. So perhaps it is the Spirit who conducts. Even if we could agree on who the conductor is, we still have the problem of the orchestra rebelling against the conductor's direction. A good symphony follows the conductor's lead. If they don't, the orchestra devolves into chaos and the conductor is out of a job.

Maybe the problem is solved if we shift from symphonic music to improvisational jazz. As I understand it, jazz has a core theme off of which jazz musicians improvise riffs. The riffs cannot ignore the theme, but they may oppose it and offer contrast to it. Such music is often highly discordant, and that would make the metaphor all the more apt. It is also created on the spot. In this metaphor there is no conductor, and God the Composer only sets the theme and waits to see where the musicians will take it. Maybe this is why God refers to Himself in Exodus as *Ehyeh asher Ehyeh*, I will be what I will be. Even God is surprised by where the music goes.

What I like most about the music metaphor (regardless of musical style) is the need for rests and the goal-lessness of play. Music without the silence of the rests is just noise. Organized religion (as opposed to mysticism) makes little room for the deep silence that frees us from the fixed notations of theology and ritual. The music metaphor would allow us to honor the silence more.

As for the sheer joy of playing, unlike most things we humans do in life, getting to the end of a piece of music is never the goal. The play is the goal; the journey is the thing. Otherwise the best symphonies would be those that played the fastest, and the greatest composers would only write endings.

Mike: Aside from your (occasional) penchant to try to treat a metaphor as a subject for scientific inquiry, I think your "improvisational jazz" suggestion is useful. It certainly provides a metaphor of life and creation as experienced in any given moment. When my sense of humor kicks in, I sometimes imagine an encounter with God when all history has played out. He greets us and agrees to take a few questions. When we mention the various music metaphors, God exclaims, "Music! What music? Me, I'm a gardener!"

Rami: God is a gardener? No way! Genesis 2:4-5, "When the God made earth and heaven—when no shrub of the field was yet on earth and no grasses of the field had yet sprouted, because the LORD God had not sent rain upon the earth and there was no earthling to till the earth . . . ." So much for God the Gardener. God had to invent that job and then create humanity to do it. Enough levity. Back to the text.

Chapter 28

Floods and Heavy Rain

"Everyone then who hears these words of mine and acts on them will be like a wise man who built his house on rock. The rain fell, the floods came, and the winds blew and beat on that house, but it did not fall. And everyone who hears these words of mine and does not act on them will be like a foolish man who built his house on sand. The rain fell, and the floods came, and the winds blew and beat against that house, and it fell— and great was the fall." Now when Jesus had finished saying these things, the crowds were astounded at his teaching, for he taught them as one having authority, and not as their scribes. (Matthew 7:24-29, NRSV)

Mike: We've arrived at the final paragraph of the Sermon on the Mount. A childhood chorus first imprinted the story on my mind. Repeating lines about the falling rain and the rising flood, coupled with appropriate body movements, led to a conclusion in which the wise man's house stood but the foolish man's house "came tumbling down." We were easily entertained in that era!

In the context of the Sermon on the Mount, Jesus' words here constitute both warning and invitation. Listening to, digesting, and attempting to structure life in accordance with his words matters. Many Christians over the centuries have taken the injunction to imply that the Sermon on the Mount is the literary core of Christianity. Those who do so tend to read the remainder of the Gospels and the rest of the New Testament in light of the Sermon on the Mount. In short, the sermon becomes a "canon within the canon."

It's worth recalling how counterintuitive the sermon feels to most of us. In an era when many, perhaps most, believe that safety is found in violence, even preemptive violence, the sermon speaks of loving an enemy, of doing unto others as we would have them do unto us, and the like. At almost any point in the sermon, we find ourselves confronted by an alternative vision of personal and community life. Frankly, it requires a leap of faith to attempt to embrace and practice the sermon's core teachings.

With regard to the parable itself, it assumes a setting in which heavy rain and floods are rare enough to encourage shortcuts or complacency. The parable's images are heavy-handed, designed to contrast the stark difference between foolishness and wisdom. As I have noted before, it seems to me that Jesus draws from the tradition of the two ways, in this case clothing it in talk of two ways of selecting a home site.

The Sermon on the Mount closes with a summary statement of the crowd's reaction to the entire speech. Christian scholars have invested a great deal of ink and paper in the attempt to understand the text's contrast between the scribes' and Jesus' approaches to teaching. More often than not, they suggest that the "scribes" tended to teach on the basis of an inherited tradition, relying on the authority of those cited. The same scholars suggest that Jesus, in contrast, spoke as one with a word from God, whether in a sense similar to that of earlier prophets or as the Messiah. Frankly, I doubt we can discern the Gospel writer's intent at this historical distance, other than to say that he believed Jesus taught with an authority his listeners found novel.

Rami: I cannot read this parable of the builders without thinking that Jesus is retelling the teaching found in the prophet Ezekiel (13:10-16, NRSV):

> Because, in truth, because they have misled my people, saying, "Peace," when there is no peace; and because, when the people build a wall, these prophets smear whitewash on it. Say to those who smear whitewash on it that it shall fall. There will be a deluge of rain, great hailstones will fall, and a stormy wind will break out. When the wall falls, will it not be said to you, "Where is the whitewash you smeared on it?" Therefore thus says the Lord GOD: "In my wrath I will make a stormy wind break out, and in my anger there shall be a deluge of rain, and hailstones in wrath to destroy it. I will break down the wall that you have smeared with whitewash, and bring it to the ground, so that its foundation will be laid bare; when it falls, you shall perish within it; and you shall know that I am the LORD. Thus I will spend my wrath upon the wall, and upon those who have smeared it with whitewash; and I will say to you, The wall is no more, nor those who smeared it—the prophets of Israel who prophesied concerning Jerusalem and saw visions of peace for it, when there was no peace, says the Lord GOD."

The "whitewash" is a coating that gives the illusion of strength, like the houses of those who build on sand. Jesus' rabbinic contemporaries made the same point. In *Avot de Rabbi Nathan* Rabbi Elisha ben Avuyah says, "A man who does good deeds and diligently studies Torah is like a man building a house with a stone foundation and a shingled roof. . . . When a flood comes the house does not move. But a man who studies and yet does evil, is like one who builds a house with shingles for a foundation and rock for a roof. Even a slight rain causes the house to collapse" (*Avot de Rabbi Nathan*, 24).

What interests me is that Jesus is, like the rabbis before and after him, preaching the gospel of the deed rather than the gospel of faith. It isn't enough to hear the words of Jesus or even to believe them; one must live them, do them, for it is our action that is the rock while mere faith is sand. Luke makes the point even more clearly when his Jesus says that anyone who hears his words and lives them is like the builder whose foundation is rock, but anyone who hears his words and does not live them is building a house on sand (Luke 6:47-49). Most of us build on sand.

The closing part of the sermon is challenging to me personally: "Now when Jesus had finished saying these things, the crowds were astounded at his teaching, for he taught them as one having authority, and not as their scribes" (vv. 28-29).

The first thing I notice here is that Matthew seems to have forgotten that Jesus withdrew from the crowd and spoke the sermon to his inner circle: "When Jesus saw the crowds, he went up the mountain; and after he sat down, his disciples came to him. Then he began to speak, and taught them," i.e., the disciples not the crowd (Matt 5:1-2).

If this is true, the crowd never heard the Sermon on the Mount, and this closing line is a later editorial gloss added to the text to highlight the idea (false in my opinion) that Jesus taught something drastically new. While Jesus puts his own unique spin on his teachings, he is still teaching Torah whether or not Jews and Christians want to admit it.

As to his manner of teaching, Jesus does violate a major tenet of Judaism: cite your source. While rabbis can be innovative in their interpretations of Scripture and law, we consider it an act of respect to honor those teachers who came before us by citing their teachings in their name. This continues today. We delight in showing the evolution of our thinking by quoting our teachers, even when we know we are going to put a spin on the teaching that these teachers never imagined and with which they might not even agree.

So, yes, Jesus' seeming lack of respect for his rabbis would shock people. It still bothers me today, which is why I spent much of our conversation citing sources that may have been in Jesus' mind when he taught. I say his "seeming" lack of respect because it is hard for me to imagine him not citing sources. It was and is such a central part of rabbinic culture that I cannot help believing that Jesus did honor his rabbis and that the Gospel writers simply chose not to include those references.

The reason the Gospel writers would make this choice is not hard to fathom. To them, Jesus was not speaking for an ancient tradition but for God, perhaps as God. God is the source of these teachings, and since God is speaking them there is no reason to cite sources. If they were to include the early teachings from which Jesus shaped his own message, this would tie Jesus too strongly to Judaism and make the emergence of a largely non-Jewish church all the more difficult. Once again, politics shapes religion.

I like way you sum up your take on the sermon, Mike. You seem to suggest that it is, in today's world no less than the world of Jesus' time, countercultural. I heartily agree. What would it be like if people built their homes on rock and actually lived the sermon rather than building on the sands of power, politics, and the theological veneer that seek to pass as religion?

Prophetic religion should always be countercultural when the culture is rooted in exploitation, greed, ignorance, anger, and violence. Judaism, Christianity, and Islam all started out as countercultural revolutions and each ended up as the bearers of culture and excusers of the violence to which their respective cultures fell prey. For example, a 2009 Pew Forum on Religion and Public Life poll found that 60 percent of Evangelical Christians supported torture of terror suspects while only 40 percent of the unchurched did so. We have to wonder if Christianity is still countercultural.

As always, Mike, you are clear and insightful: it does take a leap of faith to embrace and live the teachings of Jesus in the Sermon on the Mount. The leap is not so much the belief in the divinity of Jesus but the possibility of mere humans being capable of living the life he prescribed for us. With the rise of fundamentalism in all three Abrahamic religions, I am doubtful that any of us have this faith.

On the contrary, our faith is in the very things Jesus rejected, the very things that are bringing us and our civilization to the brink of disaster. We need to do more than hear the Sermon on the Mount. We need to live it.

Afterword

Rami: At the heart of rabbinic Judaism is the notion that the reader co-creates the text with the author. While it may be that the Torah comes from God, its meaning comes from us. I am not inclined to take this literally. I don't think God writes books. But as a metaphor it is a powerful insight.

There are some texts that come from the highest levels of human spiritual consciousness, pointing (given the limitations of the author's time, space, and cultural biases) directly to timeless principles that need to be applied in each generation. In the two volumes of *Mount and Mountain*, we have been dealing with two of these texts: the Ten Commandments and the Sermon on the Mount. While each speaks in a specific language, Hebrew, Aramaic, and Greek, and to a specific people, the Jews, both boldly articulate some of the timeless principles by which all peoples in all times can live effectively with love, compassion, and justice.

What made this project so rich for me, Mike, was having the opportunity to hear these texts filtered through your heart and mind. If it is true that we co-create the texts we read by interpreting them in light of our own experience and knowledge (as well as our own ignorance and bias), then the pleasure I have found in reading these texts with you was in discovering your version of them.

But there is something else to be found in this conversation, something that is far more important.

Interfaith dialogue is not new, but most of it takes place on the level of doctrine. Rarely do you find people of different faiths reading one another's holy books together. Granted, the Ten Commandments are no less a part of Christianity than they are of Judaism, but our traditions do understand them differently. And when it comes to the Sermon on the Mount, the rarity and import of our dialogue becomes all the more clear.

What I hope we have modeled here is a new avenue for interfaith conversation: trusted friends reading, wrestling with, and commenting on each other's sacred texts. I would like to see this repeated over and over again with clergy and texts from as broad a religious spectrum as can be mustered.

When we started this project so many months ago, I had no idea where it would take us, and I have been surprised by some of the avenues we have traveled together. I was also taken with how clearly our two voices emerged. There is a consistency in our respective approaches that reflects the fundamental differences between our traditions and yet suggests that no one way is sufficient. We balanced one another, I think, and did so in ways that enriched my understanding of the text and our traditions. It has been a blessing and an honor to work on this with you, Mike. What's next?

Mike: Do you remember the genesis of *Mount and Mountain*? We fell to talking about how we might partner to write about the Ten Commandments and the Sermon on the Mount. We knew, I think, what we did not want to attempt: yet another doctrinal study, diatribe, or something suitable only for academics. Instead, we wanted to practice and model a genuine conversation between two friends from quite different yet historically intertwined religious traditions.

At some point in the conversation, one of us mentioned reading the collected letters of a well-known author from another era. Many of the letters featured the author's ongoing conversations with close friends. The conversations ranged over a host of topics. Each matter received serious treatment. Sometimes the author or his correspondent changed their minds in light of a given argument. More often, they simply enriched one another's thought and deepened their understanding and appreciation for one another.

We knew we had found our model. So began the exchange that became *Mount and Mountain.*

I've learned a few things along the way.

First, I believe you're correct. Trusted friends reading, wrestling with, and commenting on each other's sacred texts may prove to be the most fruitful model for interfaith conversation in the years to come. For one thing, friendship may enable us to hear some things we would rather not hear! Perhaps friendship should become the prerequisite to interfaith conversation.

Second, our two voices emerged and took on consistency, even as we sought to remain open to one another's insights. We often discovered that we have much in common, especially with regard to the power of story, ethical and other practical applications of a given text, and recognition of the complexity of humans. Differences also emerged, ranging from the nature of God and the identity of Jesus to how hard to press a metaphor.

Third, I suspect that our respect for and knowledge of one another's traditions grew. The journey taught us, I think, that we need one another's perspective(s) if we are to find our way through our complicated lives and complex world.

Thank you, Rami, for investing so much of yourself in the conversation. No doubt, the two of us will continue the conversation, albeit in other ways.

Beyond the American Dream
Millard Fuller

In 1968, Millard finished the story of his journey from pauper to millionaire to home builder. His wife, Linda, occasionally would ask him about getting it published, but Millard would reply, "Not now. I'm too busy." This is that story. *978-1-57312-563-5 272 pages/pb* **$20.00**

The Black Church
Relevant or Irrelevant in the 21st Century?
Reginald F. Davis

The Black Church contends that a relevant church struggles to correct oppression, not maintain it. How can the black church focus on the liberation of the black community, thereby reclaiming the loyalty and respect of the black community? *978-1-57312-557-4 144 pages/pb* **$15.00**

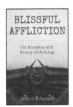

Blissful Affliction
The Ministry and Misery of Writing
Judson Edwards

Edwards draws from more than forty years of writing experience to explore why we use the written word to change lives and how to improve the writing craft. *978-1-57312-594-9 144 pages/pb* **$15.00**

Bottom Line Beliefs
Twelve Doctrines All Christians Hold in Common (Sort of)
Michael B. Brown

Despite our differences, there are principles that are bedrock to the Christian faith. These are the subject of Michael Brown's *Bottom Line Beliefs*. *978-1-57312-520-8 112 pages/pb* **$15.00**

Christian Civility in an Uncivil World
Mitch Carnell, ed.

When we encounter a Christian who thinks and believes differently, we often experience that difference as an attack on the principles upon which we have built our lives and as a betrayal to the faith. However, it is possible for Christians to retain their differences and yet unite in respect for each other. It is possible to love one another and at the same time retain our individual beliefs.

978-1-57312-537-6 160 pages/pb **$17.00**

Choosing Gratitude
Learning to Love the Life You Have

James A. Autry

Autry reminds us that gratitude is a choice, a spiritual—not social—process. He suggests that if we cultivate gratitude as a way of being, we may not change the world and its ills, but we can change our response to the world. If we fill our lives with moments of gratitude, we will indeed love the life we have.   *978-1-57312-614-4 144 pages/pb* **$15.00**

Contextualizing the Gospel
A Homiletic Commentary on 1 Corinthians

Brian L. Harbour

Harbour examines every part of Paul's letter, providing a rich resource for those who want to struggle with the difficult texts as well as the simple texts, who want to know how God's word—all of it—intersects with their lives today. *978-1-57312-589-5 240 pages/pb* **$19.00**

Dance Lessons
Moving to the Beat of God's Heart

Jeanie Miley

Miley shares her joys and struggles a she learns to "dance" with the Spirit of the Living God.   *978-1-57312-622-9 240 pages/pb* **$19.00**

The Disturbing Galilean
Essays About Jesus

Malcolm Tolbert

In this captivating collection of essays, Dr. Malcolm Tolbert reflects on nearly two dozen stories taken largely from the Synoptic Gospels. Those stories range from Jesus' birth, temptation, teaching, anguish at Gethsemane, and crucifixion.   *978-1-57312-530-7 140 pages/pb* **$15.00**

Divorce Ministry
A Guidebook

Charles Qualls

This book shares with the reader the value of establishing a divorce recovery ministry while also offering practical insights on establishing your own unique church-affiliated program. Whether you are working individually with one divorced person or leading a large group, *Divorce Ministry: A Guidebook* provides helpful resources to guide you through the emotional and relational issues divorced people often encounter.

978-1-57312-588-8 156 pages/pb **$16.00**

The Enoch Factor
The Sacred Art of Knowing God

Steve McSwain

The Enoch Factor is a persuasive argument for a more enlightened religious dialogue in America, one that affirms the goals of all religions—guiding followers in self-awareness, finding serenity and happiness, and discovering what the author describes as "the sacred art of knowing God."

978-1-57312-556-7 256 pages/pb **$21.00**

Faith Postures
Cultivating Christian Mindfulness

Holly Sprink

Sprink guides readers through her own growing awareness of God's desire for relationship and of developing the emotional, physical, spiritual postures that enable us to learn to be still, to listen, to be mindful of the One outside ourselves.

1-978-57312-547-5 160 pages/pb **$16.00**

The Good News According to Jesus
A New Kind of Christianity for a New Kind of Christian

Chuck Queen

In *The Good News According to Jesus*, Chuck Queen contends that when we broaden our study of Jesus, the result is a richer, deeper, healthier, more relevant and holistic gospel, a Christianity that can transform this world into God's new world.

978-1-57312-528-4 216 pages/pb **$18.00**

Healing Our Hurts
Coping with Difficult Emotions

Daniel Bagby

In *Healing Our Hurts*, Daniel Bagby identifies and explains all the dynamics at play in these complex emotions. Offering practical biblical insights to these feelings, he interprets faith-based responses to separate overly religious piety from true, natural human emotion. This book helps us learn how to deal with life's difficult emotions in a redemptive and responsible way.

978-1-57312-613-7 144 pages/pb **$15.00**

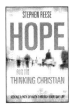

Hope for the Thinking Christian
Seeking a Path of Faith through Everyday Life

Stephen Reese

Readers who want to confront their faith more directly, to think it through and be open to God in an individual, authentic, spiritual encounter will find a resonant voice in Stephen Reese.

978-1-57312-553-6 160 pages/pb **$16.00**

Hoping Liberia
Stories of Civil War from Africa's First Republic
John Michael Helms

Through historical narrative, theological ponderings, personal confession, and thoughtful questions, Helms immerses readers in a period of political turmoil and violence, a devastating civil war, and the immeasurable suffering experienced by the Liberian people.

978-1-57312-544-4 208 pages/pb **$18.00**

A Hungry Soul Desperate to Taste God's Grace
Honest Prayers for Life
Charles Qualls

Part of how we *see* God is determined by how we *listen* to God. There is so much noise and movement in the world that competes with images of God. This noise would drown out God's beckoning voice and distract us. We may not sense what spiritual directors refer to as the *thin place*—God come near. Charles Qualls's newest book offers readers prayers for that journey toward the meaning and mystery of God.

978-1-57312-648-9 152 pages/pb **$14.00**

James (Smyth & Helwys Annual Bible Study series)
Being Right in a Wrong World
Michael D. McCullar

Unlike Paul, who wrote primarily to congregations defined by Gentile believers, James wrote to a dispersed and persecuted fellowship of Hebrew Christians who would soon endure even more difficulty in the coming years.

Teaching Guide 1-57312-604-5 160 pages/ pb **$14.00**
Study Guide 1-57312-605-2 96 pages/pb **$6.00**

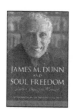

James M. Dunn and Soul Freedom
Aaron Douglas Weaver

James Milton Dunn, over the last fifty years, has been the most aggressive Baptist proponent for religious liberty in the United States. Soul freedom—voluntary, uncoerced faith and an unfettered individual conscience before God—is the basis of his understanding of church-state separation and the historic Baptist basis of religious liberty.

978-1-57312-590-1 224 pages/pb **$18.00**

The Jesus Tribe
Following Christ in the Land of the Empire

Ronnie McBrayer

The Jesus Tribe fleshes out the implications, possibilities, contradictions, and complexities of what it means to live within the Jesus Tribe and in the shadow of the American Empire.

978-1-57312-592-5 208 pages/pb **$17.00**

Joint Venture

Jeanie Miley

Joint Venture is a memoir of the author's journey to find and express her inner, authentic self, not as an egotistical venture, but as a sacred responsibility and partnership with God. Miley's quest for Christian wholeness is a rich resource for other seekers.

978-1-57312-581-9 224 pages/pb **$17.00**

Let Me More of Their Beauty See
Reading Familiar Verses in Context

Diane G. Chen

Let Me More of Their Beauty See offers eight examples of how attention to the historical and literary settings can safeguard against taking a text out of context, bring out its transforming power in greater dimension, and help us apply Scripture appropriately in our daily lives.

978-1-57312-564-2 160 pages/pb **$17.00**

Looking Around for God
The Strangely Reverent Observations of an Unconventional Christian

James A. Autry

Looking Around for God, Autry's tenth book, is in many ways his most personal. In it he considers his unique life of faith and belief in God. Autry is a former Fortune 500 executive, author, poet, and consultant whose work has had a significant influence on leadership thinking.

978-157312-484-3 144 pages/pb **$16.00**

Maggie Lee for Good

Jinny and John Hinson

Maggie Lee for Good captures the essence of a young girl's boundless faith and spirit. Her parents' moving story of the accident that took her life will inspire readers who are facing loss, looking for evidence of God's sustaining grace, or searching for ways to make a meaningful difference in the lives of others.

978-1-57312-630-4 144 pages/pb **$15.00**

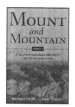

Mount and Mountain
Vol. 1: A Reverend and a Rabbi Talk About the Ten Commandments
Rami Shapiro and Michael Smith

Mount and Mountain represents the first half of an interfaith dialogue—a dialogue that neither preaches nor placates but challenges its participants to work both singly and together in the task of reinterpreting sacred texts. Mike and Rami discuss the nature of divinity, the power of faith, the beauty of myth and story, the necessity of doubt, the achievements, failings, and future of religion, and, above all, the struggle to live ethically and in harmony with the way of God. 978-1-57312-612-0 144 pages/pb **$15.00**

Overcoming Adolescence
Growing Beyond Childhood into Maturity
Marion D. Aldridge

In *Overcoming Adolescence*, Marion Aldridge poses questions for adults of all ages to consider. His challenge to readers is one he has personally worked to confront: to grow up *all the way*—mentally, physically, academically, socially, emotionally, and spiritually. The key involves not only knowing how to work through the process but also how to recognize what may be contributing to our perpetual adolescence.

978-1-57312-577-2 156 pages/pb **$17.00**

Psychic Pancakes & Communion Pizza
More Musings and Mutterings of a Church Misfit
Bert Montgomery

Psychic Pancakes & Communion Pizza is Bert Montgomery's highly anticipated follow-up to *Elvis, Willie, Jesus & Me* and contains further reflections on music, film, culture, life, and finding Jesus in the midst of it all. 978-1-57312-578-9 160 pages/pb **$16.00**

Reading Job (Reading the Old Testament series)
A Literary and Theological Commentary
James L. Crenshaw

At issue in the Book of Job is a question with which most all of us struggle at some point in life, "Why do bad things happen to good people?" James Crenshaw has devoted his life to studying the disturbing matter of theodicy—divine justice—that troubles many people of faith.

978-1-57312-574-1 192 pages/pb **$22.00**

Reading Samuel (Reading the Old Testament series)
A Literary and Theological Commentary
Johanna W. H. van Wijk-Bos

Interpreted masterfully by preeminent Old Testament scholar
Johanna W. H. van Wijk-Bos, the story of Samuel touches on a vast
array of subjects that make up the rich fabric of human life. The
reader gains an inside look at leadership, royal intrigue, military campaigns, occult
practices, and the significance of religious objects of veneration.

978-1-57312-607-6 272 pages/pb **$22.00**

The Role of the Minister in a Dying Congregation
Lynwood B. Jenkins

In *The Role of the Minister in a Dying Congregation* Jenkins provides a
courageous and responsible resource on one of the most critical
issues in congregational life: how to help a congregation conclude
its ministry life cycle with dignity and meaning.

978-1-57312-571-0 96 pages/pb **$14.00**

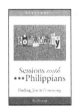

Sessions with Philippians (Session Bible Studies series)
Finding Joy in Community
Bo Prosser

In this brief letter to the Philippians, Paul makes clear the centrality
of his faith in Jesus Christ, his love for the Philippian church, and
his joy in serving both Christ and their church.

978-1-57312-579-6 112 pages/pb **$13.00**

Sessions with Samuel (Session Bible Studies series)
Stories from the Edge
Tony W. Cartledge

In these stories, Israel faces one crisis after another, a people con-
stantly on the edge. Individuals such as Saul and David find
themselves on the edge as well, facing troubles of leadership and
personal struggle. Yet, each crisis becomes a gateway for learning that God is
always present, that hope remains. *978-1-57312-555-0 112 pages/pb* **$13.00**

Silver Linings
My Life Before and After Challenger 7
June Scobee Rodgers

We know the public story of *Challenger 7*'s tragic destruction.
That day, June's life took a new direction that ultimately led to the
creation of the Challenger Center and to new life and new love.
Her story of Christian faith and triumph over adversity will inspire readers of
every age. *978-1-57312-570-3 352 pages/hc* **$28.00**

Spacious
Exploring Faith and Place
Holly Sprink

Exploring where we are and why that matters to God is an incredible, ongoing process. If we are present and attentive, God creatively and continuously widens our view of the world, whether we live in the Amazon or in our own hometown.

978-1-57312-649-6 156 pages/pb **$16.00**

This Is What a Preacher Looks Like
Sermons by Baptist Women in Ministry
Pamela Durso, ed.

In this collection of sermons by thirty-six Baptist women, their voices are soft and loud, prophetic and pastoral, humorous and sincere. They are African American, Asian, Latina, and Caucasian. They are sisters, wives, mothers, grandmothers, aunts, and friends.

978-1-57312-554-3 144 pages/pb **$18.00**

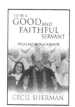

To Be a Good and Faithful Servant
The Life and Work of a Minister
Cecil Sherman

This book offers a window into how one pastor navigated the many daily challenges and opportunities of ministerial life and shares that wisdom with church leaders wherever they are in life—whether serving as lay leaders or as ministers just out of seminary, midway through a career, or seeking renewal after many years of service.   978-1-57312-559-8 208 pages/pb **$20.00**

Transformational Leadership
Leading with Integrity
Charles B. Bugg

"Transformational" leadership involves understanding and growing so that we can help create positive change in the world. This book encourages leaders to be willing to change if *they* want to help transform the world. They are honest about their personal strengths and weaknesses, and are not afraid of doing a fearless moral inventory of themselves.

978-1-57312-558-1 112 pages/pb **$14.00**

Written on My Heart
Daily Devotions for Your Journey through the Bible
Ann H. Smith

Smith takes readers on a fresh and exciting journey of daily readings of the Bible that will change, surprise, and renew you.

978-1-57312-549-9 288 pages/pb **$18.00**

When Crisis Comes Home
Revised and Expanded

John Lepper

The Bible is full of examples of how God's people, with homes grounded in the faith, faced crisis after crisis. These biblical personalities and families were not hopeless in the face of catastrophe— instead, their faith in God buoyed them, giving them hope for the future and strength to cope in the present. John Lepper will help you and your family prepare for, deal with, and learn from crises in your home.   *978-1-57312-539-0 152 pages/pb* **$17.00**

Cecil Sherman Formations Commentary

Add the wit and wisdom of Cecil Sherman to your library. He wrote the Smyth & Helwys Formations Commentary for 15 years; now you can purchase the 5-volume compilation covering the best of Cecil Sherman from Genesis to Revelation.

Vol. 1: Genesis–Job   *1-57312-476-1 208 pages/pb* **$17.00**

Vol. 2: Psalms–Malachi   *1-57312-477-X 208 pages/pb* **$17.00**

Vol. 3: Matthew–Mark   *1-57312-478-8 208 pages/pb* **$17.00**

Vol. 4: Luke–Acts   *1-57312-479-6 208 pages/pb* **$17.00**

Vol. 5: Romans–Revelation *1-57312-480-X 208 pages/pb* **$17.00**